②

The Eye

Opening

As I saw

The Eye Opening

As I saw

Admiral Vishnu Bhagwat, PVSM
(Former Chief of the Naval Staff)

Manas Publications
New Delhi-110002 (INDIA)

MANAS PUBLICATIONS

(Publishers for Defence, IFS, IAS, IPS, IRS, Press, Judges etc)

4402/ 5-A, Opp HDFC Bank, Ansari Road,
Darya Ganj, New Delhi - 110 002 (INDIA)

Ph.: 23260783, 23265523(O); 23842660 (R)
Fax: 011 - 23272766
E-mail: manaspublications@vsnl.com
manaspublications@gmail.com
www.manaspublications.in
www.manasdefenceyearbook.com

2nd Impression 2010 (2006)

ISBN 81-7049-267-X

Rs. 495/-

Typeset at
Manas Publications

Printed in India at
R.K. Offset Process, Delhi
and Published by Mrs. Suman Lata for
Manas Publications, 4402/ 5-A, Opp HDFC Bank,
Ansari Road, Daryaganj, New Delhi 110002 (INDIA)

Contents

Preface 7

1. Unlimited Militarisation: Delusions of World Hegemony 11
2. War, at the Speed of Thought 27
3. National Security: The Contemporary Context 34
4. Changing Nature of Warfare 52
5. Is the Tide Turning? 63
6. Indo-US Military-to-Military Relations 69
7. US Force Architecture — In the Coming Years 83
8. Great Game-II 90
9. China — Possibilities and Perspectives 99
10. China's Military Power—An Eagle's Eye View 107
11. Whither Self-Reliance 114

12. Kashmir: The Kernel of Our National Security 126

13. Oil Resources: Strategy and Defence Policies 136

14. Corporate Globalization, Its Militarisation and Possible Response of a United People 143

15. Silent WMDs — Effects of Depleted Uranium Munitions on Asian People & Their Future 164

16. The Intelligence Business 172

17. Signing Away Vital National Interests 181

18. Design to Cost Approach in Military Systems 191

19. Decision Making : Force Architecture & National Defence Capability 197

20. Perpetual War for Perpetual Peace : Limits to Power 205

21. Credible Nuclear Deterrance : Seven Years After 215

22. Private Military Companies in the New World Order 222

Index *229*

Preface

Public discourse amongst the intelligentsia appears to be increasingly circumscribed by the 'Washington Consensus' even though the project ostensibly pertains to the 'Reforms' agenda and determination of economic policies of Governments and parties who subscribe to it. The 'Consensus' confines the boundaries of discussion, debate, and polite conversation, specially in the Capital, New Delhi, within these parameters.

Corporate media, both TV and the 'mainstream' press and magazines, have been only too willing to publicize and endorse, throwing overboard objectivity and balance, the line with respect to issues and events, echoing and reflecting the propaganda emanating from Washington and the briefs issued from South Block.

TV personalities appear on evening shows to put the 'spin'. The subjects cover the entire spectrum: Iraq, vote on Iran, Indo-US Nuclear Agreement, July and Indo-US Defense Framework Agreement, June 2005, or even the insignificant and irrelevant Volcker Report, to cite just a few examples. Our deprived millions, their livelihood and security are of little concern to Corporate media which is eager to highlight the agenda of International Finance Capital and its junior partners. The global debate appears to camouflage the operation to capture and control the world's energy and mineral resources, simultaneously as MNCs and Banks pry open the markets. 'Democracy' and 'Freedom' also provide a convenient façade for this purpose. If Globalization is an imperialist enterprise, this is transparent.

There is only one correct assessment, one viewpoint, one perspective, and one vision. Issues which are vital to the people and the nation are seen only through the prism of the 'reforms' project . Everything is described as ' strategic'. That was once a word used on very rare occasions .

Where policies and statements of intent, in Parliament or outside, are indicative of a clear violation of the Constitution and the Directive Principles to uphold the common good, to prevent the concentration of wealth and monopoly, to provide for the well-being of all the people through state intervention, employment, equality of opportunity through equal education; all these and more are no longer considered of any relevance. 'Growth Rate' is the only coinage.

An independent foreign policy, non-alignment and self-reliance have been jettisoned. Principles of governance as laid out in the Constitution are similarly sidelined. Hence the public discourse is one sided. Any differing viewpoint is simply ignored as unwanted or summarily rejected and often suppressed in subtle and not so subtle ways .

These articles, present assessments and perspectives at variance with the 'accepted and patronized wisdom' in the Capital. An establishment may want to bury its head in the sand, like an ostrich, on grounds of pragmatism and expediency that we have to 'deviate and accept', because we are 'economically' weak and 'vulnerable', however, it should not for its own survival ignore alternative viewpoints and assessments. We were 'economically weak' from 1947 to

1984, due to the legacy of colonialism, but we did not look overseas for advise to chart our path of autonomous development with all its thorns. Consultants, country Directors, and interfering ambassadors were few and far between.

The book is intended to widen and deepen public discourse (though over the last few years or so the articles have been published in smaller circulated magazines, language newspapers, and in some widely-read international websites).

The author warmly appreciates the initiative and support of Shri Vivek Garg of Manas Publications in this attempt, to reach a wider circle of discerning and concerned fellow citizens.

1

Unlimited Militarisation

Delusions of World Hegemony

"There will be no peace. At any given moment for the rest of our life-time; there will be multiple conflicts in mutating forms around the globe ... violent conflicts will dominate the headlines ..." Paul Wolfowitz and Richard Perle wrote in the preamble, to the draft of the Project for the New American Century (PNAC), in 1992, during the heady days when the CIA's project for subversion of the Soviet Union had borne fruit.

The establishment of the New World Order demands coercion and force, preceded by the subversion of the targeted countries (mainly those with oil and mineral resources or large markets) which in the scale of its operations is unprecedented in history; hence the precise formulation of 'multiple conflicts in mutating forms around the globe', spelt out by Wolfowitz (now president of the World Bank). The warning has been sounded in the public domain. Third world ruling elites shutting their eyes and ears to this warning is another matter, perhaps in deference to their own class interests.

The Defence Planning Guidance, 1992, goes on to state, "The foreign policy of the US must be unapologetic, idealistic and well-funded. America must not only be the world's policeman or its sheriff, it must be its beacon and guide (sweeteners aplenty and democracy too, for civilisations five millennia old!) ... Our first objective must be to prevent the reemergence of a new rival. This is a dominant consideration underlying the new regional defence strategy and requires that we endeavour to prevent any hostile power from dominating a region whose resources would, under consolidated control, be sufficient to generate global power (The New Energy Policy Document 2001 is an adjunct to the PNAC). These regions include Western Europe, East Asia, the territory of the former Soviet Union and Southwest Asia (China has since been categorised as a strategic competitor) ..."

> In Washington DC in September 2005 US Vice President Cheney asserted that the 'War (on terror) could go on for several decades' reflecting the Bush Administration's commitment to global warfare.

"There are three additional objectives to this objective: First the US must show the leadership necessary to establish and protect a new order that holds the promise of convincing potential competitors that they need not aspire to a greater role or pursue a more aggressive posture to protect their legitimate interests; second, in the non-defence areas, we must account sufficiently for the interests of the advanced industrial nations, to discourage them from challenging our leadership or seeking to overturn the established political and economic order. Finally, we must maintain the mechanisms for deterring potential competitors from aspiring to a larger regional or global role."

One would have anticipated that there would be a comprehensive top-level review in view of the stalemate in Afghanistan and Iraq. Quite the contrary, if we are to go by the assertions of the National Security Strategy Document promulgated on March 1, 2005 by the Pentagon. It boldly states, "America is a Nation at war". 'New capabilities-based planning focuses more on how adversaries may challenge us than on whom those adversaries may be or where we might face them. We were in a time of unconventional challenges and strategic uncertainty'... The NSSD 2005 addresses the security of the American people, strengthening the comity of free nations, advancing democratic reforms and economic well-being around the world. The department of Defence is implementing the US president's commitment to the forward defense of freedom. The strategy emphasises the importance of influencing events before they become more dangerous and less manageable. Hence the doctrine of pre-emptive wars.

Addressing the Association of the US Army Sustaining Members in Washington DC in September 2005 US Vice-President Cheney asserted that the 'War (on terror) could go on for several decades' reflecting the Bush Administration's commitment to global warfare. Cheney said, "Like the great duties of history, it will require decades of patient effort and it will be resisted by those whose only hope is through the spread of violence." It requires, according to Cheney, the deployment of US forces worldwide in more than 100 countries rather than a select number of military bases, (watch the stationing of US forces in West Asia, creeping into Afghanistan, Pakistan, Nepal, Bangladesh and India, under cover). Cheney continues prognosticating, 'The US will be involved in military actions against 'failed states' and 'unstable states' a definition that will include not only the 'oil and mineral' states, but any and all member states of the UN! There is, as he says, 'terrorism to fight and protect the 'civilised states', promote democracy, spread 'Free Market' reforms worldwide.' However apart from the rhetoric that frequently adorns such doctrines and policy statements, the US military is focusing on operations by restructuring and redeploying its forces and intelligence assets for a long conflict in the Middle East, Central Asia and Russia, where nearly 70 per cent of the economically recoverable hydrocarbons lie. Hence the sustained complementary campaign to bring 'democracy' and hasten 'free-market economic reforms'.

> In 2006, US defence spending will exceed the total spending on defence of the rest of the world put together. Yet its soldiers had to buy their own Global Positioning System (GPS) fixing gadgets and in some cases bullet proof vests.

This is the context and the framework that is before us when we embark on a review of the changing nature of warfare, to make sense of the bewildering array of contradictions that confront us. Do we have a clear picture of our national interests? Do we appreciate sufficiently that the livelihoods and well-being of our 1050 million people (not just the creamy layer) is dependent on an independent, not dependent, balanced mix of political, economic, foreign/defence and S&T policies, not just the neo-liberal mantra advocated by the Washington Consensus and Wall Street? Military Commanders cannot lead their forces to victory if the nation has been economically hollowed out, as modern wars represent the will and resources of the nation in their totality.

In the US itself the social and financial downslide appears to be unstoppable. A fiscal deficit of $500 billion; a current account deficit of $700 billion; a nation in debt for trillions of dollars (7.7 trillions soaring by $2.3 billion daily with no savings), living on 80 per cent of the world's savings, borrowing almost $3 billion every day, having lost its once leading manufacturing base, spends more than $500 billion a year on the Defence budget, (with unfunded military procurement liabilities of more than a trillion dollars), and another $100 billion on Intelligence operations, maintains nearly 700 military bases globally and yet has its Army mired in Iraq and Afghanistan. In 2006, US defence spending will exceed the total spending on defence of the rest of the world put together. Yet its soldiers had to buy their own Global Positioning System (GPS) fixing gadgets and in some cases bullet proof vests too. When they return home with injuries or DU afflictions they have to partly pay for their treatment and meals at the hospitals!

> Several scientific papers assert that the AIDS virus was introduced into Africa, riding on the back of vaccine inoculations, as a part of the drive to reduce population, originating in the Army's Bio-warfare laboratory in Fort Detrick, Maryland.

The US's NATO allies spend another $225 billion on the military. Compare this with the defence spending of the three target countries, Syria, Iran and North Korea, the 'Axis of Evil' who together spend $8.5 billion, which is less than two per cent of the US defence budget! This is a strange paradox. These predatory wars are being financed by China, Japan, Taiwan, South Korea and petro-dollars from West Asia. Dollar-denominated oil trade upholds the dollar when the dollar is in reality of notional value and at risk. Yet it funds militarisation of space for first strikes with 'air burst' electronics disabling big bombs and neutron bombs to incapacitate people, SDI, new micro-nuke programmes, bio-chemical warfare (BCW) weapons, war-breaker strategies and cyber warfare to paralyse an adversary's central nervous systems like command and communications, power, telecom and water supply.

Weaponisation of the sea bed, Depleted Uranium munitions, new attack systems to achieve information and full spectrum dominance weather/climate warfare which experts call the 'ultimate WMD' and which Zbigniew Brzezinski advocated long ago as National Security Adviser to be part of National Security Policy, are also products of those war research programmes, as well as the High Frequency Active Auroral Research programme (HAARP), gene warfare applications (genetic bombs) to attack specific gene types (based on the complete cataloguing of the human gene sequence expressed as DNA/RNA), courtesy directions given by Wolfowitz and Kristol.

Several scientific papers assert that the AIDS virus was introduced into Africa, riding on the back of vaccine inoculations, as a part of the drive to reduce population, originating in the Army's Bio-warfare laboratory in Port Detrick, Maryland. As for the extensive use of Depleted Uranium munitions in Gulf War 1991, Kosovo, Afghanistan and Iraq the US Uranium Medical Research Center, Washington DC and the Bulletin of Atomic Scientists have published extensive reports by field teams in Afghanistan. The European Parliament Report, (ECRR) 2003, has documented the contamination of water systems,

> The media orchestration of a coming cancer epidemic in India to smoke-screen DU munitions effect is part of the cover up on DU.

ground and air environment, that can cause cancer, gene mutation, heart disease, autism, Parkinson's, asthma, chronic fatigue syndrome, slow destruction of the body's immunity. Countries lying within a 1000 mile radius of Kabul and Baghdad are being affected by radiation poisoning. The media orchestration of a coming cancer epidemic in India to smoke-screen DU munitions effect is part of the cover up on DU. If we think cancer is a problem, much worse lies ahead when more DU is released in the course of 'wars against terror' and for regime change based on 'mistaken' intelligence reports.

The use of DU in the Gulf War/Kosovo and now in Afghanistan and Iraq has already back-fired on US soldiers, their families and offspring. Bio-warfare agents have demonstrated themselves to generate their own blowback. The officer son of General Westmoreland, the Commanding General of the US Army in Vietnam, was afflicted by cancer after the use of Agent Orange. The US President is now requesting some $4 billion from Congress to prepare for quarantine arrangements under the control of the army (until now not allowed to deploy at home by the US Constitution) in anticipation of the mutated gene Avian Bird Flu pandemic, presented as an internal threat requiring military quarantine of regions and cities as per the statements emanating from White House.

The policy for targeting with micro-nukes was jointly decided by corporate heads and senior military general officers at the US Air Force Strategic Command Headquarters, Offut Airforce Base, Nebraska, in August 2002. The CIA's covert operations responsibilities have been transferred to the Pentagon. The CIA was assessed to be too timid in the 'War on Terror' regimes! This signals a dramatic shift in the character of the US military, the consequences of which will become apparent to developing country elites in the immediate future.

"These robots do not get hungry. They are not afraid, they do not forget their orders. They don't care if the guy next to them has just been shot. They are far cheaper and yes they do a better job than human soldiers", a stinging indictment of the US soldiers in Iraq and Afghanistan!

Robotised warfare is expected to be waged by an "Unbeatable Robotic Army" entitled 'Future Combat System'. Says General Gordon Johnson of the US Joint Force Command, of the robots born of nano-technology, "These robots do not get hungry. They are not afraid, they do not forget their orders. They don't care if the guy next to them has just been shot. They are far cheaper and yes they do a better job than human soldiers"; a stinging indictment of the US soldiers in Iraq and Afghanistan! Unmanned Aerial Vehicles (UAVs), getting increasingly versatile, also fall in the category of 'robots' in the air.

The US Defence Advanced Research Projects Agency (DARPA) has programmes and contracts running in hundreds of universities, research labs, private military companies (PMCs), and think-tanks also in foreign countries. DARPA synergises the combined R&D budgets of the civilian and military sectors as integration of the two is facilitated by micro-electronics, micro-electro-mechanical systems (MEMS) and nano-technologies, all of which have military applications in software and hardware. Laser weapons, charged particle beam or directed electro-magnetic weapons (E-Bombs), 'Black-out bombs' (incapacitating agents), mind-control, psycho-pharmacology agents, acoustic weapons, optical/visual weapons are some of the projects in various stages of operationalisation.

When serving Indian military commanders speak, after they take over as chiefs of 'Network Centric Warfare' (NCW) one only hopes they are not merely echoing out of context their counterparts in the West. Just to take this as an example, 'NCW' has its pitfalls like overload, slow response to military operations other than war. NCW favours the mean and cheap force structure, "shoot first asks questions later" approach and resurrects old myths like 'strategic bombing'. What did second generation warfare achieve in Korea or Vietnam? What will fourth generation warfare achieve in Iraq?

Yet in the face of these esoteric weapon systems, the fact is that nations and peoples which refuse to accept defeat cannot be vanquished. In this context it is relevant to quote the Iraqi Resistance. It may be recalled that Iraq was supplied with weapons by the West for the duration of its war with Iran which weakened both nations. Thereafter it faced the 1991 Gulf War, 12 years of crippling sanctions, 'no fly zones' in its own airspace, half a million children died, its water supply was denied simple bacteria-killing medicines, machinery spare parts were prohibited for import, oil revenues curtailed and oil infrastructure adversely affected. The invasion and the occupation's devastating damage to basic civic services, and its long suffering people notwithstanding, the spirit of the Iraqi nation lives and has driven a super power's army into a quagmire. The Iraqi Resistance has taken on this Hi-tech Coalition armed force, and its statement reads "Over two million innocents died waiting for the light at the end of the tunnel. It is our duty as well as our right, to beat back the occupation, whose nations will be held morally accountable. We did not cross the oceans to occupy Britain and the United States. And we are not responsible for 9/11. These are only a few of the horrid lies that these criminals brandish to cover their true plans for the pillage of our country's energy resources. We thank all those, including those in Britain, the USA and elsewhere who took to the streets to protest against the war. We do not require arms or fighters. We have plenty. We are asking you to form a worldwide front against the war, occupation, and sanctions. The enemy is on the run. They have no place to hide. Like rats they are being driven into the corner. They are in fear of the Resistance fighters every moment of their lives. They can neither see nor predict. We can now choose when, where and how to strike; in much the same way as our ancestors harnessed the first sparks of civilisation. We shall now proceed to define the word 'conquest'. At present we are writing a new chapter in the arts of urban and rural resistance warfare."

> 'Peaking of Oil', however much it may be underplayed, impinges on military planning underpinning geo-political moves on the global chessboard.

There are some overarching features that have to be kept in mind in assessing the situation:

1. That the US by sheer dint of military presence and capability has become a neighbour to all States.
2. 'Peaking of Oil', however much it may be underplayed, impinges on military planning underpinning geo-political moves on the global chessboard.
3. Vastly telescoped time-periods of development of systems from the lab to the field and rapid obsolescence of military technology *per se* are creating imbalances and bursting of planned budgets due to over-reliance on technical gadgets and under-confidence in leadership and strategy.
4. A recent example of this is how the operationalisation of the Russian Topol-M, also designated as the SS XN 30/27, (*Baluva* in the submarine version, with a manoeuvrable, MIRV, electronic-cum-laser and heat shielded warhead, and a 10,000 km range), supersonic missile has put a spanner in the SDI or Star Wars and ABM Defence works on which a decade and more of research and hundreds of billions of dollars appear to have been wasted.
5. Only for a few years of this decade will the only Super Power get away with military invasion, capture and occupation of a country or region. The roll-back has begun from forces of resistance, the anti-war movement of the people of the United States and the horrific consequences of global warming on the coast and mainland of the US taking a heavy toll, equivalent to a military invasion or attack which HAARP and all the technologies of weather warfare are unable to prevent. A flu pandemic of the kind referred to by the White House, requiring military-imposed quarantine would be catastrophic in terms of the political fall-out effect, apart from straining the budget of the United States, its organisation and resources already depleted by the wars in Afghanistan and Iraq and covert operations across the globe.

> Hence, war plans will have to be recast and reoriented to rapidly inflict the maximum damage to the adversary's military assets and selected economic targets.

The cost of future military invasions and sustained occupations is beyond the financial and organisational capacity of the US, affected by the insecurity of supplies of hydrocarbon resources from the affected regions. Other countries will have to give up any plans for annexation of territory in a conventional offensive. This option is foreclosed by UN actions which will force a cease-fire in most cases within 4/5 days. Hence, war plans will have to be recast and reoriented to rapidly inflict the maximum damage to the adversary's military assets and selected economic targets. This reality has to be appreciated by the political and military establishments; otherwise we may end up in the stalemate of India's 'Operation Parakrama' which began with the bombastic assertion of 'teaching a lesson' and ended up with a whimper and attrition losses running into thousands of crores of Rupees (hundreds of millions of dollars), in replacement costs of equipment and machines, tanks and aircraft engines. The then Army Chief General S Padmanabhan reports in his interviews and books that when he asked the Prime Minister to explain to the Armed Forces the political objectives to be achieved with a given time frame, the latter replied *Woh Baad Mein Batayenge* (That we will communicate later); a clarification that never came during the ten months that the largest mobilisation since 1971, was maintained!

'Economic warfare' and subversion of the economy chart a steady path to political alienation and break-up of federal structures. A popular quote says it all: 'a banker is more feared than a whole army division'.

Such is the political leadership that happily sanctions US$30 billion for conventional arms imports, and spends US$5 to 7 billion annually to defend the borders, while at the same time opening up the country to big ticket privatisation and foreign ownership, and capital outflows, unmindful of the sobering experiences of Latin American nations, Indonesia, Turkey, Eastern Europe, post-1991 Russia, and now Africa. It simply refuses to acknowledge that 'economic warfare' and subversion of the economy chart a steady path to political alienation and break-up of federal structures. A popular quote says it all 'a banker is more feared than a whole army division'.

6) The triad of narcotics, gun running and terrorism is as ruinous as an armed insurgency, the latter often being sustained by all three. Proxy war is usually a concurrent activity.

7) Middle-men in the Arms trade are the carriers on which subversion of key officials of the defence establishment rides.

8) The subversion of the civil and military structures and their infiltration by counter-intelligence is often the first objective of foreign penetration of targeted countries. The rules of the game and *modus operandi* have changed a little in past centuries as Lawrence Lifschultz so well puts it in his book. "Just over two centuries ago a contingent of 800 irregular soldiers faced an army of nearly 80,000 troops from the Nawab of Bengal's standing forces. Not only was there numerical superiority on the Bengal side, but in this instance artillery and technical supremacy were also against the European force. Nevertheless in the most miserable skirmish ever to be called a decisive battle the Europeans walked off with a victory which would change world history. That was the Battle of Plassey. The date was June 23, 1757." (Lawrence Lifeschultz, *Bangladesh: The Unfinished Revolution,* London, Zed Books, 1979).

All sorts of racial, national and historical myths developed out of this event, but the story of the conquest of Bengal was no mystery. In the modern parlance of the Western Intelligence community, what happened was a classic 'covert' operation carried through with great clandestine success. There never was a military defeat of the Nawab of Bengal's army. The method of securing victory was much simpler: the Commander of the Nawab's armed forces had secretly been bought off by the British before either side had reached the mango groves around Plassey.

> From the incident at Plassey onwards, the British waged more or less continuous war against the Indian people 'consolidating their power' in India while conquering other regions, breaking up the old systems of self-sufficient villages, and supporting an elite whose self-interest would harmonise with British rule.

Through an astute and subtle understanding of the political factions within the Bengali leadership and ruling class; by carefully distinguishing the patriotic from the corrupt; and through an unabashed capacity to buy and sell *comprador* loyalty from those who deal in ambitions of power, the small British expeditionary force under Robert Clive secured its military triumph by a neat gamble on prior political arrangement. From the incident at Plassey onwards, the British waged more or less continuous war against the Indian people, 'consolidating their power' in India while conquering other regions, breaking up the old systems of self-sufficient villages, and supporting an elite whose self-interest would harmonise with British rule.

Over the next century an entire world was remade and reshaped by the expansion of the British empire. In Bengal a pre-capitalist mode of production was totally transformed. Indigo, jute, tea, opium, private property of land, *Zamindari* landlordism, land tax, and the right to buy and sell a peasant's property, to extract debt from him were all introduced. From its staging post in South Asia, the new Europe-based epoch of commerce and modern industry broke open markets throughout Asia with the rumble of war and the 'right' to an open door.

After Vietnam, the prevailing environment is once again beset with unforeseen problems as the situation in Afghanistan and Iraq is stalemated; the military-technological prowess is impressive, 'State to State' contests having been easily won, but the people and their quaint nationalism stands unvanquished. The phoenix of the 'end of history' has risen from the ashes to haunt the victors, leaving little space for an honourable retreat, without irreparable loss of prestige which may foreclose possibilities for other such adventures, predicated on military dominance alone. Some blame is sought to be placed on insufficient

The situation in Afghanistan and Iraq is stalemated; the military-technological prowess is impressive, 'State to State' contests having been easily won, but the people and their quaint nationalism stands unvanquished.

priority given to 'Stability and Support Operations' (SASO) and the civil-military mix of the SASO. Such superficial understanding betrays a total disregard for Afghan and Iraqi nationalism. Surprises happen. In this case the surprise is the people. Regime changes with imposed NRAs or NRIs who have lived and worked for Western establishments are usually not bought by the people. A mix of 'throw-away' soldiers, mercenaries supplied by private military companies, special forces working *incognito* behind the scenes and local armies hastily assembled can hardly face 'assymetric warfare' by people's militias with the will to do or die.

The expanding role of NATO eastwards to Central Asia, Afghanistan, Africa and possibly West Asia cannot be a cause of comfort to anyone who has studied their thinking and planning processes. A repeat of the Iraq process to capture some of the largest energy resources outside the control of the US, concerns all who have an interest in accessing on strictly commercial terms, Iran's surplus energy resources for export. Iran is India's neighbour and in the eventuality of its invasion, occupation and loot of its resources under the pretext of stopping its nuclear development programme, the entire West Asian region and the Indian sub-continent are likely to become cauldrons that will boil over with unpredictable consequences and which the US and its allies can hardly hope to keep under control.

The people of the United States themselves are realising the diabolical game of 'war on terror' at home and abroad, a war for the profits of certain corporations, entailing criminal neglect of the majority of the unemployed and low wage work force.

The people of the United States themselves are realising the diabolical game of 'war on terror' at home and abroad, a war for the profits of certain corporations, entailing criminal neglect of the majority of the unemployed and low wage work-force at home left without healthcare, medicare, decent housing and education. They have begun to see through such hollow initiatives as the 'Africa opportunity and growth act', another name for neo-colonial capture of resources and markets.

American Presidents in the past sounded alarm bells about increasing Corporate and Big Business influence. General Dwight Eisenhower's warning, near the term of his presidency on the 'military-industrial complex' is well known. Since then corporations in the advanced capitalist nations have not only installed their men in leading positions in the state's apparatus, they have also taken an increasing share of the orders for new military acquisitions, logistics contracts and R&D budgets. The 'revolving door' policy for civilian and military personnel in the Pentagon and in defence-related companies enables the Generals and Admirals to secure lucrative second careers in the corporate sector and the think-tanks funded by it. Is it any surprise therefore, that the essential ethos and character of the military leadership has changed from 'Duty, Honour, Country' to the pursuit of private gain, specially in the years approaching retirement? The corporate quest for oil, minerals and markets has never before so openly determined the agenda, and the time-table for invasions, regime changes, occupation and plunder. It may well be that behind the public façade of the Pentagon and Whitehall, the direction for this century's military emanates, without any fuss from the Corporate Board Rooms.

It is appropriate to quote the eminent historian Michael Howard, since most men in power are forgetful of history... He writes: "Let me repeat the analogy about the drunk who lost his watch in a dark alley, but was found looking for it under a lamp-post because there was more light there. The light provided by our knowledge of technological capabilities and our capacity for strategic analysis is so dazzling as to be almost hypnotic; but it is in those shadowy regions of human understanding based on our knowledge (and understanding) of social development, cultural diversity and patterns of human behaviour that we have to look for the answers." If one may say 'men and women willing to sacrifice all for a cause'!

Corporations in the advanced capitalist nations have not only installed their men in leading positions in the state's apparatus, they have also taken an increasing share of the orders for new military acquisitions, logistics contracts and R&D budgets.

To conclude with an observation attributed to a school teacher who turned into the greatest General of the last century, Vo Nguyen Giap, whom I had the honour of meeting, in 1990, in Mumbai: "McNamara and his advisers have raised the numbers of invaders to around half a million. What are the consequences? They have vastly deployed chemical defoliants (Agent Orange *et al*) and other terrible engines of mass destruction. Certainly these will vastly increase the number of deaths and impose additional, appalling sufferings on our people. It will not however loosen the grip of our fight for freedom. It will enhance it. In the end our resistance fighters will triumph."

Essentially as Harold Pinter, the Nobel Prize winner said in his speech in the House of Commons, it is the US (and its allies) versus the rest of the world. Media reports quote India's Prime Minister Dr. Manmohan Singh as saying that "it was necessary to arrive at the truth from the facts", an unexceptionable principle. The question is which facts and which reality one is looking at—the picture of truth and reality that the leaders of the US, UK and their corporate media paint or the reality of millions of women and children trampled upon, mutilated, mass murdered, tortured and of deformed babies born in the cradle of the world's civilisation? The consequences of pre-emptive, unilateral war, integral to the PNAC, outside the UN system, cannot be passed over as 'a mistake'. More such 'mistakes' are on the anvil as India has signed up for joint operations, logistics and material support with the 'super-power'; a power in precipitous economic and social decline. The June 2005 Indo-US Defence pact/agreement and the August 2005 Indo-US 'strategic' pact appear at first to rely on tenuous logic and 'thin' facts. However they are a natural, pre-meditated consequence of the privatisation/de-nationalisation of key public enterprises, at first to be taken over by 'Indian' companies with loans from public sector banks and then by foreign financial interests via the 'acquisitions and mergers' process enabled by FDI. Foreign military intervention to 'save' these now foreign-owned assets from the people who first created them with their savings is not uncommon. There is still time to ensure the security of the overwhelming majority of the Indian people from this disastrous course but this would require a different focus and orientation.

The strategic course of US militarisation unmistakenly leads to a *cul-de-sac*. However, given the frenetic and unlimited funding for new and deadlier weapon systems (specially bio and gene warfare) which will kill people in the millions or billions, these are issues that cannot be ignored. Th basis for weapons development is political and military, hence a closer focus is required when concerns nearer home are reflected as in the speech of the US Ambassador to NATO at Brussels on September 22, 2005 "... Afghanistan would remain NATO's most important mission"... for the foreseeable future. Add to this the designation of Pakistan as 'the Most Important Non-NATO Ally' and 'India chosen as the US-supported, budding Big Power of the Region' according to the Bush-Manmohan Singh Strategic alliance Agreement.

> Foreign military intervention to 'save' these now foreign-owned assets from the people who first created them with their savings is not uncommon.

Yet the strategic demands of the twenty first century lie exactly in the opposite direction.

2

War, at the Speed of Thought

Cyber War is not coming, it is here; and we are burying our heads like ostrich, not wanting to prepare ourselves for it. This is a civil-military combined system of systems, and its cutting edges are usually defined in terms of microprocessors, telecommunications and even more importantly, software algorithms, both in the offensive and defensive roles. Its conflict zone is not confined by terrestrial space and since it is technology-driven, its onward march cannot be halted. We can be the new 'slaves' in the new world order if we ignore it, or at least reasonably incharge of our destiny if we grasp it in the mind and rationalize in operationalizing this novel dimension.

It is neither an invention nor a discovery; there was no *eureka,* but it did gain momentum from President Reagan's Strategic Defence Initiative, popularly known as the Star Wars, the Defense Advanced Research Projects Agency (DARPA), and to driving strategies, conceived and conceptualized by the Pentagon which acted as a stimulus to a very large civilian sector R&D innovative, creative, and adaptive culture whose architecture considered necessary (appropriately named Coppernicus), subsequent to its first *nom-de-plume* 'Sonata' by its conceptualizer Admiral William Owens, Vice Chairman, US Joint Chiefs of Staff until 1996. The hierarchical command and staff chain of information flow was broken in favour of mission achievement. The multi-path flow of information became instantaneous, sensor to shooter connectivity put in place in the

Gulf War, in days, what could not be done earlier in NATO, in the preceding four decades. The other major objective — 'War Breaker Technology', which aims at completely paralyzing, the command and control networks, telecommunications and transportation centres, energy nodes, and even the water supplies, in the first 72 hours from the decision point. So, not only was the 'Orient, Observe, Decision and Action' cycle put in a near instantaneous loop but whether in war, short of war or no-war-no-peace, the punishment meted out could be catastrophic, measured, and calibrated by the political requirements in the new world order.

I have used the word 'Rev—Evolution' because this whole new 'System', or the concept is both Revolutionary and Evolutionary, depending on how we wish to approach or pursue it.

The General Communication Headquarters (GCHQ), Cheltenham, UK; and the largest surveillance agency (much larger than the CIA), the National Security Agency, USA; with its two supporting pillars, the National Geospatial Agency and the National Mapping Agency, have been running this business successfully, with the Third World leaderships and elites, unaware, unmindful and deliberately neglectful, that every CCB telegram, all transmissions in the ether, across the entire frequency spectrum, telecom centres, secrecy (scrambling) devices and even their secret rendezvous and pillow-talks are digitized, video-recorded, available for blackmail or pressure, with the help of sophisticated Voice Recognition Transcripts, on call.

Only China, amongst the 'target' countries, appears to be taking resolute steps on this front *per se*. Brilliant papers in the public domain, by the Chinese institutes, pushing for the common but parallel telecom backbone, with interconnecting nodes, indigenous software switching protocols, to overcome riding on imported or assembled computer systems, increasing lengths in the countrywide system, being connected by fibre optics, are systematically being used to decrease their vulnerability. The Chinese are there in the US, studying in situ. In 1985, Shen Weiguang, a 25 year-old Chinese soldier, serving the PLA, wrote a monograph on Information Warfare. His work foresaw Information as an over-arching feature of society across the spectrum of the civil and the military. In 1996, China established a top-secret Information Warfare Centre which comes under the direct control of the Central Committee, with representatives from every important department.

The American Government and those responsible for Counter Computer Warfare Systems, are no doubt aware of all this. While the Presidential Commission on Infrastructure Vulnerability, is meticulously working to reduce their own vulnerabilities, all 'export' systems have 'trap-doors', 'virus' and 'sleepers', with compliments of the exporters; and no amount of fire-walls will protect the 'target country', unless it has itself devised indigenous algorithms and protocols which are impenetrable; and that is a tall order... a long, hard road.

Other accompanying 'Revolutions' the Micro-Electronic Mechanical Systems (MEMs), Unmanned Aerial Vehicles (UAVs), Electronic Detecting Devices, the size of silent beatles, Microprocessors, Miniaturized Trans-Receivers, the GPS, Virtual Reality Displays (VRDs) on the forearm, Robot-Bugs instead of Grenades, which can put a missile system to 'sleep', Head Up Displays (HUDs), which can be slashed on to local or the tactical pictures to see what is happening behind the hill or round the corner. This is not fantasy, it is happening in the labs; and the labs to production cycle are now highly telescoped and, therefore, economical. The 'Competition' is here.

There is a whole gigantic mass of inertia in the General Staff, Naval Staff and Air Staff. It is not that people have not known that winning demands 50 per cent of the financial resources to be allocated to 'Support Systems'. There were the Sail Battleships, then came the 'Iron-Clads', the Horse Cavalry—replaced by Tanks, the old War-Ships by Aircraft Carriers and Submarines, and the Manned Aircraft, if not wholly replaceable for the next two decades, need imagery 'while on mission' targeting data 'while on mission' damage assessment, from the previous strikes, AWACs support, Land Attack Cruise Missiles with revisit facility—none of these will work with the designed level of effectiveness and efficiency against a real Cyber Competitor, nor deter it. The US Military is not going to permit any nation to come within one million steps from the lead it holds, and the bag of tricks it has has developed in its advanced laboratories. Even without Cyber War and Cyber Space, they know that the fourth largest Air Force, that is the IAF, lacks both the sub-systems, the support systems and the personnel planning and career-cum-professional structure, that will make it an all-weather Air Force, capable of fighting at night. So, the simple thumb rule—since the Third World Air Forces are not trained or equipped to fly at night, in actual fact, their effective fighting strength is not more than 30 per cent of their holdings, if the fighting is concentrated in the dark hours. This calculation is without counting the multipliers in support systems like AWACs, Electronic Warfare, Digital Data Warfare and countless other devices that exist, in the inventory of the United States, to make deaf, dumb and blind, those who do not heed the call of the times or were only partially doing so. Or those who just do lip service, calculate and depend on the 'bean-count'—a self-styled 'regional superpower' cannot emerge without matching capabilities. Chanting 'National Security, unthinkingly, increase Defence Budgets for hardware, result in *all the King's men and all the King's horses cannot put Humpty Dumpty together again'.*

The start-up on Information Warfare or Cyber Warfare has been made in our Navy, but this is not a part of any national priority, as there is no national priority. It is not just the size of the Defence Budget, as the BJP manifesto in January 1998 alleged, which came down from 3.4 per cent of GDP in 1989-'90 to 2.2 per cent in 1997-'98, that imperils national security. We can allocate 5 per cent or even 10 per cent of the GDP to Defence. Will that serve national security? If we do not know where to go, which direction, what will make the difference, and do not re-capitalize our Defence holdings, replacing the same old things with more of the same, albeit with a new model and number plate, does not enhance national security. At the best it provides an illusory security. In the times ahead, it may just mean more tracked motor vehicles stopped dead on their tracks! Cyber War capabilities drastically reduce the fog and fiction of war.

If we forge the essential capabilities in Cyber War, it will leverage both our foreign and domestic policies and security, otherwise we will be constantly blackmailed and *de facto,* enslaved. War has been described as a human contest that rewards innovation, learning, adaptability and flexibility. Peace demands even more of these virtues, and more so, when the survival of one billion people is at stake.

The US Military conceived, funded, and operationalized the Internet as a redundancy, against a catastrophic attack on the country's capital city and key population centres. Now, the Internet is a kind of a Trojan Horse! The US Military is operationalizing an advanced Internet, wholly dedicated to the US 'command and control' functions. Cyber War is also described as War by Other Means (WBOM), through control of the electronic or the electromagnetic medium/space.

If we want to fight and defend ourselves at our doorstep, we may continue to do what we have been doing. If we want to reach out to fight in the adversary's backyard and further want to reach out to our strategic frontiers, then it really is the last call for the Generals and Admirals, who regrettably have been planning wars, that they have known of.

General Colin Powell succinctly defined this 'command and control' warfare, C2W, because it is aimed at the brain (or Cyber Centre) of the Enemy and his central nervous system or means for the Central Direction of War. The military and the civilian leaderships, both have to educate the present and future establishments, not to hold on to the anachronism of the past. Today, product creation to delivery, to market times of as little as six months are becoming common, particularly in computational systems and software.

For the Military Commanders, the questions were defined by General Franks, in TRADOC, in 1994:

> What is my Mission?
> What is the enemy doing (Planning)?
> How can I keep him from knowing what I'm 'doing' and lead him to believe that what I'm doing is something else?

Where am I vulnerable, and does the enemy know it? Where is the enemy vulnerable, and how can I exploit it and win, at least cost?

A powerful and determined school of scholar-warriors are set to take forward the Cyber Warriors. The United States would never fight a war where two armies meet on a battlefield. Instead, wars would be fought through Cyber Space, Computer Bugs, Viruses designed to paralyze an enemy, and bring him to his knees without firing a shot. These Armed Forces are addressing a change through Special Task Groups. The Pentagon is proceeding systematically to invest in the future and reduce costs on present assets and replacements. While it will not be one long leap to Cyber War, the process has to move forward, balancing the conventional with the new path, until the new pathway is completed to face the challenges of 2010 and 2020. Advanced Distribution Simulation and Virtual Reality engines or VR responsive workbenches will prove and justify such fundings. A career invested in the status quo cannot stop the 'Rev-Evolution'. The military mindset is being changed by the speed of innovation, by MEMs, with engineering, at the microscopic level. Competent munitions, a marriage of dumb shells and guidance through control surfaces driven by the GPS, improve accuracy by 90 per cent. This has already happened, and I am mentioning just one very small area.

In Information Warfare and Counter Information Warfare, as James Adams perceptively commends, "Government groups based on conservatism, conformity and stability of tenure, cannot match hackers who exist on wits, adrenaline and iconoclasm." So, not only have the Cyber Terrorists to be neutralized, wherever possible, they may have to be co-opted as partners. President Clinton's Commission on Critical Infrastructure Protection had also been tasked with reporting on the Threat to America's Computer Systems and Networks, particularly those, Governing Telecommunications, Oil and Gas, Electricity, Banks and Financial Operations, Transportation, Water Supplies, Critical Emergency Response and Government. The RED team was recently put into action by the US Joint Chiefs of Staff to test the ability of the military and political structures to withstand a concerted Cyber

Attack, in an exercise called 'Eligible Receiver' which disrupted logistics, plans, crisis response sub-systems, Central Direction of War—and this was done by young hired hackers, using commercially available information, and constrained by the rules of the game... and not surprisingly, they surprised quite a few. Empowered Robotic Agents, supplied with the systems embedded, could be used to take autonomous actions, as programmed against the Host or remote systems or networks. Network Penetration could achieve the ends for both, whoever is more competent and capable, the Attacker or the Defender. To quote Admiral Cebrowski, who previously headed the US Navy's Space and Electronic Warfare Division and also served as Director, Command, Control, Communications and Intelligence, C4I, for the Joint Chiefs of Staff, "Offensive Information Warfare, the ability to destroy an enemy's Information Systems, is pivotal to future deterrence and defense... The strategic landscape, is forever changed, he said, like when nuclear weapons appeared".

With or without the Cyber War capability, we need to be warned against the National Security Agency, which has "the biggest and the best ears in the world". There is nothing that it doesn't hear. Way back, in 1993, when I was the Deputy Chief; the United States knew in advance, through intercepts, that we were secretly carrying out an anti-hijacking drill, on a particular Indian Airlines flight, Delhi-Bhopal, and we can be sure that with our unshielded, open-wire systems, everything of interest, in the North and South Block, and even the Prime Minister's residence, is listened into, and confirmed by Humint sources. 'Back doors' are an integral part of our PCs in the offices and homes.

We have outstanding people in the IITs and in our country, but they are generally kept outside the DRDO system on the specious ground of security. The DRDO, with its unstable, constantly shifting personnel in the software groups, who leave at will, cannot serve our full spectrum needs, especially in this dynamically shifting area.

3

National Security

The Contemporary Context

National Security is no longer defined in unidimensional terms, as a Military endeavour. It now embraces a framework which is multidimensional, stretching from the Security of citizens across the spectrum, to Energy Security, and the Security of Financial Systems.

The National Security Policy Document of the United States, published by the White House, in December 1999 (again revised in 2002, 2005 and March 2006), comprises some 50,000 words, but the word, 'Military' is mentioned only about five to six times. This speaks for itself.

Just seven years ago, when the present President, Dr. A.P.J. Abdul Kalam, was spending an evening in our house, my wife put to him the proposition that, while he had led his team to engineer Ballistic Missiles to put fright into nations across our borders, had he thought of providing systems, which would protect and defend ordinary citizens on the streets, in their villages! Dr. Kalam was dumbstruck and remained silent, lost in thoughts!

This trend of thinking was once again reflected in a Report, rendered by one of my Officers, deputed for a course of study, at the US East-West Centre at Honolulu, where a group was diligently at work, on a study entitled, *'Conflicts Over Food and Water in South Asia'*. It is such Papers, that form essential inputs into the National Security scenario-building and contingency planning in the United States. Take the Case Study of Imposition of Sanctions, pertaining to Export of Chemicals and Equipment, required for Water Purification Plants for Iraq. The US has been responsible for the death of nearly a million children, according to the UNICEF, but it does not demur. Inter-state disputes over sharing of River Waters, the recently foisted agenda of Public-Private Partnership, and Privatization of Water, by the World Bank-Transnationals, is an extension of such Studies. The call for review of the Indus Waters Treaty, the unending discussions with Nepal, on Joint-Control of Anti-Flood Schemes in Nepal, and the outstanding issues of Water and Water Transportation, carry the potential for future conflicts. Conflicts over Water are nowadays a daily feature in our media; between the States, in the Villages, between the haves and the have nots, and in the Urban Areas, where a single tap with few hours of water supply, is the cause of violence. At the same time, the new craze for 'Privatization', is being extended to Water Resources. Lengths of Rivers, Dams, Water Bodies and City Water Supply Systems, in 40 cities, have already been handed over to Private interests. If the objective is to build a cohesive society, in which we participate in common endeavour to create Security for all, then this Policy is fundamentally disruptive for the Security of the people.

The 'Food' Weapon has been a part of the Western Arsenal, for decades. It was articulated in 'public domain', by Henry Kissinger, during the then President of USA, Nixon's Presidency. Diverse tactics have been used; be it the seduction of countries like Nigeria, Mali, Malawi, or the efforts which are on, in India, to switch from Food-crops to Cash-crops (despite the steadily falling prices of Cash-crops), rendering them vulnerable to Food Shortages, and consequently, accepting dumping of imported GM Food-grains, to impoverish people, deprive them of their meagre livelihoods, and cause ruination of agricultural economies, so as to destabilize these countries.

Nutrition Security relates to Health and Development of the Child in particular, and if, as the saying goes, 'A Chain Is as Strong, as Its Weakest Link', then we are hardly embarked on the path of becoming a 'Developed' Nation, or strengthening the foundations of National Security, in which the people's stake and participation is the central concern.

While the Edible Oil Technology Mission, and Dr. Kurien's White Revolution, contributed to National Security in a big way, the post-reform years are demolishing these great achievements. The progressive dismantling of the PDS, the FCI, and plans to privatize them, and active encouragement to creation of monopoly of the traders, is placing the majority of our people into the hands of profiteers, hoarders, and black marketeers, who have little respect or regard for human life. We should be building on Edible Oil Banks, Grain Banks, and Seed Banks, supplemented by a Food for Work Programmes, to renew land, water, forest, fisheries, livestock assets instead, which will all contribute towards People's Security, Economic Security and building of a cohesive society.

In a deteriorating social, economic and political environment, lawless groups seem to be increasingly beyond the reach of law; in fact, many a times they tacitly work in collusion with the police, and effectively subvert the criminal-justice system. Be it the underworld or the mafias, the safety and security of the citizen, his home, family, neighbourhood, village, street and city, are increasingly under siege. Armies secure the country's Borders, based on the presumption that, their rear areas are strong and secure.

The Security of Energy Supplies is vital for an Energy Deficient country, like ours. The bulk of our Energy Fuels are imported across the seas, and whether it is power-generation, national transportation network, industry, agriculture, or the home-fires, they are all import-dependent.

The Financial and Currency System is increasingly subjected to the new predator — International, Speculative Finance Capital, the big Currency Traders (George Soros *et al*) , who wrecked the South-East Asian economies, only nine years ago, and are in an invisible league with the new local parasitical class, which exports money, Rupees for Dollars. Fortunately, while countries across the globe have been raided, we have been partially saved because we have resisted 'Full Currency Convertibility'. Money laundering, whether through *"Hawala"* channels, or 'Private Banking' facilities, illegal outflow money in our system are a menace. The Collection Centres, hosted by many countries, are called 'Offshore Corporate Bodies', or OCBs and tax havens.

An important dimension of Contemporary Security Concern, is the threat to a country's sovereignty, from what Prof. Chussodovsky calls, "Economic Terrorism", arising from 'Restructuring and Stabilization' Programmes, which have just the opposite effect, forced down by the IMF and World Bank-IFC, on behalf of the NATO and G-7. They act on behalf of the US and other MNCs. The National Security establishment in India appears to be, or rather pretends to be, wholly innocent about this.

One of the most tragic victims of this Economic Terrorism, is former Yugoslavia, though the cases of former USSR, East Europe, and down the line--of Latin America, Africa, and some Asian countries, are also similar. The global and national mass media have concealed more than they have revealed: the forcible, stage-by-stage break up of Yugoslavia, is a consequence of the SAP imposed on Yugoslavia, by its Western Creditors, the London and Paris Clubs, followings the IMF Loan, taken by Yugoslavia. This led to the brutal impoverishment and unemployment of its once prosperous people. This programme, deliberately imposed, created and fostered ethnic hatred and cleansing, pursuant to the objective of the National Security Decision Directive (NSDD 133), titled: *'US Policy towards Yugoslavia',* a censored version of which was later declassified, and which envisaged the break-up of the Balkans, and its integration into the 'Free-Market' Economy, for the benefit of the MNCs, Western Banks, and financial institutions.

It is necessary to refer to some of these acts of Economic Terrorism, as these have implications on our Security and Integrity:

1. Run away Import Liberalization which devastated the Yugoslav industry.

2. The Central Government, in view of the pressure on Debt Servicing, was directed by the IMF, and World Bank, on behalf of Creditor Nations, to suspend payments, due to the Federated Republics and regions, which fuelled the process of 'Balkanization' and Secession, as resentment mounted in various regions, and created a De-facto Secession by Croatia and Slovenia, in June 1991, egged on by NATO.
3. Massive Privatization of all Socially Owned, or State Sector Enterprises and sale to Western Purchasers, was insisted on, at nominal book value, as part of the Restructuring Programme.
4. Supporting Legislation, drawn by Western Financial Consultants and Lawyers, to safeguard the rights of Foreign Creditors, was hastily introduced, and unrestricted entry to foreigners was permitted, not only in industry, but also in banking, insurance, and service sectors.
5. The entire Nationalized Banking Sector was dismantled.
6. Practically one-half of the Work Force, or more, was laid off, due to privatization.
7. Ethnic strife and ethnic cleansing, with the strategic objective of breaking up of Yugoslavia, was actively supported, by funding and supporting violent Secessionist Groups, by Western Intelligence Agencies, by training and hiring mercenaries. Bosnia was turned into a base, by hiring Arab / Afghan fighters, trained in the killing fields of Afghanistan; and the Kosovo Liberation Army, and its *Al-Qaeda* arm, financed through drug trafficking, white slave trafficking, and supplied with unlimited arms.
8. The November 1995, *Dayton Accord,* initiated by the US and EU, installed a full-fledged Colonial Administration (*a la* Andhra Pradesh 1999-2004) in Bosnia with expatriates. Article VII of the *Dayton Accord,* stipulates that, the first Governor of the

Bosnian Central Bank will be appointed by the IMF, and will not be a citizen of Bosnia, or Herzegovinia.

9. The entire inflated so-called Peace-Keeping Expenses were to be paid for by the now autonomous Republics and the debt has been proportionately divided between them. Oil Exploration has been started in Bosnia by the American Oil Company, AMOCO.

10. The territorial division, under the *Dayton Accord* of 1995, sanctions the partition on ethnic lines, for which nine heavily armed brigades, termed 'Peace-Keepers', were to ensure ethnic division of Yugoslavia, have been deployed.

In sum, Economic Security, or the lack of it, as emphasized even in the US President's National Security Document of December 1999, is the central issue of our times.

No longer are Armies, Navies, or Air Forces going to march, sail or fly, under the foreign flags, to invade countries as big as India, though military coercion and blackmailing will remain on the horizon. Nuclear and Conventional Forces stalemate, generally prevents shooting Wars, especially as Superpower Surveillance, Monitoring, Diplomatic Intervention is in real time.

At the same time, the Global Criminal Economy runs a Parallel Government, and the Police is nurtured by a Parallel or Black Money Economy. The big players are Mafias or Criminal Gangs, Businessmen, Politicians, Police-Customs-Excise-Tax Officials, and Bureaucrats, in key positions at various points, in the decision-making apparatus. While countries in Latin America, and the declining Soviet State in 1987-93, are the more talked about examples, documented in the Report of the *"Anti-Mafia Commission"*, to the Italian Parliament, to the United Nations General Assembly, March 20, 1990, India is no longer an exception. Terrorist outfits have established well-oiled Narcotics and Gun-Running Networks in almost all the

States of India. There can be no terrorist activity, without money-laundering, be it through *Hawala* or the more sophisticated Foreign Bank's Private Banking Operations, connected to OCBs. The standard operating procedure for local Mafias, connected to the International Criminal and Corruption Network, is well illustrated in Italy, by the Kosovo Liberation Army, and the countries in and around 'The Golden Triangle'. Penetration or subversion of the Police, Para-Military Forces (including the Army) and the Judicial and Political systems have changed Latin American politics. The Drug Lords or Drug Kings are confident of their relative control over the Judges, Police, and the Penal System, in their own countries. The process of deposits of $ 9,999 is known as 'Smurfing' (sic), to evade the $10,000 Reporting System. The question for us remains, whether we are repeating the dramatic errors of Gorbachev, of first disorganizing the Soviet Systems, without replacing it, and of the Yeltsin Regime, in pushing Privatization with the Mafia, as intermediaries, without social and institutional control, creating conditions for take over by the Global Criminal Economy, of what was one of the largest, and naturally the wealthiest country in the world. As Marshal Akhromeyev, and the senior most officers of the Armed Forces of the former Soviet Union wrote, in their letter to Gorbachev, and the Members of Parliament — 'Hitler could not achieve with all his military mass, what Gorbachev was doing to break-up the Soviet Economy and Polity'.

Unchecked, unpunished, Economic Offences, Black Money Economy, and Money Laundering, usually seduce the political class, to build a mutually beneficial relationship with business interests, and, since Profit and Greed are the only surviving Value Systems of society, the State and its Democratic Institutions erode and decay, through subversion.

The new threats to countries like India are analysed and discussed in the book by Susan George, *Lugano Report.* For the twenty-first century Capitalist order, Democracy is but an interregnum. The post-Bretton Woods, post-Uruguay Round negotiations, and the birth of the WTO, on the advice of the

MNCs, is rapidly intervening, in establishing a Western-dominated Global Economy, International Trade, Food trade, using Food as a Weapon; TRIPS seek to put in place Globalization (a New-world Empire of Finance Capital). Liberalization (which Joseph Stiglitz, Nobel Prize Winner, and former Economic Advisor to President Clinton calls '*Briberization*') and place public assets into the hands of one's private friends. The WTO is aggressively pursuing a Global Economic Agenda, which includes Government Contracts, Competition Policy, Labour Policy, and a legal framework, to be made applicable to all countries, except the US, where domestic laws supersede any international obligation. The WTO is staffed by non-elected officials, who are approved by the IMF and the MNCs. The MNCs globally employ only 28 million people. There are 15 million new entrants of working age in India every year. Excluded from this statement of the Indian reality, are the 741 million village folks, who are steadily being impoverished, both due to internal neglect, and the coming GM seeds/agri-exports, from the rich countries. If this, in sum, does not lead to a disastrous assault on the already low levels of Economic Security, which our country is in, then what else will?

Steadily increasing expenditure on the Armed Forces, Paramilitary Forces, and the Police, now approaching Rs 1,50,000 crores annually, is hardly protective of India's Security. The slogan given by our then late Prime Minister, Lal Bahadur Shastri, in 1965, *"Jai Jawan - Jai Kisan"*, (Hail the Soldier, Hail the Farmer), had a deeper message, which appears to have got lost. Ninety per cent of our Soldiers come from the villages and are, therefore, closely related to their villages, where they will return to, on completion of their service. When they see the growing poverty, impoverishment, unemployment and destitution in the villages, they are bound to think and reason, why? The spending on the Armed Forces, Paramilitary and the Police, cannot be at the cost of the 70 crore people who live in the villages. Geo-economics in the contemporary world overshadows Geo-politics.

Briefly, the *Lugano Report* emphasizes a steadily increasing surrender of Economic Decision-Making, by the Nation-State, which amounts to surrender of Sovereignty. Politics and political processes, including the much discussed issue that 'Governance' cannot operate in vacuum. While some elements of law and order, jails and judiciary will remain out of control of WTO; in the New World Banks, Currency, Financial Institutions, Industry, and even Intelligence Agencies are increasingly going out of control of the elected Government. The *Lugano Report* rightly states, "any political order requires a Military enforcement mechanism. The Pentagon, with the National Security Agency, and an enlarged NATO, seem destined to play such a role. It is envisaged that it will maintain trustworthy, second-tier, military establishments, in certain Client States, in the culturally diverse Non-Western civilizational areas." The Report further goes on to suggest that, Information Technologies will be paramount in the construction and consolidation of a renovated world order. Elites are already linked through dedicated networks, and these links will be necessarily reinforced, as the need for Global Political Consultations and Management becomes even more apparent. Information technology will enhance Surveillance, Infiltration and Disruption of any nascent opposition. Budgets and fiscal deficits, investment and trade-policies are out of the ambit of the Central Government. As this is happening, the Political Class, and those in power, at the Centre, and in the States, are increasingly resorting directly or indirectly, to Divisive Politics, based on religion, caste, perceptions of real or imaginary historical grievances, which are being encouraged by Hate-Politics. In this concept, ideally, individuals everywhere should identify with an ethnic, linguistic, racial, or religious sub-group, to the detriment of self-definition, as a 'part of the human race'. The notion of 'Citizenship' at any level, is to be actively discouraged. These narrowly defined groups have general access to communications media, with group-specific outlets, established and financed, wherever they do not occur spontaneously. All fundamentalists, separatists, and supremacists, and the Hindus, Sikhs, Muslims, Christians, Jews and others, with all their newspapers, magazines, radio, TV, and websites, are pre-occupied with their 'Rights', including the Right to a Separate

State. The goal is to reinforce fragmentation, to underscore differences with others, and erect ghettos, whether they have any basis in fact or tradition. Contrary to received opinion, most identities, particularly the so-called ethnic ones, have shallow historical roots, and are more often than not, of recent construction. Their identities are very much like the Gods of the mythological tales, even if they do not exist, they are extremely powerful—so much so that, people will kill each other, in their name. This has very grave consequences for the integrity of the country, as our Secular fabric is a real guarantor of peace and development, and the essence of our National Security.

The conventional concept of National Security is at the crossroads. The ideas enunciated by Jaswant Singh, the then Foreign Minister of India and, briefly then Defence Minister, in his book *'Defending India'*, recommends an alliance with the US. There cannot be an alliance between two parties which are unequal. That would be a surrender of India's Independence and its subscription to the New Empire, about which Tony Blair's Chief Foreign Policy Advisor, Robert Cooper, has written in a recent Paper published in London by the Foreign Policy, Centre, set up by Tony Blair, of which he remains the Patron. Robert Cooper calls for a 'New Imperialism', to the Post September 11 World. The call for a 'Defensive Imperialism', with Western Countries, particularly Britain, and the EU, intervening abroad to restore order, comes in a pamphlet with a foreword by Blair himself. Cooper argues for a "Post-Modern", apartheid like duality of laws and systems, to deal with "ourselves and the Pre-Modern World", and adds that the West will have to employ "double standards". Later, the British Foreign Secretary declared that, "UK is not a Superpower, but we have continuously shown that we play a pivotal role. We can make a big difference. Our challenge is to stave off the 'Afghanistans' of the future", In this country, we know that role played by UK, in Kashmir, and elsewhere, presently perhaps, subdued, in the interests of the *Hawk AJT deal.* (since concluded in 2003)

We were following a policy of ambivalence in regard to our Nuclear Weapon's Status, prior to May '98. There have been, after *Pokhran-2*, a succession of confused and damaging posturing. Instead of gaining self-confidence, reducing our Military Conventional Forces Budget, and building up the Nuclear Command and Control System, we went into a state of nervousness, and one half year of humiliating talks, between Jaswant Singh and Strobe Talbot; publicly stating, at the level of the PM that India will sign the CTBT (fortunately the voting out of the CTBT in the US Senate and Congress saved us). This was followed by a Nuclear Doctrine, which subscribes to a "No First Strike" Policy, without having in place, a credible Second-Strike capability. This is, doctrine and strategy at its worst, so far as defending India is concerned.

The substantive threat to a nation also emanates from wherever the Technology level is higher. It is difficult to appreciate how the current dispensation has been encouraging people in the media, academia and the intelligentsia to think that the US and India are 'natural allies'. This is just wishful thinking. There can be no genuine shared relationship or goals between nations, so unequal, and having disparate, vital national interests, be it the market, energy resources, or the geographical assets, that help in attainment of national goals.

We have tried, in the last seven years, to plead with the US to declare Pakistan as a 'Terrorist State'. This has not happened, nor is it likely to happen. If China is perceived as the Main Enemy by our Government, the US has a different strategy in place, to subvert the Chinese political system, in much the same manner, as they did in the USSR. Kashmir remains a Disputed Territory for the US, as it was in 1948, and they would like to see the Kashmir Valley detached, as in the KSG, (Kashmir Study Group) Report, December 1998. "An independent entity, without an international personality". The US is a major partner in Pakistan, and their own regime is in place, in Afghanistan, whereas our natural frontiers lie in the Hindukush. Beyond, in Central Asia and the Caspian Oil Region, it has Military bases, and pre-positioned facilities that have elbowed out the Successor State, Russia, and any real hopes that China dreamt of (Though this balance is changing since 2005). In the subcontinent, in Sri

Lanka, the Norwegians work the US game plan. In Bangladesh, its partners Saudi Arabia to hold decision-making in its hands.

In Nepal, the old 'India-Nepal Relationship' is now subservient, to US dictates. The US has overt military presence at crucial levels. (At the time of going to the press a revolutionary tide is underway in Nepal). However the new Prime Minister Mr. Girija Prasad Koirala may bring peace in the country.

At one stage, the present Government in Delhi, under its own illusions, dreamt of and put all its political efforts to forge an Anti-Islamic Coalition with the US. The US is for 'Energy and Oil', and not for any religious crusade. The Islamic countries are distributed in a varied mosaic, most of them drawn by the US and its old Anglo-Saxon cousin, the UK. Only Iraq, Iran, and the Palestinians, remain apart for the present. Until the Oil and Gas lasts, and the Petro Dollars flow into their banks, any anti-Islam noises are just atmospherics. The Islamic regimes will have the direct support of the US, as hitherto, and the 'Nationalists' in Delhi need to do their sums again. In other words, this is not a favourable scenario for India, where the US is strongly ensconced all around us, not withstanding the June 2005 Indo-US Defence Framework Agreement and the July 2005 Indo-US Civilian Nuclear Energy Agreement at the apex level which includes suggestions to support India's bid to became a Regional Big Parex.

We have witnessed in the last few years, a series of self-deluding moves by ourselves, on the chessboard, first the Structural Adjustment Programme, which binds us internally and is destroying the vast network of Public Sector / Financial/ Industrial Institutions. Then, since 1998, a series of self annihilating manoeuvres; the KSG; moratoriums on nuclear tests after *Pokhran II,* two years of one-sided bargaining on CTBT; Lahore, Kargil and internationalization of Kashmir; intrusive and endless visits and briefings with the US and Israeli Intelligence teams, permitted to operate freely in Delhi and J&K; formalized presence and activity of the FBI, and the US Drug Enforcement Agency; overseeing and advice from US Intelligence to our Military and Civil Intelligence Agencies, and the building of too close a relationship between individuals and Institutions; the *Sangh Parivar's* support to 'Trifurcation of J&K' on communal grounds; destabilizing the State and subverting the entire basis of the J&K to meet the *Hurriyat* — a US supported outfit; and the latest charade of Demarcating territory for US experts to install, operate, train and maintain the latest ground-sensors fad, (a thin end of the wedge, if you like), tried and rejected earlier by the BSF, and with a poor track record on the US-Mexican Border, where even after intensive Aerial and Ground Surveillance and Sensors, Drugs and Human Trafficking continues, since these were put in place more than 15 years ago, as seen first hand and in the official briefings. Look at the Ocean scenario. Navies do not patrol Malacca Straits in peace time as part of Anti-Piracy Patrols; because that is the job of the Coast Guard. We are working with the US Navy and laying bare our electronic order of battle, much as Iraq did, with fatal consequences, in the 1980s.

Instant welcome to an National Missile Defence Project 'NMD' announcement by the US President, in a University campus, setting aside the entire staff system on the MEA, MOD, COSC, PMO, NSAB and CCS, without any discussion or debate, is symptomatic of erosion of self-confidence; offers of Avantipur, Adampur and Bhuj, Nallaya Military Airfields; the US disdainfully turning down the offer and choosing its old and trusted ally, Pakistan, demonstrates a psychology of dependency to the people. It appears Foreign, and Defence Ministry appreciations were naive in ignoring that, both the US and Pakistani establishments had together nurtured the *Taliban,* and had a deep relationship with it.

We should steadily and persistently work in the economic and political spheres, to extend the concept of India's strategic frontiers, along the Indian Ocean Rim, in the West and the East. This would secure a Defence-in-Depth. We are hemmed into our Borders and cannot think and articulate anything else, except Cross-Border Terrorism and Pakistan, which suits everybody in the international community — a nation of over1000 millions, busily preoccupied in defending a Border and its courtyard. As recently as 1996, our Military presence was sought in the Gulf and the African near East regions, but we dithered, awaiting a green signal from 'Big Brother', which never came.

Divisive, denominational politics weakens our country, and when it does, as much as in Gujarat, our ability to defend India weakens in direct proportion. The accession of J&K, it is worth reiteration, was predicated on a Secular India. When India's Secular fabric is under assault, the country's unity and integrity is weakened. We then have to ask ourselves whether we are wittingly or unwittingly driving ourselves towards the Yugoslavia/ Bosnia, and former Soviet Union/EE scenario. Rapidly increasing Defence Budgets and Resource Allocations are an inadequate response to answer such a developing situation, anywhere in the world. And when an erstwhile Superpower humbled itself, by choosing a suicidal path of political surrender, what chance do the big, bloated Indian Armed Forces have?

The 'Natural Allies' syndrome had earlier led us to signing a contract with an unregistered US company, to implement a project as sensitive as the 'Sankhya Vahini', or de facto, handing over our National Telecom Network, our central nervous system, to that company's total control. Fortunately cancelled due to internal pressure in 2003. At the drop of a hat, Mumbai, and Delhi Police, and 64 Intelligence Officers, are off to Tel Aviv and Langley, to learn Anti-Terrorist Operations. This is symptomatic of the new wave, whether relevant or irrelevant to our scenario.

We have given up almost entirely on our earlier strategy of Self-Reliance in Defence — be it Software, Humanware, or Hardware. Instead of quickly setting up a Command and Control System, post-Pokhran, conducting the minimum, necessary tests to establish a credible, Missile Delivery System and production, with the essential support systems, we went into a nervous freeze. We have recently undertaken to expend over one lakh crores on Imports of Defence Hardware, with the additional bluff that CKD /SKD Imports mean Transfer of Technology. Imports worth nearly two lakh crores are in the pipeline as of 2005. They, in fact, kill indigenous design, R&D, skill, industry, and the thousands of ancillary industries, that are the backbone of a nation's capability. China called its ship-building industry in 1978, as the 'spring-board' of the Nation's development. In India, Defence Ministers preach to us the CKD/SKD route, as self-reliance, and the departments of the MOD, DRDO, and the Services, meekly follow the sermon.

The last CVC, classified the findings of the MOD Deals, on the plea that they derived from classified files, which is a wholly worthless reasoning, because a summary of findings and recommendations should have been shared with the Parliament and the people. The originator of any document in our Government system, has the right to decide on the classification that he gives to a document, suitably paraphrasing it as 'unclassified', if he wishes to do so. Shri Vittal, CVC damaged the system by recommending the abrogation of the Government Order, approved at the level of the Prime Minister, in 1989, banning Middlemen in Defence deals. By no stretch of imagination, are Middlemen essential, or even desirable, in Defence deals. When we buy a Defence System or equipment from a foreign company, all the commercial details are at best classified as 'Commercial Confidential'. They have already been, most probably, communicated to other countries/buyers previously, or this would occur soon. In this age of modern communications, there is no query of the Ministry, or the General staff, which requires the services of Middlemen or Agents in New Delhi to obtain answers. *Admiral Nanda and Sons* are incidentally the honourable Middlemen, in a top-secret project, and several other acquisitions, and Nanda-Junior is based in London. Yet, if the *Babus* insist, the information required can be communicated, to and fro, through hand of Pilot, special messengers, or the Military Attaches, without any delay or problems. The Intelligence Agencies of many countries use Middlemen, not only to buy off Politicians, Civilian and Military Bureaucrats, but also subvert them, as 'Sleepers', and thereby nurture *'Trojan Horses'*. It is surprising that people had to wait to see the *Tehalka Tapes,* to wake up to this reality. This methodology is described in several authoritative bestsellers, on the subject. (As the well-known author of the book, *'The Arms*

Bazaar' noted, that he was not surprised, that people in the decision-making chain, were amenable to being bribed in Defence deals, what surprised him was that, their price was so low).

Twenty-six per cent stake by foreign companies in Defence PSUs, has the wink and the nod of the Cabinet Committee on Security in 2005!

Extension of US Presidential Doctrine No. 59, arrogating to the US, the right to attack Non-nuclear Weapon States NNWS, is now operationalized, and declared as such in 2002, by Donald Rumsfeld as, "Useable"/Micro nukes against the "Axis of Evil", and for that matter, anyone else who is not with the US.

Refusal by the US to sign the International Criminal Court Resolution, and signing of the Presidential Order of November 2001, giving one's own Service Personnel Immunity, under the Servicemen Protection Act, are indicators of the New World Order. At the same time, anyone classified as a Terrorist, Supporter or Sympathiser, will simply be taken from any country, tried, and then thrown overboard.

There is an argument, repeated faithfully, by those close to the establishment that time does not stand still; that the world has changed; and there is now a single Superpower, with whom we have no choice but to deal. One of our former Prime Ministers, P.V. Narsimha Rao, in a mid-term review of National Security and Economic Policies, had advised that India can deal with this Superpower, keeping its vital national interests, intact. It need not go so far, as to tightly do an *aalingan* (embrace) the deity. That was good advice, and like all good advice, it was simply ignored, in preference to individual self-interest.

The Cabinet Committee in Security CCS has been concerned with Cross-Border Terrorism, Border Deployment, etc., that it hardly ever dwells on the 'Grand Strategy' of the country, looking at a 50 or a 100 years perspective. It is poorly staffed, supported by viewpoints of Ministries, Departments and Agencies, and receives no comprehensive assessments and National Intelligence Estimates, that are a pre-requisite. A National Security Adviser or a Cabinet Secretary's wisdom, is not a substitute for a Multi-disciplinary Staff System, as recommended by K.C. Pant, Chairman of a Committee in 1998 to suggest a National Security setup (a former Defence Minister) in June 1998, to provide Staff Support to the CCS, as in the United State. Instead of a National Vision, we are therefore afflicted with myopia.

The United States, UK, and the countries of the G-7, pursue their respective National Interests, notwithstanding any provision of International Law, obligations of International/Bilateral Treaties or Agreements, quoting their National Interests to the advantage of their own people. Even recent examples on patents, bio-diversity, the Kyoto Protocol, the International Law of the Sea, UNCLOS, Resolutions of the United Nations' Assembly Security Council, the International Court of Justice and the International Criminal Court (signed by a majority of the countries), to name only a few, are simply disregarded. Take the example of the ICJ's Award, in favour of Nicaragua, as penalty for mining its harbours, or the War damages reparations, due to Vietnam, which have been turned on their heads.

The most dangerous threat is that of subversion of people in the highest places (list the Bureaucrats and Ministers, who are in key-posts in the Central Government, and who have the pre-certification of the World Bank—IMF).

What happened in the former Soviet Union was the subversion/surrender of just the top few, and it is well recorded in the 1997 book, *In Highest Places,* by Bechloss and Strobe Talbot. Installation of regimes through the Electoral System, is now a perfected art, *a la* Russia in 1990s. Subversion of the Constitution, rendering a Parliament ineffective, bypassing it on all vital treaties, agreements and protocols, often claiming secrecy, has become part of the process.

Bypassing the Parliament or its established committees, violates the basic principle of Accontablility of the Cabinet to the Parliament, and through it, to the people. Secret diplomacy does not absolve the Government of the day, from taking the Parliament or its select committees into confidence, and where necessary, obtaining its approval. Subverting of the Democratic

Machinery is proceeding unchecked, at a faster pace than what was alleged in the *Shah Commission*, and where the Nuremburg Principle of 'Superior's Orders', was held not to be a protection for the Judges and Public Servants.

Will we rise to these threats and challenges to India's Security, or be apathetic, as we have been, on recent occasions in the past, when such dangers visited us? To reiterate the danger, subversion is a silent virus, which penetrates the top echelons at the very start.

4

Changing Nature of Warfare

"Let me repeat the analogy about the drunk who lost his watch in a dark alley, but was found looking for it under a lamp post because there was more light there. The light, provided by our knowledge of technological capabilities and our capacity for strategic analysis, is so dazzling, as to be almost hypnotic; but it is in those shadowy regions of human understanding, based on our knowledge of social development, cultural diversity and patterns of human behaviour, that we have to look for the answers." (Eminent historian, Michael Howard)

19 Discussion Papers by Warfare Analysts were presented at the National Intelligence Council, convened by the Central Intelligence Agency, in May 2004, on 'The Changing Nature of Warfare – 2020'. These Papers, it is specifically noted, do not represent the views of the US Government. Nevertheless, they deserve the attention of specialists and agencies in Governments, as the United States has in fact become the 'neighbour' of all nations. It also has established over 700 military and military-logistic bases and facilities, in more than a hundred countries, far and near. It would be a fair assumption that the US has also entered into dormant arrangements with a number of Governments in secret, to be activated on an as required basis, in an emergency, considering the sensitivities of local populations in some Democracies. It is for this very purpose and intent that 'Military-to-Military' or 'Mil-to-Mil' relationships are fostered, 'inter-operability' is practiced and foreign training assistance

programmes nurtured, like the Pentagon Project for the Indonesian Military, designated JCET (Joint Combined Education & Training), the 'School for Americas', and so on. They are founded on the belief of 'Strategic Convergence' and 'Strategic Partnership'.

After Vietnam, the prevailing environment is once again beset with unforeseen problems, as the situation in Afghanistan and Iraq is stalemated; the Military-technological prowess in impressive, 'State-to-State' contests having been won so easily, but the people and their quaint nationalism stands unvanquished. The Phoenix has risen from the ashes to haunt the victors, leaving little space for a honorable retreat, without irreparable loss of prestige which may foreclose other such adventures for unilateral, pre-emptive invasions, predicated on Military predominance alone.

This tentative 'halt' has of course not halted the onward march to threaten the rogue States and 'failed' States; some of whom have been labeled as 'The Axis of Evil'. The Central Intelligence Agency, its Covert Operations Wing apart, deserves respect for its thoroughness in analysis and its intellectual resources which have so brilliantly succeeded in the past, whenever it is considered inputs have been permitted to aid policy formulation and implementation. Hence, studies presented by Warfare Analysts stymied somewhat by the reverses in Afghanistan and Iraq, need to be studied on their own merits.

Except for one Paper by Ralph Peters, 'Virtuous Destruction, Decisive Speed', which advocates that unmindful of collateral damage to unarmed civilians and property, the speed of use of 'maximum' weapons is a must and was a must in Iraq, for example; all other Papers suggest a cool, sober, calculated response to challenges in the next 15 years or so, though the instruments, strategies, tactics and mix of resources, recommended by these Experts, differ according to their historical experiences, the availability of technological means, the costs, economic consequences based on their individual perspectives and what they have analyzed in their respective perspectives, and interactions with their respective institutions, and their Armed Forces.

Most Papers presented are of the view that occasions for 'State-versus-State', conventional wars are either diminishing or that the Superpower and its allies (principally the UK) have a one-sided capability to bring it to a quick decisive end, against most States with rich resources but with little organization and strength to fight and hold back the invader. Others deduce that Special Forces, like the Seals, SAS etc., having a decisive surgical capability to destroy specially selected targets, have been effective, but cannot be a replacement for capabilities and Forces required to ensure the 'desired peace' objectives, even with better puppets and expatriates, re-injected with bagful of Dollars, as the Northern Alliance, a few Kurdish factions, the *Challabis* and *Allawis* have shown. Special Forces did a brilliant job in coordinating anti-*Taliban* forces, in homing air strikes with precision guided munitions, and are still doing so in both countries, but are too expensive in manpower and equipment, to substitute a mix of conventional Ground Forces, Police and 'pioneer/reconstruction' corps, of the type deployed in Japan, and FRG, post-1945. There is still no solution to the policies that must govern 'Stability and Support Operations' (SASO) and the Civil-Military mix for the SASO. If the 'one hundred orders' of Paul Bremer foul up the situation, as these orders, *de jure* and *de facto*, sold out Iraqi national assets to foreigners, placed 'above and outside domestic jurisdiction'; with 67 per cent Iraqis out of work, and nightly attacks on their homes, hearths, women and children, then no 'mix' can deliver. There was of course no resistance to the Allied Armies after V-Day. So while the fourth generation, mini nukes are one option in the arsenal, it has implications on domestic and world public opinion, which has the possibilities to turn counter-productive, in these days of the internet and wars/violence brought into homes instantly, across the globe.

That the Superpower's Mighty Military machine may face 'empty battle-fields', has been suggested in a Paper "Special Forces and the Future of Warfare", by Stephen Biddle, of the Strategic Studies Institute of the US Army War College, from where have emanated a number of other studies in the past, pre-2001. Special Operations Command (SOCOM) may of course play a leading part in the 'War on Terror' in the future, but the problem with the War on Terror is that, it singles out *Jehadi* Forces, nurtured by 'Radical Islam', in part *Wahabis,* financed and supported by the US itself, in 1979, in Pakistan, to oust a local 'Communist' Government in Afghanistan, and now the spawning ground for hundreds of disparate terrorist groups, notwithstanding President Musharraf's claims to the contrary.

Dr. Maniel Marston of the Royal Military Academy, Sandhurst, in recommending a Force Structure for high and low intensity, is of the view that the British experience of 35 years, in Northern Islands, would suggest that the whole Army needs training in Low Intensity Warfare which already forms one-third of the syllabus for the British Army. He says, of course, that while the Americans may need to learn from the British in this area, they have their own mentality and organization to adapt it in part. Stated here is the example of the initial days in the siege of Basra, in April 2003, where the British Commander moved very slowly, until he had gained the confidence of the city's population. Now, that confidence lies shattered, as Basra is now a hostile city and the Southern Oil Pipelines are frequently shut, blocking Iraq's major oil artery!

Daniel J. Whiteneck of the CNA Corporation, in presenting the 'Alternative Futures for the Next Decade', describes three 'Futures' : The Cooperative Future, (uncomplicated by the discontents of globalization, more aptly described as the 'Globalization of Poverty and the Globalization of Inequality'), where Third World markets are 'integrated' in the 'functional core', as discussed in the article, "Is the Tide Turning?", or a Competitive Future, where there are strong States of the Western alliance system : an absence of major theatre wars, but increased tensions, divergent security interests and policies among Western Powers, leading to renationalization, machinations and manipulations of conflicts in the Third World by the US and aspiring regional powers, increased economic competition between First World States, while the Third World stagnates; alternatively, a 'Chaotic Future,' where the global economic system is disrupted by a breakdown of prevailing regimes, in the financial sector, the trade sector, and development security. The Author has made a significant omission, in failing to mention the two most vital issues of the day: Peaking of Oil and the unsustainable Debt of the US (financed by China, Japan, UK, Petro-Dollars and the Central Bank reserves, kept in Dollar accounts, Capital Flight Dollars etc.)

In a detailed Paper on the RMA and the Middle-East, Dr. Zeev Maoz of the Tel Aviv University and the University of Michigan, makes an interesting point that there is a major discrepancy between the size and sophistication of the Saudi Armed Forces and the amount of money spent on Defence. (Saudi Arabia, with only 10 million people, is the biggest importer of Arms in the world, most of them lying in crates since arrival, and this may be, in part, due to some 'creative' accounting, in the re-cycling of Petro-Dollars.)

The Middle-East or West Asia pervades the thinking of most participants, and many, like Dr. Kurt Campbell, Senior Vice President, Henry A. Kissinger Chairman and Director of the International Security Program, Centre for Strategic and International Studies (CSIS), Washington D.C., assesses the Middle-East to be the "headquarters" of the most immediate and intractable threats to American security, in the world today. Israel is a robust ally, to be supported at any cost. Asia, he assesses, 'stands on the cusp of significant strategic change...some of this could lead to Big Power competition and even overt conflict ...(who these Big Powers may be, is not described...) ... Perhaps the rise of China, perhaps historical rivalries and endemic political distrust among the leading states, Dr. Campbell says, can break out on the surface...contradictions in the Asian attitude towards the US will likely be a continuing feature of Asian Security Diplomacy. Dr. Campbell cautions: it is difficult to imagine the US, retaining its influence, or recovering its prestige in the Middle-East, should the US suffer a similar strategic fate in Iraq (as in Vietnam).

'American Way of War' (AWW), while it has familiar connotations, is a new terminology to most of us. H.H. Gaffney rightly points out that it is not detached from the American political leadership and their political choices (and preferences, one may add). Global War on Terror and Nation Building in the occupied nations/regimes, change victims, which the author of this Paper surprisingly adds, he 'suspects that the US does not quite have the guts or the resources to undertake.' The US Corporations with their separate and growing Private Military Companies, claim to do, under the benign dispensations of the likes of Paul Bremmer's 'Hundred Orders'! Gaffney is fearful that a faltering economic situation and demands of an ageing US population will take away funds for social security and medicare. 'America's new Borders are at a great distance from her shores. A Military Force engaged there can only be effective, if it has the staying power, through a moral 'intimidation' and patient engagement, rather than continuous combat. That can only happen, if the purpose is just'.

Professor Colin S. Gray of the Reading University, UK, in discussing the issue of 'Has the War Changed Since the End of the "Cold war", enters the discussions with four caveats: Do not neglect war's political, social and cultural caveats (In Iraq, it means, don't forget 1920). Defense establishments prepare for the problems they prefer to solve, rather than those that a cunning enemy might pose. Trend spotting is not a good guide to the future. Surprises happen. Perhaps, the 'SURPRISE' is the people. Prof. Gray makes the important point that, "Pre-eminently, warfare should always be waged with as much regard to the character of the subsequent peace, as the immediate Military necessity allows". Right ...but what happens when there are no roses to greet the liberators?

John B. Alexander, in his Paper on 'Demands on Personnel, Machines and Missions', focuses on 'Types of Future Wars', and it may be worthwhile quoting him in full, on what he describes as "Outsourced War' (The article on 'Private Military Companies'). Even in the space of seven months, the PMCs have gained what appears to be unstoppable momentum, as the MNCs find their use and flexibility, of profit. Alexander says, "Outsourced wars have begun in earnest. There have always been mercenaries, but future conflicts will take the concept to new levels. During the Cold War proxies, fought as Client-States of the East and West, the US frequently provided assistance to forces, opposing those supported by the Soviets, in order to strain their Military resources. However, Proxy Wars are undergoing a metamorphosis and will emerge in the form of non-Governmental, outsourced wars. This trend can already be observed in contracting of services, traditionally done by Military Forces, in both Iraq and Afghanistan (elsewhere in Latin America, East Timor, Kosovo and West Africa; Mark Thatcher of 'Operations Executive' of South Africa *et al*)...Examples include the Americans who provide protection for President Karzai, Allawi, Advisors to Foreign Senior Military Officers, and private guards for building and convoy security. Many of these contractors are heavily armed and have used deadly force on several occasions. Use of contractors in sensitive situations, including interrogation of prisoners at Abu Ghraib, near Baghdad, and other secret locations has raised serious issues regarding both ethical and legal responsibilities (Washington Post, May 11, 2004). Large Transnational Companies, routinely engage Contracted Security. Many of these contractors look like executive class mercenaries, but with a professional imprimatur (ex-Generals and Admirals). They are often subsidiaries of well-established and respected companies. In Corporate Boardrooms, around the world, the image of the Rogue Soldier of fortune, is being transformed into that of Elite Master Craftsmen. The impact will be profound for the US military.

The corollary to this trend is seen in protection afforded within the United States, where the ratio of Private Security Guards to sworn Law Enforcement Officers is 5:1 and is increasing (same as in India)... Some of these private organizations provide security for the most sensitive Government sites and are prepared to engage protective service that equate to military operations. The internationalization of Private Security in the US has happened. As an example, Wackenhut, formerly an American company, is now a subsidiary of Group 4 Falck of Copenhagen (Imagine the situation in India where the Intelligence and Security Agencies seldom have an idea of who is who, except if he or she is of a particular denomination).

Legal frameworks/limits have not been set. (They are not intended to be set, as the Corporations pay for it and are rarely not the friends of the Regulators.) Outsourcing of Military Services has been embraced by the US, as a means to minimize exposure of troops and acquire services, currently not available, due to personnel resource constraints ... The issue of preemptive operations by contract organizations, the key to counter terrorism, is totally unbounded. The institutional and ethical boundaries have not been tested as to what operations are appropriate. The question is whether or not the 'Pandora's Box' has been opened?"

It was, in fact, opened long ago in Argentina, Chile, Colombia in Central America, Indonesia, Timor and Southern Africa. Only, it was then under 'D' Notice for the corporate media. Alexander concludes on this issue by stating, "because of the superiority and success, of US Forces potential adversaries now concentrate, on Asymmetric Warfare."

The most useful contribution to the 'National Intelligence Council' comes from Dr Andrea Ellner, Lecturer in International Relations University of Reading, and Centre for International Security and Defence Studies, UK, Dr Ellner weaves through the Interactions and Dialogues, Policy Agreements and some operations on the grounds in the Balkans, the Middle-East and Africa. She does not mention NATO operations in Afghanistan, nor the tacit understanding that NATO will deploy by common assent in Africa and Asia, when imperative, to safeguard their financial and energy interests, as they did, for example, in 1917, pre-NATO, in Russia. Dr. Ellner refers to the 'break up' of Yugoslavia, (as if it happened, on its own!), the St. Malo Process in 1998, when the UK and France took the lead in promoting a 'Common Foreign and Security Policy (CFSP), including the provision of Military capabilities, which led a rather dormant life since inception, with the Masstricht Treaty. At the Thessaloniki European Council, in June 2003, the EU's Special Representative for CFSP, Javier Solana, proposed Strategy Papers on both Security and WMD Proliferation, respectively. Both documents were adopted officially as, "A Secure Europe in a Better World—Europe Security Strategy" and 'Fight Against the Proliferation of WMDs-EU Strategy against Proliferation of WMDs in December 2003'. (EU neatly pretends Israel is not a Nuclear Weapons State, but promptly picks on Iran to warn it of the "use of other mechanisms", *a la* Iraq (As reported by BBC, on September 21, 2004).

Dr. Ellner neatly summarises...The security concepts of the EU and UK, "the security strategy conceptualizes Future Security Challenges as negative effects of globalization and is deeply wedded to the concept of 'human security' and 'global common good', which must be protected or enhanced through a mix of political, economic and, if necessary military means (in line with Petersburg Tasks). It emphasizes multi-lateral cooperation with and within, especially the UN, the WTO or the IAEA, in conjunction with NATO, especially the US, but also Russia. The Trans-Atlantic Relationship is identified as a core element of the International System...." Highly nuanced, but where does it leave the former Colonial World, on whose past exploitation, and present resources, the prosperity of the West rests?

Dr. Ellner goes on to say later that ..."weakening of the State System, organized crime and the privatization of forces ...combine to present a very radical threat indeed." Yet, there is a contradiction, as all of them are the by products of globalization, whose application has been highlighted by many... Joseph Stiglitz, Buddhoo, James Petras, Chossudovsky, Raymond Baker and hundreds of other eminent thinkers.

After 'The Helsinki Headline Goals, 1999', which were to enable the EU to deploy an autonomous Force of 50,000 to 60,000 with their equipment and logistics, in May 2004, days before the CIA Workshop of the Council of Europe approved 'Headline Goals 2010' (6309/6/04) which incorporates the capabilities of Member States, and defines more clearly the levels of rapid reaction to be achieved. (The 'reaction' need not always be after the event, as it also implicitly implies pre-emption).... within five days of the EU decision of the approval Crisis Management Concept, having been approved by the EU Council (note: not the UN Security Council) This will be available in 2005, with full capability in 2007...for Peace Making, Joint

Disarmament Operations, the Support for Third World Countries, Combating Terrorism and Security Sector Reforms...the commitment is for the EU to "share the responsibility for Global Security". Shades of 'Project for the New European Century'?

Shortly, thereafter, followed the establishment of the European Armaments, Research and Military Capabilities Agency (Head, Nick Whitney of UK), to harmonize their future requirements by 2010. Dr Eller informs that there are several highly capital intensive items in the pipeline and the 2003 Defence White Paper Projects, and further integration with the US. Is the Boeing-Airbus fight then, just shadow boxing? The EU is awaiting to fulfill requests from the President of Azerbaijan, a greater engagement in the Balkans and the Caucasus...back to 1900 AD! It undertook 'Operation Artemis', in the Republic of Congo, in 2003. It is looking beyond in the whole of Sub Saharan Africa. The June 2004, EU Council in Brussels, was expected to take over the duties of SFOR, coordinate with the NATO, as proposed jointly by France and UK. Where 'Artemis' involved 400 troops, the EUFOR Mission slated for Bosnia – Herzegovinia would be the largest and most demanding operation of the EU, with US presence continuing there. It will be conducted under 'Berlin Plus Arrangements', that is with NATO's assistance. The German approach to Security Policy is highly compatible with EU, and it is only a matter of time that the Bundeswehr becomes a professional Army. Germany has made significant progress in developing new organizational and conceptual tools for the Civil and Military in peacekeeping and long-term conflict resolution and conflict prevention. This includes enhancing the coordination between Ministries and other organizations and the establishment of a Centre for International Peace Operations (Zentrum fur Internationale Friedeseinsatze) in Berlin. "Prevention as the New Rationale for German Foreign Policy: Peace Policy by Civilian and Military Means", Sebastian Hanisch, 2004, in Deutsche Sicherheitspolitik. "In sum, the assessment is that, the failure to resolve the crisis in Iraq, is too grave, not to make a renewed attempt," says Dr. Andria Ellner. (In other words, Iraqi oil output and giant oil reserves are too great a prize to give up now!)

Dr. Ellner is candid in suggesting that one of the reasons for the Caucasus build-up for EUFOR, is the Caspian Sea Basin Region Energy Finds/reserves, as throughout the 1990s, according to her, Russia has been reluctant to allow the EU and the West to access its potentially sensitive sites. Which, of course, has already been pre-empted by numerous US military bases, established from Georgia, Azerbaijan to Khazakstan, Uzbekistan, Turkmenistan and Kirgizia. The US continues, according to Dr. Ellner, as the guarantor of European security (there and beyond).

Why is it that the Indian Security and Intelligence establishment do not inform the Political Leadership/decision-makers of the NSSDs, the Presidential doctrines, Senate and Congressional Committee proceedings, EU Council and Parliamentary Committee proceedings, to name only a few, on subjects relevant to India's vital interests, from food security to patents, to NATO's and EUFOR's plans, to subjects as in this article, when they have such vast resources and funds, their brilliant ones posted in every Embassy abroad. The experience of the Chiefs of Staff Committee and the Strategic Planning Group, chaired by the Cabinet Secretary, reports by insiders in the National Security Advisory Board and the Joint Intelligence Committee, which is the Secretariat to the National Security Advisor and the Cabinet Committee on Security (CCS), are not reassuring for a nation that has set itself, higher goals for the wellbeing of its people. Strobe Talbot's assurances to or praise for Mr. Jaswant Singh, in his recent book, are not substitutes enough for 'hard assessments' or meandering through the 'Next Step in Strategic Partnership', 'NSSP, February 2004, or the hurriedly inked 28 June, 2005. Indo-US Defense Framework Agreement, when one is dealing with the Republican's Elephant or even the Democrat's Donkey!

5

Is the Tide Turning?

Admirable traditions of scholarship, learning and access to information, were established by the founders of the great Universities in the United States. This was followed up by the establishment of academic 'thinktanks', consulted by successive US Administrations, interacting on Policy with the Administration, on a regular basis, commissioned through endowments and contracts from public funds, supplementing funds, of the private foundations which seeded them. Heads of Corporations and big Capitalist Enterprises considered these 'thinktanks' as the fountain-head of ideas, that would initially influence and later, drive foreign, economic and military policies, as a logical follow up of the post World War II Bretton Woods Institutions in alliance with Corporate-owned media, these foundations and 'thinktanks' began to influence policy, information and entertainment/culture.

The major ones to start off were, the Trilateral Commission, the Council on Foreign Relations, the Carnegie Endowment for Peace and later the most dynamic and expanding Rand Corporation, which has established 'sub-contracted' centres, all over the world, and has a very loyal clientele of analysts, thinkers, professors and media people, who have signed various contracts. Rand, of course, is involved in multifarious studies and reports, at any point of time, for almost every department of the US Administration. There are tens of prestigious institutions, including the American Enterprise Institute, and the National Endowment for Democracy, besides, several private initiatives, like one steered by George Soros, which operated in East Europe in the 1980s and today, to spread 'democracy'. The past shows that 'fellows' and insiders walk in and out of the thinktanks, into middle and high level posts in the US Administrations, just as they do from being CEOs to Cabinet posts and back, through revolving doors.

Globally, these thinktanks have an expanding network and have over the years, incorporated in the process, people from every nation and elites who serve their purpose and help to raise both new ideas and generate a favourable environment for 'Globalization' and the 'Project for the New American Century'. The agenda for the debate is set by such works, as Francis Fukiyama's *'The End of History'*, *'The Lexus and the Olive Tree'* by Thomas L. Friedman, *'Clash of Civilizations'* by Samuel Huntington and now the resurrected works of Brzezinski, *'The Grand Chessboard'*. A deeper analysis of the media and information network and opinion making programmes would indicate the underlying influence of such works, in setting the agenda of debates, discussions, both public and private. Ultimately, these find themselves at the operational levels by being incorporated into the 'syllabus' and projects of the Army/Air Force/Navy War Colleges and the NDU in the US and the corresponding institutions in the English-speaking nations in the world. They thereafter, become the catalysts for operational doctrines and devices, 'Military-to-Military' cooperation/relations, which is the facilitating process for many future agendas, and which the political leadership of India never permitted upto the 1980s for good reason (Secretary of State, Colin Powell, recently hailed the 'Military-to-Military 'relationship between the US and India as most important and the 'cornerstone' of Indo-US relations). Intelligence cooperation falls in the same category of relationships though it has been nurtured under the cover of cooperation in the 'War on Terror' and all fire walls in the Indian Intelligence Agencies, in effect are removed.

The sole Superpower status has also generated internal dynamics in the United States itself, which mitigate against the objectivity and independence of its own Intelligence establishments. Intellectuals and strategic thinkers are realizing and expressing 'shock' that it is now the 'policy' that determines 'Intelligence' reports, not the hard Intelligence inputs and facts, which influence the making of policy, and high level policy decisions'. This, of course, cuts at the very roots of real national interest. The line on Iraq has lost all credibility. It may be conceded that Gorbachev was a great 'asset' in bringing about the dissolution of the USSR, but the installation of Karzais and Allawis, and the hunt for the replacement of Chavez, should objectively limit itself at some point. NATO is stuck in Afghanistan and the US in Iraq (for four years, says the Democratic Party Presidential candidate), despite clear indications that this military occupation will not work. In Palestine, helicopter gun-ships have only succeeded in destroying homes and killing women and children, not the spirit of the Palestinian nation. In Iraq, even with overwhelming military technical superiority, the Coalition Forces and the Iraqi Police, are not in control. The reality becomes grimmer with every passing day. Yet, there are more Position Papers appearing at the Military War Colleges and the Pentagon which are looking out for 'little newer versions of Gorbachev's' and extending the war into Iran, based on the Intelligence Reports of the Iranian immigrants/expatriates of the Shah's regime. To describe the Iran Government as a '*Mullah*' regime, awaiting its execution and death is self-delusion. Just as the recognition of Iraqi Nationalism was sidelined over a year ago, not by the successors of Kermit Roosevelt (CIA), but Wall Street bankers who have closed their eyes to the grit, determination and fierce nationalism of the Iraqi people, in their hurry to grab Iran's oil! Military weaponry will indeed bomb out the infrastructure and the Government, but after that what US Military Policy will face, is another Iraq and another Afghanistan in Iran. Whatever their religious motivations, Iran's leadership has many wise people in their midst. They have a dialogue going on through back channels with the United States, and at the same time, they would be preparing for an Iraq-type invasion. That would be a reasonable expectation and assumption even for their enemies to make.

Typical of this approach and thinking, is a recently published book, '*The Pentagon's New Map*', by Thomas P.M. Burnett. The author is a Professor of Warfare Analysis at the US Naval War College, Newport, Rhode Islands. Burnett is also an Advisor to the Pentagon and the Defence Secretary, Rumsfeld, gives them and the Intelligence community, presentations on current US concerns, namely, an 'Operating Theory of the World – and a Military Strategy to Accompany it'. This involves identifying the problem parts of the world and aggressively shrinking them.

Burnett divides and categorizes the world into two: the Functional Core, or the 'Core', with 'globalization connectivity'; and the non-integrating 'Functional Gap or Gap', disconnected from globalization. The Gap is the strategic threat to the US, in his words. Global connectivity means, the US (and the MNCs) connected to the markets with reducing tariffs and customs barriers, trade laws drafted by Corporate Lawyers for permissive and full access to banks, insurance and financial markets. India and China (emerging markets) are included in the 'Core' category. He elaborates: "A country's potential to warrant US Military intervention is inversely related to its globalization connectivity." That is a clear signal, 'fall in line or else!'

Burnett articulates his thesis with unshakable conviction : "Show me a part of the world that is secure in its peace and I will show you strong or growing ties between the local military and the US Military... Show me the regions where war is inconceivable, and I will show you permanent military bases and long term security alliances ....Show me the strongest investment relationship in the global economy and I will show you two post-war occupations, remade Europe and Japan, following World War II"; (an old, outdated argument, no longer relevant, when the engine of growth has turned into the world's largest debtor, living on borrowed money). But Burnett's warnings cannot be disregarded, he writes, "In sum, it is always possible to fall off this bandwagon, called globalization (specially directed at Argentina, Brazil, Venezuela, Bolivia and Uruguay, who are cool to the US proposed Free Trade Agreement). And when you do, bloodshed will follow. If you are lucky, so will the American troops!"

Burnett advocates that the 'gaps' are shrunk, as they are non-integrating with the markets and the 'Functional Core' is enlarged and incorporated into the Western Alliance System, albeit, as markets for the goods and services of the Western dominated and controlled economic system, being steadily put in place, for the American century. "Our next war in the Gulf will be a historical tipping point—the moment when Washington (read Wall Street and the Bankers) takes real ownership of strategic security, in the age of globalization". Bremer's famous '100 Orders' on behalf of the Coalition Provisional Authority, in force, under Allawi, places all Iraqi national assets for privatization, with no legal encumbrances and liability and full immunity Iraqi and by Presidential decrees, issued in Washington, in the American Courts of Law.

Returning to Burnett's 'Pentagon's New Plan', he continues in similar vein, "Freedom cannot blossom in the Middle-east without the US provided Security and Security is the country's (US) most influential public sector export. By that, I do not mean Arms Exports (possibly that goes without saying), but basically the attention paid by our Security Forces to any region's potential, for mass violence. We are the only nation on earth capable of exporting security, in a sustained manner, and we have a very good track record of doing it". Even as the people of Iraq and Afghanistan experienced the worst insecurity in their history!

Burnett and his friends in Washington and the Wall Street are no cold war warriors; they are cool, calculating and hard-boiled, who help determine the new Agenda for overwhelming, pre-dominance of the world, the 'hand on the spigot', global finance capital. Their job is to influence the Officer Corps around the world, that all that they are commanded to pursue, is vital to US national interests, 'no matter what it takes'. The Armed Forces as instruments of State Policy, now more than ever before, have to understand, and further the announced and planned force, being repositioned around global trouble-spots, in the main, where rich global resources lie.

The major problem in the hypothesis, advanced by Professor Burnett, is that, the quality of life to be sought after by a US citizen, held out as an attainable ideal by the American citizen is unsustainable in the global economy, in view of the paucity of resources, foremost amongst them Oil or Energy equivalents. Oil has already peaked, according to top experts and the few who do not concur, also agree that it will peak, latest by 2010, in the face of consumption exceeding new finds, and the established reserves exhausting themselves. Secondly, even after the Petro-Dollars in the Dollar denominated trade are parked in major US banks, that still does not prevent the fiscal crisis in the US Government and Corporations. Additionally, the Saudi Arabian ruling family has parked one trillion Dollars, in US Treasury bonds, and another one trillion Dollars in US banks, along with China, Japan, South Korea, Taiwan, who have almost all their surpluses in US Treasury bonds, Pension Funds and Housing Mortgages and other Paper-Securities. So, we have the Government, the Corporate sector and household debt, in trillions of Dollars which is unsustainable even after delinking the world's reserve, from 'Gold' in 1973. Hence, there is likely to be more loss of jobs, not less, lowered wages, lack of medicare and housing, fewer opportunities in education and inequality in the homeland, in the days ahead. Globalization is not working even for the average American.

Hence, Globalization (privatization and liberalization) would open and capture new markets: manufactures, services and agriculture products. That brings us to the old world of the 18th and 19th century, when colonies were the order of the day. The Papal Bull had divided up the world for that version of 'Globalization,' termed 'Colonization'. Now, we have the 'Functional Core' and the 'Functional Gap' with the self-given mandate, to squeeze out the 'Gap', what the UK foreign policy experts have defined as 'New Empire'; hence, the increasing Militarization of Globalization. Private Military Companies (PMCs) are adjuncts to regular Armed Forces, local militias are growing under various labels to support the local nominees or potentates/war-lords.

Defence and Security Establishments, including the Armed Forces, are increasingly being told to devote their intellectual resources to other than 'State vs State war/conflict scenarios to interventions of an altogether different kind. It is true that major Military systems and newer fourth generation, micro nuke weapons are also on order, but they will be used as blackmail or in blitzkreig invasions, should other attempts at regime change fail.

6

Indo-US Military-to-Military Relations

Military-to-Military relationships, usually have as their underlying basis, the tacit approval of the 'limiting boundaries,' set by the political leadership of the two countries involved. The United States has a long and a somewhat controversial history of such relationships that it has forged with countries around the world, particularly in the Philippines, South Korea, Japan, Indonesia, Egypt, Nigeria and Latin America, and nearer home, in Pakistan, Iran, Saudi Arabia, Iraq, Turkey and now, in East Europe and the Central Asian and Caspian Sea region. Its Military-to-Military relationships with European nations have been of a different character, though immediately after World War II, they had a very large covert undercover objective, that of the elimination of the Communist Resistance which had gained popular acceptance in countries, such as France, Italy and Greece, to give some examples, in view of their anti-Fascist people's movements and militia organizations at a time when most Governments had capitulated to the Nazi /Fascist atrocities.

Overthrow of democratically elected Civilian Governments was routine in Brazil, Argentina, Chile and Pakistan, if it served the political and economic interests of the US. The School for Americas, identified, groomed and trained Military and Police Officers to assume such leadership roles in their home countries. The International Police Academy groomed up the coming Police and Intelligence Officers of the developing countries and gave them the political orientation of the free world, free market economies etc., and of 'Democracy' oriented to this model. India had stayed largely clear of such joint Military/ Police ventures, having a broad understanding of the policy objectives of a Non-Aligned State. With the spread of such an all-encompassing concept as 'Globalization' with policies oriented towards the political and economic objectives of the Nation-State, all but remaining in name, with arms expenditures of all countries concurrently escalating, in an arms race, fuelled by antagonisms, the orchestrated 'War on Terror', fueled among others by Oil Giants and arms manufacturing conglomerates, in need of subsidies from national exchequers, strange undercurrents seem to be at play.

In the introduction to a recent publication, '*People, Progress, Partnership — The Transformation of US – India Relations'*, the outgoing US Secretary of State, General Colin Powell, recalls former Prime Minister Vajpayee's words that India and the US are 'natural allies'. In this context, the question arises, "Who are the "natural enemies" of these "natural allies"? This document has an entire chapter on 'Defence Relations – Shared Strategic Future'. During General Colin Powell's last visit to New Delhi, the Secretary of State of the Bush-administration, spoke glowingly of 'Military-to-Military' relations progressing, and being the cornerstone of growing Indo-US relations, in this fundamental transformation in relations between the United States and India. Powell underlined that, 'together', we have opened new levels of co-operation, on law enforcement and intelligence sharing.

It is worthwhile summarizing the major thrust areas of this chapter, on **'Defence Relations—Shared Strategic Future',** which are as follows:

1. The key word in the ever expanding lexicon of the US-India Defence Relationship is, "inter-operability"...It portrays a future in which the two countries share strategic doctrines and operations, in order to tackle the challenges of a new century.

2. It was India's swift response to the September 11, 2001 terrorist attacks on the US and its unconditional support for the War on Terrorism that galvanized the change in US-India Military Relations.

3. That, the first steps had already been taken months earlier, when India endorsed the National Missile Defence programme unveiled by President Bush, in his speech at the National Defence University, in May, 2001.

4. The announcement of removal of sanctions against India, in September, 2001 helped to identify mutually overlapping National Security Goals and gave a new impetus to Military ties.

5. The aim of the burgeoning military ties, is to develop capabilities and confidence, jointly confront Multilateral Security issues, such as protection of energy supplies and sea lanes, conduct peace-keeping and combat Terrorism. The Military establishments of both the countries have much to gain from strengthening this relationship.

6. The development of inter-operable procedures, communications and doctrines is only possible through familiarization, understanding and confidence building, focusing on areas of mutual interest and enhancing the professional development of personnel.

7. Fast paced developments in Military-to-Military ("Mil-to-Mil") Relations have been most visible aspect of transforming the bilateral relationship. This is evident from the growing frequency of bilateral exercises, seminars, personnel exchanges, high level and unit visits and exchanges, as well as military technology sales and cooperation, "and can play an important part in contributing to peace, security and freedom" in Asia . Admiral Blair, former C-in-C, US Pacific Fleet, emphasized during his visit to India, "We will develop our relationship with India on the basis of India's emergence as a rising global power."

8. The guidance document of the US-India Defence Relationship, is the 'Agreed Minute of Defence Relations of 1995. However, the relationship has since then acquired many dimensions and progressed towards working together in real situations and when the need arises. A key element of the engagement process is the enlarged 'International Military Education and Training' (IMET), programme which has a questionable record and history, in the role that some of the US-trained and sponsored officers have subsequently played, in overturning democratically elected governments, replacing them with Military *juntas* or in allying with civil servants who subtly further the US interests in their home countries.

9. Joint operations and joint exercises will, it is argued in the document under reference, necessitate India possessing compatible equipment and technology. (Even though, Electronic Sensors were marginally effective to check Mexican infiltration across the flat lands, into the US, India has inducted the same Sensors on the LoC in J&K and stationed US technical personnel to install and maintain these Sensors).

10. The document quotes the former US Ambassador, Blackwell, as saying, "The US will be a reliable provider of defence commodities to India, because a strengthened, capable and effective Indian Military is in America's national interests."

11. The last refrain for 'Mil-to-Mil' relationship is of course combating the regional and global challenges of Terrorism.

Two of the initiatives in the recently accelerated relationship, have invited reactions which need to be addressed, in the background of the continuity and clarity of the definition of what are the vital national interests of the US. These are not subject to changes, based on the incumbent holding the Presidency of the US, or whether he is a Republican or a Democrat. These are spelt out in the National Security Strategy documents, promulgated periodically. Therefore, several media commentators, who take the trouble to comment on President Bush being 'good for India', are simply adding to the obfuscation of the core issues. US Presidents uphold and relentlessly pursue Corporate America's interests, though their style and rhetoric in public speech may differ. The control of oil and key mineral resources in West/Central Asia, West Africa and Latin America is the number one priority of the US policy and nothing will permit a deviation. If 'Rebuilding America's Defence: Strategy, Forces and Resources', have to be reassessed, that is done in the framework of the 'Project for the New American Century' (PNAC). If the criticality of the 'Resource-rich' areas is geo-politically necessary, a "Force Posture Review' is undertaken without fuss. US policy is not influenced by sentimentality, or even such values frequently resorted to as 'Freedom and Democracy', though they may be frequently cited to camouflage Corporate interests. It is hardly necessary to quote examples, in different parts of the world. Democracy plays a second fiddle, in pursuit of the US global interests. Some may say that, this is 'real-politik' and it has always been so, specially so where imperial interests are to be secured. The problem is not with the United States which has a clear global vision, all spelt out. The real problem lies in the minds of the spin doctors who are out to confuse the public interest, the people of India, as to where lies our vital national interests.

November 2004 saw some inspired writing in the mainstream media and some TV channels painting a doomsday scenario, for the most important non-NATO ally, MINNA, Pakistan. It is being visualized in this scenario that Pakistan, is all on the way to 'cracking up'/or breaking up, (despite the US economic aid of US$ 3 billion, and Military Supplies, already in the pipeline, of US$ 1 billion), US Military forward operating bases in Pakistan, a pervasive influence and control of the ISI, and close relationships with the Pak Military. Following the break up, it is projected that US and India will intervene to eliminate the *Jehadi* forces in Pakistan. This scenario is unrealistic and ignores the military strategic objective of the United States in the region, with large, debilitating US Forces, committed in Iraq, preparing for similar action in Iran, and the Axis of Evil; the Military Forces, redeployment to West Africa, and stretched out from Georgia-Azerbaijan to Khazakistan, Uzbekistan, Kyrgyzia, Turkmenistan, not to mention the over 700 bases around the world. With this reality, Ops "Save Pakistani Freedom" does not appear to be a probable one, with 'Save Nepal, Bangladesh, Myanmar and Sri Lanka,' on the anvil! The security management issues confronting us are such that we are in no position to consider interventions outside. The BJP led Government's policy announcements, articulated by L. K. Advani and Brajesh Mishra, "about the same source of Terror", will have to rest, while the present Government devotes itself to pursuing a fragile energy security scenario to keep the people, industry and agriculture going, rather than chasing Terrorists in foreign lands.

It is the same type of thinking of there being joint security interests, that commits the Indian Navy to 'joint anti-piracy' patrolling, with the US Navy in Malacca Straits, without the prior concurrence and participation of Malaysia and Indonesia, the other two nations on the Straits.

The Proliferation Security Initiative is a laudable idea, but it needs the UN approval. After all, the IAEA is UN instrument. The US and India, unilaterally intercepting, searching and detaining merchant ships in international waters could become a messy business and cause avoidable friction and tension, specially when the Intelligence is poor, as it was in Iraq and the Niger Uranium and the Aluminium Rods case, and wholly fabricated, in pursuit of the US Military objectives, in other Sovereign States.

Any objective analysis will demonstrate that US global designs, plans, preparations and operations have an altogether different dimension, and there is very little, by way of convergence, between a Superpower and India, whose main challenge is to maintain its unity and lift its billions of people, out of misery and poverty – to feed, clothe, house, educate, and provide employment to about 18 million young people, entering the working age, each new year, apart from the responsibility of nearly six hundred million people who are unemployed or under-unemployed and, therefore, suffer serious malnutrition. A former Prime Minister, Shri PV Narsimha Rao himself forced to sign the IMF loan and conditionalities and subsequently the Uruguay GATT Agreements, and the US Treasury Sponsored 'Reforms', and its consequences spoke of the 'middle path' and cautioned his Government and the country, against too close an embrace or an "*Alingan*".

We now have a situation where the US Armed Forces, a hitherto highly professional institution, has turned itself deliberately and openly into a killing machine, to impress the world with diabolical cruelty, mass murdering of men, women and children, sparing no one, not even the ill, maimed or the old people, in the Iraqi cities, much of it shown on video tapes. Civilians have been bombarded, indescribable methods of torture have been used even on children, women, and civilians at Abu Gharaib city and elsewhere; the infrastructure of cities and towns, including water, sanitation, electricity and hospitals, have been destroyed for the world to see. The resistance of the people of Iraq to the invasion and occupation of their country, and seizure by military means of the Oil resources, is being described as "Insurgency" and "Terrorism." We are witnessing a Nazi assault and holocaust again, and a replay of the Vietnam on video in the scenes of killings by the Occupation Forces emerging from Iraq.

Within the United States, the US Administration having politicized the CIA, even more than ever before has resulted in a revolt amongst the CIA personnel, at various levels and departments, including Analysts, and personnel in Overt and Covert Operations. To sideline this dissent, the US Secretary of Defence had already created a Special Intelligence Group, Strategic Support Branch in January 2005, in the Pentagon, reporting directly to the Secretary of Defence, to provide Intelligence and to justify policy decisions, already made for Iraq and elsewhere.

The latest news leaks are reporting that Covert Operations or 'War in the Shadows', in foreign countries, will henceforth be carried out by the US Armed Forces, the CIA, having been divested of this responsibility, due to lack of confidence (and trust) in its personnel. This fundamentally changes the character of the Armed Forces who now become the preferred and sole instrument of the Administration in planning and executing covert operations, which also includes assassinations of Heads of States, and political leaders, subversion of local militias and their bosses, to serve such political objectives as 'Regime Change' or the blackmailing Governments. In other words, the deployments on the battlefield can change into covert deployments in another country's political arena and its internal affairs, as per requirement. That transforms the Generals, Admirals and Air Marshals, into secret operatives who will stop at nothing and to whom no rules of engagement will apply. They already enjoy, by the US President's executive order, immunity from the International Criminal Court and the Geneva Conventions, as interpreted by the President of the United States.

What must be squarely faced, is, whether 'Mil-to-Mil' relations, therefore, will generate a similar psyche in the Indian Armed Forces and whether, we can remain immune to the example that is being demonstrated, in the name of Anti-Insurgency and Counter Terror Operations, on daily show in Iraq and Palestine. Will this influence not lead to a blow-back that will completely destabilize a nation with a diversity, presently mutually reinforcing in India? In fact, these objectives, if emulated of the US strategic Military Covert Doctrine, could turn India's direction to a theocracy with a contrived 'Internal Enemy'. Importantly, will such close relations with the US Military Forces, mandated to carry out Covert Operations against people of Sovereign nations, not alter the apolitical and hitherto Secular and professional character of our much respected Armed Forces? Will it not result in India's objectives being questioned in the region and globally? Are we not then, playing with fire?

The world is witnessing a fragile 'energy security' situation, which many experts in and conferences on 'Peak Oil' have categorized as, the "End of the Age of Oil". We are witnessing a volatile Dollar on a steady decline, with countries, companies and individuals switching to the Euro and gold, having earlier given life support to the US economy, hitherto, regarded as a Global Power House. Today, its Government, Corporate, and household debt is in trillions and every day it is the injection of US $ 2.6 billion a day, and 80 per cent of the world's savings that enables the US economy to manage to survive, holding in hostage, the Chinese and Japanese economies, East Asia and Europe and the Central Banks, including India. All those who have parked their Dollars in US Treasury Bonds! (The Prime Minister, Dr. Manmohan Singh, known for his understatements, underlined at the Senior Commanders Conference, on October 26, 2004, the "imperatives of the increasingly unstable international environment.") However, in October 2005 (reports *The Hindu*) the PM directed the Indian Navy go ahead to forge "workable alliances" to safeguard 'Energy Security' (supplies) (in the Arabian Sea, Indian Ocean and Malacca Straits)!

Very few nations would survive this economic time-bomb that is ticking relentlessly. Therefore, to talk of the 'War on Terror', which is a cover up for the war to capture resources, is brinkmanship on a global scale.

India has tackled Terrorism and Insurgency, encouraged by the same external forces which now wage a fraudulent 'War on Terror', with political acumen and sagacity; through reconciliation, bringing about peace in very difficult circumstances. Narcotics, Gun Running and Terrorism, together, have been and are our foes, aimed at corroding the independence of our economic and political policies within and in the International fora.

In February 2004, the 'Next Step in Strategic Partnership' (NSSP), was hailed by the BJP leadership, as a precursor to the bonanza of hi-tech that would follow. The last BJP led Government sold out India's vital national interests (see article in this book), and brought no major gains. It consistently by-passed Parliament, hid its inter-governmental and agreements from the people and the Parliament, wholly in violation of the Republican form of Government, which mandates open policies.

Former Foreign Secretary, Shri Kanwal Sibal, now our Ambassador in Moscow, as reported in *The Hindu,* dated

October 28, 2005 said, "India and the United States are not strategic partners, and have a long way to go before they become that ....NSSD 2001 describes India as the US Strategic partner, Ignoring the harsh reality that India and the United States cannot be strategic partners until issues related to nuclear power, missiles and dual technologies are resolved. Sibal further quoted that, "India was still subject to US sanctions."

In a recent interview to *The Hindu* in October 2004, Dr Anil Kakodkar, Chairman, Atomic Energy Commission in reply to the question, "Will the dialogue on with the US Next Steps in Strategic Partnership, be of any use to India, for developing our nuclear power technology? answered, "I don't think so." However, it is an irony that Dr Kakodkar reversed this earlier stand in the July 2005 Indo-US Nuclear Agreement signed in Washington DC.

A lot of water has flowed down the Ganga, since the days the BJP-led Government went on an imaginary honeymoon to distant shores. On September 19, 2001, *The Times of India,* normally a cautious paper, reported on a front page dispatch, datelined, New Delhi, under the heading 'India Offers America, Use of Three Air Bases'. The report said "Even though no Military plans have been firmed up by the US, for retaliatory strikes, India has identified three Air Bases, in addition to unspecified Port Facilities, on the western seaboard, as part of its operational support to the US. The Air Bases are, Avantipur in Jammu & Kashmir (next to Srinagar, to be more precise), Adampur in Punjab, and Jamnagar, to the US. A senior security (Defence) official told *TNN* that the offer was conveyed to the US after it was approved by the Cabinet Committee on Security last Thursday (i.e. around September 14, 2001, three days after 9/11, a record of sorts), after consultations with the three Service Chiefs, who unanimously agreed on the need to support the US action (without knowing its contours and dimensions)... According to the officials, "The Chiefs felt that the Americans had joined 'our' War against Terrorism and we must naturally be the first ones to offer them help." The officials stated that the Defence Minister, Jaswant Singh's articulation of the

Government's stand, was motivated by a desire to ensure that Pakistan does not gain by India's default... The officials said, India has already begun "operational cooperation" by providing US officials with intelligence on Afghan camps and on the Taliban. The Research and Analysis Wing (RAW) has gathered a wealth of detail on Pakistani Military assistance to the Taliban, in the last few years (US Ambassador Blackwill, meets Defence Chiefs, page 7 the *Times of India* report concludes).

It is hardly necessary to add that the United States preferred to operate, from and within Pakistan. The CCS had made decisions, without waiting to pause, in a record 72 hours. 'Our War on Terrorism', as the Service Chiefs reportedly described it, continued against Cross Border terrorism exported by Pakistan, as here to before, with little or no assistance from the US, except to nudge and cajole us to sit for talks with MINNA. The 'attack' on Parliament House, on December 13, 2002, led to the 'goofed up' Operation *Parakrama* (when the Army Chief asked the Prime Minister, what expected from the war or in other words, what the political objective of the unprecedented mobilization or "Stand to" of the Armed Forces was, to achieve; all he got as a reply was: "*Woh Baad Mein Batayenge*" (that will be told later).

As for which is ever ready with 'details' for the US, and hardly ever for our own Defence Forces, we have the following, on record, from an intelligence official, after *l'affaire* Ravinder Singh, in May 2004.... *The Hindu* reported, in a series of articles, the failure to issue directions by the National Security Adviser, Brajesh Mishra, while he was in the know and while the file was with him, for some days 'instructions even to prevent the CIA asset to fly out of the country' (He was reportedly under surveillance). Why did Mishra hold back a decision and Why was Ravinder Singh erstwhile in Joint Secretary in RAW headquarter, New Delhi so important to the Americans is what the Intelligence Adviser, in the PMO, wants to find out!

The Hindu report, dated August 20, 2004, under banner headlines, "Why was Terror Intelligence withheld," reports and quotes in extenso, Indian intelligence officials, as expressing 'concern over the withholding of terrorism-related information, by the United States Information Centre, New Delhi believes could be key to saving lives 'Specific instances of non-sharing of information, gained through interrogations of Al-Qaeda operatives, like Muhammad Khan, arrested on July 13, with respect to Al-Qaeda operatives in India, as this organization shares infrastructure with Pak-based Terrorist Groups, operating in India. Various arrests of key people in Afghanistan and Pakistan, charged with aiding the Taliban, also ran extensive Terror Networks in India. Cases, with names running Harkat-ul-Ansar, like Akhtar, interrogated and detained, have been cited at the Counter Terror meetings in New Delhi in July 2004 but Indian Intelligence has been kept in the dark. "The US assets, which are part of the extensive technical and human intelligence of the US in Pakistan pick up enormous communication intelligence on the activities of terrorist organizations based in Pakistan." Our Intelligence Officials have been cited in *the Hindu* report, as saying, "that not one single piece of Intelligence has ever been passed on to us. By contrast, are being regularly mined for. whatever we know, about these groups." Washington has also been unwilling to facilitate on going CBI investigations, into the 1999 Hijacking of Indian Airlines Flight IC-814.

A senior Intelligence official told *The Hindu*, that while Counter-Terrorism has expanded greatly in recent years, much of what was passed on was, "vague in the extreme and almost never of operational use." Are we to assume that knowing this state of play, the Cabinet Committee on Security and the three Service Chiefs, have played a game from 1999 to May 2004, which is fraught with grave consequences, in opening the doors of Civil and Military Intelligence, the sanctum sanctorum, to US and Israeli Intelligence? This bonhomie and casualness has extended to joint exercises in J&K and the North East, where not only are assets recruited but the 'ground truth' of Spy Satellite Imagery is verified.

All the joint exercises, primarily provide windows to probe our Electronic Warfare and Communication vulnerabilities. Friendly countries do not launch, almost daily, intelligence flights up and down our Western and Eastern seaboards from Diego Garcia and Australian bases, nor would their Surveillance Aircraft and 'Research Ships' monitor our exercises, missile firings or take gravimetric measurements and hydrological conditions on a fairly regular basis, off sensitive Indian Vital Areas(VAs) and VPs.

The greatest opening into the previously barred areas, has been encouraged by the former Home Minister and the two Defence Ministers (Fernandes and Jaswant Singh, with the tacit concurrence, of the former PM and his NSA). Senior civil, intelligence and military intelligence officials, knowing that this was gravely jeopardizing national security, fell in line to carry favour, promotions and gubernatorial posts, like Mr Dave for example. Kashmir and the North East, specially, were up for grabs. Otherwise their jobs may have been on line.

The greatest losses have occurred as this 'bonhomie', 'trust' and unmonitored contacts, have multiplier effects, whose bounds have never been assessed. In the meanwhile, the thinktanks in New Delhi, in particular, and the media in general, have been giving encouraging, uncritical support, to such activities and individuals.

Will anyone in the new dispensation call for a review of the losses and gains and bring into force the time-tested checks and balances, in the 'Mil-to-Mil' and Civilian to Civilian Relations, at par with what the US and UK and every prudent nation has thought it appropriate–to minimally safeguard its interests.

Post Script: New Delhi, December 9 2004, *The Hindu*: Under headline, 'Arms Supplies to Pakistan'— India Conveys Concern to US. Defence Secretary talks with *Raksha Mantri* ... Sharing perspectives on "their respective ties" with Pakistan, the External Affairs Ministry Spokesman stressed that, "it was noted that the India-US Relations had seen significant transformation during President Bush's First Term and that the US was now perceived as a strategic partner."

"We attach importance to the visit of Secretary Rumsfeld. This is the first visit, at the Cabinet level, after the re-election of

President George Bush. As you know, Defence Co-operation has imparted a significant impetus to the emerging Indo-US Strategic Partnership."

The role played by the Department of Defence (US) to the growth of our bilateral ties, was recognized during the discussions today. It was also noted that India cherishes its relations that are based on our shared belief in Democracy. During the discussions, considerable emphasis was also laid on the maintenance of the strategic focus of our bilateral relationship," he said.

The spokesman also said that Rumsfeld's visit provided the two sides with an "excellent opportunity" to review Defence cooperation. Showing a visible interest in broadening Defence Cooperation, they expressed satisfaction at the rapid growth of this relationship, including the effective working of the dialogue mechanism, Military-to-Military contacts, exercises, visits, education and training.

Therefore, the big question is whether the Indian military is being nudged to reorient itself to moving away from defending India and Indian interests to such unending, quests as 'furthering 'regime changes', 'democracy' and the smoke-screen, of the 'global war on terror', under US auspices.'

That question is answered in the Indo-US Defence Framework Agreement of 28 June 2005, signed by Rumsfeld and Pranab Mukherjee in Washington, where India has agreed to 'Joint Operations' (outside the UN), if they are in 'Mutual interest' for the first time since 1947.

7

US Force Architecture – In The Coming Years

Afghanistan and Iraq may have compelled a rethink in 'Rebuilding America's Defences–Strategies, Resources and Forces', the operational architecture of the 'Project for the American Century (PNAC)' and the objectives of world dominance, spelt out in NSSD 2002.

Afghanistan is far from secured. It has the fastest growing GDP in the world; but it is based on opium production and exports, which contribute about 57 per cent of the GDP. That is under the command and control of the war-lords and effectively that is where the 'power' lies, notwithstanding the feeble 'reconstruction' of that country. NATO Forces in Afghanistan are mainly deployed on garrison duties and occasional convoy protection; UN and Western aid agencies have withdrawn from the countryside due to the insecurity of the situation.

Iraq is in a state of worsening turmoil, even if we disregard reports from well reputed, unembedded journalists. The latest CIA Reports on Iraq, in the end November 2004, have not been disputed by the Commander of the US forces in Iraq, though the US Ambassador, Negroponte, has expressed dissent. Over a hundred attacks per day, on US and its allies, including the Police, Fallujah – flattened but not won, other major Iraqi cities like Mosul, Ramadi and Najaf in disputed control even 19 months after the 'Mission Accomplished' Invasion objectives were achieved – neither freedom nor democracy was established, with a large number of children, women and civilians killed and maimed; the wanton destruction of cities, towns and villages, is all that has been achieved. Oilfields and oil pipelines are unsecured and this time, America is paying for Gulf War II, and its aftermath.

It is true that while Iraq has added US$ 80 billion to the US Defence Budget, which adds to the US$ 500 billion budget deficit and the nearly US$ 700 billion current account deficit, as of today, the US receives US$ 2.6 billion per day, or over 80 per cent of the world's savings, with which it buys goods and services and pays the public services. This bounty is voluntarily paid for by Japan, China, Korea and Taiwan, European investors, Latin American flight of capital, Petro-Dollars from Saudi Arabia, Kuwait, UAE, Nigeria, Angola and Zaire. India contributes a little by keeping over 50 per cent of its Foreign Exchange in Dollars, earning 3-4 per cent and paying out 7-8 per cent to those who have parked their money here, for higher returns. Effectively, Japan, China and South Korea are paying for the US War and Occupation in Iraq, with its over 740 Bases, in more than a hundred countries around the world.

What needs to be understood, without white-washing is that, the 'Force Posture Review', ordered a few months ago and now underway, has the sole objective of redeploying Forces, where the oil and mineral resources are. Yet, the existing mix of forces, is still largely unchanged from the Cold War stand-off, except the addition of Private Military companies, which are the *'avant-garde'* of the corporations, and also the 'cowboys' of the US Army.

The MIRV Ballistic Missiles, with mega-ton Warheads, are hardly useable against any major enemy. They are an insurance for the 'big boys'. We, therefore, have in the offing, the accelerated development and deployment of the Precision, Micro Nukes, capable of destroying small cities, where the 'Insurgents' breed! DU Weapons, fired from aircrafts and tanks, do not have immediate deterrence value. People are still ready to die for their country, for instance, the Shias, Sunnis and Kurds, who are one entity in Iraq.

Iraq has taught us that the Big Bang Wars do not vanquish people. If there is already a friendly regime, in effective control of energy and mineral resources, there still have to be Forces, a few hours away, to provide a counter to any challenger, who may have other ideas! If 'Regime Change' is necessary to secure vital national interests of the US, anywhere, anytime, the contingency must provide for effective intervention and policing/ law enforcement support, to friends and allies. Hence, the erection/establishment of four major Military Bases in Iraq, in addition to the Big Bombers in Diego Garcia, and the Carrier groups in the Gulf and the trouble spots.

Non-state actors, instability in the Islamic (Oil) World, political shifts in Asia, Africa, and the Latin American countries, and accelerated proliferation of WMDs and hence, the justification for the new targeting lists of the fourth generation weapons as pre-emptive, and justification for their first-use.

Humvees, Air Defence Weapons, and Heavy Artillery are being scaled down. Humvees with armour protection, substitute the old, light Humvees! When the emphasis has shifted to low end of the conflict spectrum and post-conflict management, it is natural that a new mix of Forces have got ready. Young 'throwaway soldiers' will be required to mop up the professional Pincers of the Marines and the Black-Watch Regiments. Special Forces launched from the sea, air and the grounds, will be required in larger numbers. They may double up for the 'War in the Shadows' covert operations, in the process of being transferred to the US Armed Forces (hitherto with the CIA). This environment, best exemplified by the Iraqi resistance, was not anticipated by the Quadrennial Defence Review and subsequent planning exercises. The Vietnam War was largely a rural-based resistance. The last such tactics and decentralized organization of resistance were seen in Algeria, Stalingrad and in the partisan resistance to the Nazi Army, when it invaded the Soviet Union and to some extant also in Yugoslavia, under the leadership of Marshal Tito; though no 'Al Tito' has been heard of, so far in Iraq! Killing the top leadership may temporarily weaken the resistance, but is unlikely to vanquish them.

The zone of instability, extending from the West coast of Africa, through the Middle-East, on to South-East Asia, is a considerable challenge to a flexible, yet quick and effective response of the US Military leadership. At this moment, the US Forces are pinned down in Iraq and the deployment of 12,000 additional troops is not likely to bring the situation to a successful solution. The mix of conventional, special operations forces and law enforcement forces is complex, with no previous experience of the current environment, in the politically unstable but resource rich areas. The European Union, with the new 'Berlin Plus' Project, is also considering such requirements and the expansion of its commitments to areas other than Europe. Through increased joint exercises, the US military is planning 'Ad-hoc' coalitions of the willing nations with such partners as India and Pakistan, and hence, the emphasis on inter-operability.

It is a topic of some importance to discuss, whether the US Military is spread out too thinly and whether the US ambitions are taking on the hue of 'imperial overstretch'. It needs to be remembered first that the US Naval and Airpower is flexible and can re-deploy within days, if not hours. So can integral 'Special Forces', which by definition are Quick Response Forces. This leaves the Infantry and the Armoured corps, which also have specialized Airborne corps and divisions, which can be re-deployed with dispatch. In essential characteristics, the US Armed Forces are capable of being 'concentrated', if the Political and Intelligence appreciation is alert and knows its mind clearly. The second part of the poser is : when is it enough and when are the Forces deemed to be insufficient, in given circumstances. Obviously, this depends on the local conditions. If the regime and its leaders are susceptible to compromise, there is no problem to start off with. However, if the people rise, with or without a strong Central Organization, as in Iraq, then even a strength of 3,00,000 will not be sufficient. This cannot be predicted, whether we take the hypothetical cases of Syria, Iran or North Korea, despite the projection of destructive power from offshore. The stabilization phase, as the Americans have termed it, is essentially a political issue and the Invasion-cum-Occupation Force, whatever its professionalism can hardly provide the answer, and as in Iraq, lose its moral and professional bearings or compass. Once this happens, the game is usually on a slippery slope. Colombia, Phillipines and perhaps, Indonesia would, therefore, require very careful execution of military operations, else, they will degenerate into a morass.

'Wars in the Shadows,' is like heady wine for the arm chair Tacticians, adorning thinktanks, but people, time and again, have emerged as 'unknown' quantities, in the neat 'operational research' modeling that both Thinktanks and 'War-gaming' Centres tend to present.

It can be argued with many illustrations and examples that, 'Wars in the Shadows' and 'Regime Change', as well as Control of the 'Oil' spigot operations, have in the past, been brought to successful conclusions by the CIA, acting in concert with multi-national oil corporations and conglomerates in many cases without the mess that has been brought on in Afghanistan and Iraq in particular, through massive, ill-timed military operations. If there is a tearing hurry, then it may lead to a tearing failure too!

Vice President Dick Cheney's 'New Energy Policy Group' did a comprehensive review of the US Energy Requirements and the Global Energy Resource Base, its present possibilities and potential. It concluded that in the current pattern of energy consumption (over two-third spent on road transportation with cars, SUVs and big trucks dominating), America would be even more dependent on imports of Oil, to the extent of about 67 per cent in another 20 years (with the Base Year 2002). The Global Energy Demand was expected to rise by 44 million barrels a day, or 57 per cent more, than the current production, after meeting local consumption. With all the technology and investment, there was little prospect that, this could be met, with no new Oil Fields on the horizon (Saudi expectations of raising Oil output, simply not materializing, Shell BP's Oil Reserves being revised 20 per cent downwards, opposition to drilling in the Alaska Natural Wild-life Reserves (ANWR) rising, and the US R&D efforts in Alternative Technologies on drip. There was as yet no mobilization to persuade people to adapt or moderate their lifestyles or for the Government to invest in mass rapid transportation means, even though the US is well endowed to permit change. If this is not happening, as it was recommended by the Cheney Energy Report 2001, then it can be due only to the profit driven myopia of the oil companies. If the oil corporate agenda drives the US government to re-deploy the Military, globally only, with the objective of having the 'hand on the spigot', all over the world then, there is a problem, because the US Military will have to comply, because the US Administration is driven by these very companies, and so is the US Congress and the Senate.

Of course, the Pentagon is doing its best to re-configure the architecture or force-mix of the Military. However, as the US State Department has, in several earlier reports, acknowledged that the US Foreign Policy and presence is generating opposition and hostility in large sections of the people everywhere, including in the West. The best Military in the world cannot be expected to create Fallujah's at will and get away with it. A Military Force, however empowered, is not capable of dealing with political fallout. An arranged election in January 2005 will not prove the thesis of the 'influentials' that 'this is the end of history'.

It was diamonds and gold in the Congo and Zaire, a half century ago (it is relevant to recall that Patrice Lumumba, the democratically elected Prime Minister of undivided Congo, was murdered at the behest of Foreign Mining interests). The companies may still be mining, but the people there have already paid the price of four million deaths, 98 percent of them being children, under the age of 5 years. Oil has cost over a hundred thousand lives and destroyed cities, towns and habitations, its health, education, water and energy supply infrastructure, not including the lives lost, under 10 years of sanctions and the first Gulf War. Extrapolated, over the same period, at the same rate, that would be more than five million, in the next few decades. Will the living beings be better off than the dead ones?

Militaries are best on the battlefield, not at homes, parks, school playgrounds, health clinics and hospitals, even if they may be trained and restructured for law enforcement, peace-making and peace-keeping. Do the armoured vehicles and armoured soldiers inspire peace and tranquility? Democracy is incompatible with such a painting on the mantle piece.

Japan is reported to have threatened to offload its dollar investments, if the US does not raise interest rates and restore minimal Japanese export value. Oil dominance is multi-dimensional in its repercussions. This is yet another dimension that the US Armed Forces cannot be expected to deliver on, no matter how exceptionally professional they may be, no matter how much their budget is enhanced, how many high school students join, or are drafted. More and more people are beginning to understand that the job losses, lower wage employment, and 'restrictions at home' are somewhere linked to the War on Terror, and that this War is likely to create more young people, who are not prepared to take more and more injustice, round the world. They have some idea of what US style democracy means; Militarization through Political and Military Methods and Processes, be it in pursuit for Oil, Minerals or other resources.

8

Great Game II

'Great Game II' is not new. It is history repeating itself. Only, it is to the power of 'n', in its scale, magnitude, frequency and spread. It is in 'War on Terror' jargon, perhaps a part of the series 'Unending War for Unending Peace'. Great Game II was the title of a perceptive article, in the *New York Times,* about three years ago, describing the Violence/Conflict laden games, to assert claims on Oil and Gas bearing fields, based on prognosticated reserves, from surveys carried out by the 'Oil Majors', in the Caspian Sea Basin.

The key players were naturally the Oil Majors, supported/ leveraged by their home-country Governments, the Successor Regimes of the USSR/CIS, mostly headed by old Communists/ Apparatchiks, who had been 'committed' Party First Secretaries of the Republics or Politbureau Members, now turned 'benevolent dictators', guiding 'democracies' and new friends of the 'free markets'. Simultaneously, new fundamentalists and their associate militias/mafias were sprouting, generously, funded by the Oil potentates, like the Saudis, be it in Kosovo, Chechnaya or to the East in Azerbaijan, Kazhakistan, Kyrgistan, Turkmenistan or Uzbekistan. Private Military Companies (PMCs), based in South Africa, UK, and the US, comprised mercenaries disbanded/ retired from regular armies, post the end of Cold War 1990, serve either the Global Oil-Mineral Conglomerates or offered their services as Advisors to Arms Merchants and local potentates (the Purulia Arms Drop Case, regular landing of arms-narcotics, by sea and overland routes to North-East; India is part of the same pattern).

Klashnikovs, land mines, helicopter gun-ships, transport and older surplus fighter aircraft, armoured cars, and communication equipment became brisk business, whether in Bougainville, Timor, Borneo, Indonesia, North-East India and Kashmir, Sub-Saharan Africa, Central Asia, Afghanistan or resource rich East Europe.

Fundamentalist groups, supposedly espousing the Great religions, or based on new found ethnic/racial/language/caste, identities secretly funded by the 'Agencies', either to dispose off 'lootable resources' to the big energy-mineral and old timber firms or to dispute 'ownership/control' of these resources by legitimate successor regimes, post the colonial era or in the case of East Europe and the erstwhile Soviet Republics, the new dispensations. Fundamentalist groups, the track record indicates are handy tools, as agents provocateurs (Osama Bin Laden types).

Hastily recreated 'ethnic' identities have often become the new allies for these big corporations, who either held century old leases or concessions, which should have lapsed at the time of Independence, or which smartly entered into new/revised, one-sided agreements, with the new rulers, who appear to have cared only for self-enrichment. The vast Global Corporate Media Network has been keeping the 'myths' of legality alive, on an unprecedented scale, 'Manufacturing Consent', in the words of Noam Chomsky and Ed Herman.

Therefore, when the Congressionally funded, 'US Institute of Peace', announces the name of a well-reputed Indian journalist as Senior Fellow, and the project for the Fellowship is 'Islam, Ethnicity and Nationalism: A History of Terrorism in Jammu & Kashmir', it ought to ring alarm bells. The people of Kashmir, over the last two thousand years, have, of their own voilation, adopted and embraced in their daily lives, from Buddhism, *Advaita* (Hindu philosophy enunciated by Adi Sankara), spiritual guidance from Central Asian Islam in the fourteenth Century, and from Sufism (in part, emanating from the Iran based *Sufis*). Above all, the Kashmiris gave themselves an Egalitarian, Democratic programme, '*Naya Kashmir*', through their own leader, Sheikh Abdullah, despite the ill-advised, separatist predelictions of Maharaja Hari Singh. Their Accession to the Indian Republic was predicated on a Secular India, whose deviation and aberrations in practice, have hurt the sentiments of the common Kashmiri. From whence Islam, ethnicity, nationalism and 'terrorism', except as a foreign funded operation by fundamentalists, using unemployed youth as cannon fodder. Apparently, there are no advertised Oil and Mineral Resources in Kashmir, though it is the underbelly or the cockpit of Central Asia, in geo-strategic terms. Mention of Kashmir was necessary, just to show that exceptions prove the rule!

Reverting to the issue of Resources; oil, minerals (including strategic minerals), diamonds, gems, timber and water — the G-7 consumes disproportionately large proportions of the world's diminishing resources. For example, the US, with a population of only four per cent of the world consumes over one-third of the energy resources, to sustain its standard of life and Military machine. With the consumption of resources, growing at double the rate of the rise of the world's population, which is growing at about 80 million a year, it will reach eight billion, from the present six billion, by 2020, building up new pressures.

An US Department of Energy Study indicates that India, Brazil, Mexico and China will require three times the Energy in 2020, than their present consumption in 1990. The competition for resources is steadily sharpening, no matter what camouflage is used, to reduce the focus or to generalize the resolution of such potential conflict, as Thomas Friedman, in the *NYT* terms it, "The One Big Thing", claiming that Major Resource disputes will be resolved, through the market mechanism, ignoring that Governments egged on by corporations, have repeatedly taken recourse to coercive diplomacy or military action, over what they define as, 'vital national interests' (for instance the Carter Doctrine 1980, which had put a new Red Line on the Persian Gulf.)

In a refreshingly candid World Bank Study (*Paul Collier and Anke Hoeffler,* in 1999) the conclusive finding is that, States with 'lootable resources' such as diamonds, timber, strategic minerals, oil and gas, are "four times more likely to experience War than a country without these primary Commodities". In different words, John C. Gammon, Deputy Director, CIA, in 1996, noted: "We have to recognize that our nation will not be secure, if Global Energy supplies are not secure. The Sovereign Independence of Saudi Arabia is of vital interest to the US, announced President Bush Sr, on August 7, 1990 (Underlining a continuity in the US policy, since 1945, post Yalta, when President F. D. Roosevelt reached a secret understanding with the Saudi rulers.")

The unimpeded acquisition of the world's Finite Resources continues, aided by legal and illegal arms flows, narcotics generated funds touching US$ 700 billion annually, and PMCs are available for deployment, as desired by corporations and dictators of all brands, the latter signing away huge public wealth while the majority of the citizens live in poverty, squalor and filth, broad brushed by new paints of AIDS, poor governance and 'corruption' in Society.

Oil accounted for 40 per cent of the World Energy Consumption, and Coal for 25 per cent. The remaining 35 per cent was divided between Natural Gas (22 per cent) Nuclear Power (6 per cent) and Hydropower and traditional fuels (7 per cent). Oil and Natural Gas are projected to provide two-third of the World's Consumption of Energy, by 2020, in the face of Oil Production and Reserves, peaking by 2007-10. (The annual US production is 2.8 billion barrels, per year, depleting the US Reserves of 28.6 billion, by 2010.) Transportation is largely driven by 'motorization' of the world, the acquisition of automobiles by individuals and companies. Albeit, with a comparatively low baseline, demand for Oil in China and India is increasing by 10 and 4 per cent respectively per annum, against the world average of 1.8 per cent as per the US Department of Energy (DOE): *'International Energy Outlook'* 1999 (China's imports will jump by 960 per cent, 2001-20 and Asia's by 115 per cent.)

Underlying statements, specially since 1973 and 1979 that the US would not hesitate to go to War, over Oil (National

Security Decision Memorandum No. 92, piloted by Kissinger, mandating an expanded US presence in the Gulf, the RDF was converted as CENTCOM in 1983, with the US 5th Fleet, based in Bahrain), the G-7 are united in their resolve, to monitor, supervise and control political developments, in key Oil producing areas, and 'will intervene' in one way or the other, when necessary. Successive US Administration have made public their policy documents, making it abundantly clear to the rest of the world's Governments and their leaders about their intentions and likely courses of action. It is just that the leaders and their staffs have chosen to sleep over these signals, overtime. (President Chavez is on notice in Venezuela). The same is true, as regards the shipment of oil, specially through the Straits of Hormuz (connecting the Gulf to the Arabian Sea-Indian Ocean) and the Malacca Straits-South China Sea, through which two-third of half of the world's 'Export-Oil' flows (The Gulf will supply one-third of the world's Oil by 2010, and 40 per cent by 2020).

Incidentally, in spite of increased Oil Revenues, the Saudi budget has deficit for nearly a decade, because of a steady 'Oil for Arms' swap, and a nation of barely 10 million people, has been the World's No.1 Arms Importer. (The Iran-Iraq War, which resulted in a million casualties and an estimated US $ 100 billion damage to infrastructure, was also a boon for the Arms Exporters).

The situation in the Caspian Sea Basin shows a similar trend in character – the prevailing concentration of Oil Wealth is in the hands of a small local elite, coupled with a cauldron of created 'ethnic' and religious strife. Chevron, with its representative, Condoleeza Rice, signed a huge US$ 20 billion Joint Venture Arrangement, in 1994, with the Kazakh Government, to develop the 'Tengiz Oil Field', on Kazhakistan's Caspian Coast.

The US has two key objectives in the area – to develop the Caspian Sea Basin, as an alternative to the Gulf (more likely as an 'additional' source) and to ensure that Caspian Oil and Gas goes to the markets in the west, without passing through Russia or Iran, the two nations, which it considers potential trouble makers. In sum, this is likely to be an area of Proxy Wars, one side on behalf of the US, and the other, allied to Russia. Except for Georgia and Azerbaijan, the other Central Asian/ Caspian Basin States, have renewed the 1992 Collective Security Treaty with Russia in 1999 (The US, on the other hand, provided over one billion Dollars to the Caspian Basin States, for regional security, arms, non-proliferation and Military training. President Shevarnadze of Georgia, later disowned and replaced, was a special US friend). Military-to-Military ties with local counterparts, provides the US with the opportunity to gain close familiarization with the terrain and operating areas of the Caspian Basin. Notwithstanding the Oil and Gas (mostly Gas), there is a pervasive bitterness and a growing sense of deprivation, that most citizens of these States feel about their deteriorating lives.

Great Game II is being played, not only in the Gulf-Caspian Sea Basin-Central Asian Region, but even more craftily in Western and Southern Africa. In the last four decades the major local actors have enjoyed political freedom but appear to have happily mortgaged their enormous wealth and resources, for a song. Perhaps due to their perception that their innings are likely to be short-lived; indeed internal, fratricidal strife is the order of the day, in almost every newly Independent Nation State, in the name of tribal and ethnic differences. There is little chance of survivability of an independent minded, elected and popular leader, as the old and new colonial powers support their Corporations, which have deep roots, to manipulate unequal trade agreements/laws, monopolise/cartelise markets, and supply arms, partly in lieu of 'lootable resources', as PMCs freely operate as advisers, specialists fly helicopters and aircraft, encouraged by their Corporate paymasters. Even where the UN Security Council Resolutions have authorized peace-making or peace-keeping, by UN or African forces their effective operations are sabotaged much as UN Special Representative Rajeshwar Dayal was in the 1960s in Congo, or Lt.Gen. Vijay Kumar Jetley recently in Sierra Leone.

Top level visits, announcements of Special Africa Fund to fight AIDS, the media suggest are altruistic and demonstrate the humanitarian concerns of the great Democracies, for the 'African

Condition', human rights, peace, security and prosperity. They may well be. However, at best, they are a single track of the multiple track, multi-dimensional operations which take away precious resources such as Oil, Diamonds, Strategic Raw Materials, and even Cocoa and Coffee, at steadily depressing prices, controlled by the London Metal Exchange, Food Conglomerates, Diamond and Precious Stones Central Exchange, at Antwerp (Belgium), the entire banking and insurance system through which transaction must be carried out.

One would have imagined that South Africa, which endured a long bloody, cruel struggle against apartheid, would have walked out of the trap, in the interests of the majority of its people. The financial structure, ownership of resources and processes, and its foreign trade, remain as it was in the apartheid era. Only the new indigenous elite have smoothly incorporated in the 'new' system, and in reality, the 'old' system controls the levers of economic power.

One of the more famous PMCs, 'Executive Outcomes' (EO), like offshoots of Halliburton, Kellog Brown Roots and other PMCs in the news in Iraq, the Gulf and the Caspian, Indonesia, Borneo, Timor etc., operates for its clients in a highly flexible and easily manipulated environment, out of South Africa. The South African Arms Manufacturers, have also shown their creativity in dealings, including with the Indian Defence Ministry.

It may be useful to mention, very briefly, a few Case Studies in Africa and in States like Indonesia, under General Suharto. Generating conflict to maintain control over Resources, or to extend control over the new Resources is described in the International media, as ethnic and sectarian conflict. Rivalries and animosities may be latent but it is the overwhelming desire to reap the financial benefits of Resource Exploitation that generally sustains the fighting.

In both Angola (UNITA) and Sierra Leone (Revolutionary United Front), it is the major Resource Conglomerates that are contributing to the persistence of violence, by purchasing diamonds, minerals, timber and other commodities from the Combatant groups. UNITA sold diamonds to buyers, working for 'De Beers,' which controls two-third of the world's diamond market. State assets are either used to buy arms in the black market or siphoned off to the proliferating Offshore Corporate Bodies or the private banking departments of the World's biggest names in banking.

Governments, elected or otherwise, go to the full extent in preserving and sustaining this relationship with the Corporations. Indonesia, under Suharto, was a classic case, whether it pertained to Gold, Copper, or Timber, in New Guinea, Borneo (Kalimantan), the involvement of the Corporations was pervasive.

Dr. Siaka Stevens in Seirra Leone and Mobutu in Zaire, siphoned off much of the national wealth, in partnership with the mining companies and the international banks. The story in Sierra Leone and West African countries became murkier, even after the 1960-1980s period. Nepalese Gurkha Soldiers dismissed from the British Army, were part of the Revolutionary United Front (RUF). Later, 'Executive Operations' (EO) led Military Forces and regained control of the Kono Diamond Region and the Rutile Sierra Mines. Angola (Oil-for-Arms Swap 2000), Brazil (pre 2002) Myanmar, Cambodia, Colombia, Congo, Indonesia, Liberia, Philippines, Equatorial Guinea, Chad, Central African Republic, Irian-Jaya (richest gold deposits in the world), even Rwanda, Mali and Kenya, etc. are part of the pattern, given some ups and downs (How deep and far the operations of arms merchants, middle-men, and the agents extend, can be illustrated by the case of a former Chief of the Indian Navy, based in London and offshore, who has the confidence of people in power, to deal with ultra top secret acquisitions/issues, in St. Petersburg, to selling his wares in Rwanda 1997-98, where a million people were killed in genocide, about whom there has been much chest-beating recently, even in the UN).

Exxon-Mobil have obtained Oil and Gas concessions in Angola, Chad, Nigeria, Congo-Brazzaville and Equatorial Guinea and the projection is that "African operations will account for a significant proportion of their worldwide production. African Oil Production (exports) are slated to constitute 11 per cent of the total world production (Iran and Iraq combined), by 2020".

Exxon has teamed up with Royal Dutch/Shell, Elf and the World Bank, despite a repressive Government in Chad.

Africa was the focus for President Clinton, in his Second Term, and President George Bush, in his First Term. Assistant Secretary of State for African Affairs, spoke of, "The US Stake in a Secure, Prosperous Africa.... We have important strategic interests in Africa (Source of 16 per cent of US Oil Imports, reliable sources for Platinum, Cobalt, Chromium, Bauxite, Manganese, and all those 90 odd exotic and rare minerals, that form the base for hi-tech products and missions) and is poised for explosive growth", she said.

Naturally, the US Military follows the US Corporate economic intent. 33 out of 48 Sub-Saharan States are provided with Military training or aid, and are involved in the efforts, to develop the African Crisis Response Force, for 'Security and Stability', hardly ever meriting a line or 'sound-byte' in the Indian media. Stepped up Military Assistance Programs, and training exercises have normally been preparatory to Military Interventions, if past precedence is to hold good.

All this predatory competition for Resources is taking place in the 'Developing World'. All of it, in the name of democracy, Human Rights, good governance, peace, security and prosperity. While a handful of individuals may profit, the majority will continue to be in want and despair. Terror and Counter-terror will fester. One-fourth of the US Defence Budget, about US $ 90 billion, is allocated to the US Forces in the Gulf. Corporations appear to be in command, because they bring revenues to the home countries. They freely engage with war lords, and rebel groups; effectively there is little check on them in long exploited and divided countries. Concurrently, the entire administrations, elected Representatives in the US Executive and Legislatures, if statistics are to be relied upon, have been in the service/ employment of the Big Corporations, or on change of an Administration, will revert to their former employees. In either case, they will serve Global Corporate Interests and those of Global Finance Capital. The destiny of the developing nations appears to be hostage to Great Game II.

9

China — Possibilities and Perspectives

Any attempt at encapsulation of the future possibilities in China, is a hazardous exercise. The amount of data, information on the country, as well as the policy pronouncements emanating at the end of the annual Chinese Party Congress, in October each year, are a guideline, but not very revealing of the inner logic or rationale of arriving at such policy statements and directives, although in recent years, there has been a level of transparency, as to the assessment of the Party, of such issues as regional disparities, growing unemployment between the coastal belt and the inner regions of China and growing income and wealth inequalities that the 'Social Market Economy' has created, making a mockery of the goals of the Chinese Agrarian based Revolution and victory over the old feudal, semi-capitalist order, pre 1948.

It was said of the former Soviet Union, by the longest serving US Ambassador in Moscow, George Keenan, that "There were only levels of ignorance about the USSR; it depended what level (of ignorance) you wished to operate from"! To the term 'Iron Curtain', was added the US propagandist term, 'Bamboo Curtain' in the 1950s to China. The US had meticulously compiled voluminous documentation on the USSR, and its Kreminologists were indeed the best informed, of all. This facilitated the CIA to completely penetrate and subvert the top Soviet leadership, epitomized by Gorbachev, and key levels in the State's bureaucracy and the KGB, '*Komitet Gosudarstvennie*

Bezopacnacti', the organization to defend the State/Government itself. In contrast, though marked by such events as the 1971 Indo-Soviet Treaty, our knowledge and grasp of the Soviet System remained at a very elementary level, and hence, our relative failure to advance mutually beneficial relations, in the opportunity window, 1960s to 1980s.

The United States has excelled in producing Sinologists over the last 90 years, helped by a formidable array of language experts, academicians, University faculties and thinktanks, which have rendered timely inputs to the Government of the United States, in deciding upon its policies of 'engagement' with China, specially since the 1960s. China has also built up a somewhat similar structure of 'institutes', small groups and big special groups, around Beijing, which provide staff support to the decision-makers, at different levels of the Party and Government. This reduces to the minimum knee-jerk responses to events and developments. The drama surrounding the periodical stand-offs on Taiwan, are perhaps put on, for the rest of the world and TV channels.

China's State-to-State relations have little to do with the CCP or its ideology, specially, since China broke away from the Soviet Union, ostensibly on the grounds of ideology, namely 'Revisionism'. In and around 1964, soon after China exploded a Nuclear Bomb, and forgot about the 'paper tiger' idiom, it allowed the United States to secretly put in place, Electronic Eves Dropping Listening Stations, in Northern China, to monitor Soviet Military activities. This was followed by a distinct coolness to Vietnamese resistance and frequent waylaying of Soviet Military supplies, intended for Hanoi. The Bamboo Curtain was certainly helpful to both China and the United States, in keeping secret preparations, for signing of the Shanghai Communique 1972, and the MFN Status to China, granted by President Nixon and his aide, Henry Kissinger (who is still greatly regarded in New Delhi). All encompassing relations accelerated between China and the United States, thereafter China has been hailed as a 'friend', notwithstanding the drama periodically staged, with respect to Democracy and Human Rights. Trade, economic ties, commercial exchanges and later, technology deals, became the order of the day. From time to time questions were raised about dual end use technology sales and transfers to China, but hard cash usually sidelined any major political or military considerations. China's position on the military coup in Indonesia, the slaughter of the PKI in 1965, the military push into Vietnam in 1978-79, and full throated opposition to the USSR, were perhaps, among the rich dividends gained by the US policies towards China.

By 1990, China had flooded the US low-end market with toys, apparels, leather goods and light engineering products, with export earnings of US$ 5 billion in each category. With steadily reducing income levels for the majority of the Americans, this availability of cheap FMCGs became a leverage factor for China, in the US economy. Trade surpluses began to grow and soon enough ran into tens of billions of Dollars in China's favour, resulting in a huge accumulation of Forex reserves (exceeding US$ 400 billion, in 2003), which China began to invest in US Treasury Bonds, learning little from the experience of Japan. Thus, China is now caught up in a reverse debt trap. China, with Japan, is the biggest holder of US Treasury Bonds and cannot withdraw now, for fear of its main market collapsing, in the face of huge US budget, trade deficits and national debt.

China's brilliantly conceived and implemented national policy of the 'Four Great Modernizations', with the Military placed as the last of the four priorities, may be headed to resolving the growing contradictions and dangers, but this is not yet apparent. True, China wisely detached itself from disputed areas, South China Sea has cooled, the Sino-Indian Border, mended relations with nearly all countries, infact expanded its economic ties and cleverly exploited the advantages of the overseas Chinese populations, in Indonesia, Malaysia, Singapore, Thailand and Phillipines etc; but has, however, become too dependent on the United States, for its economic expansion and growth and that is creating vulnerabilities, that it will find hard to shake off. However, China's very recent initiatives in Central Asia, in Latin America, with Russia, EU, and the latest 'Asia Three Plus' (Japan, South Korea and China), possible moves to diversify its foreign currency holdings, in 2005, signals changes to come. Close US relations may be subversive and damaging to its internal vitality, cohesion and unity. The co-relationship is being kept away from the Chinese people.

How many of us know that China was forced into signing an Agreement to import automobiles worth US$ 6 billion, as a price for its entry into the WTO? A great and emerging Super-power is compelled to accept such terms and face the socially disruptive inequity amongst its people, a majority of whom still use bicycles and public transport. Consumer imports for the rich will add to China's burgeoning Oil Imports and complicate its social priorities (notwithstanding its fresh investments to convert Coal into Gas and Oil). Oil, as we shall see, is a growing vulnerability for the Chinese political economy, in the years ahead. The rich, and the super rich who live in the likes of the 'White House', are great businessmen, the Chinese have always been clever businessmen outside China, and now, in the Special Economic Zones, which are full-blown Capitalist Structures, potentially full of contradictions for the people of China, specially the 240 to 300 million people, who have been pushed out of the social safety net, however meagre, created by the Chinese Revolution. The question that must arise is, can the US/Europe model of consumption be sustained, for such a large Chinese population at all?

The big limousines, which are crowding Shanghai, Guangdong, Shenzen and the coastal belt, have been paid for by the 'new class', out of funds borrowed from the Banks and export earnings. While learned Western economists are never failing to point out that the NPAs of Chinese banks have been created by uneconomical, loss making State Enterprises, they rarely mention that China's new capitalists, products of the 'social market economy', are equally guilty of contributing to the NPAs of the State Owned Banks. That, the foreign banks are playing their own games in China's hard-to-be-supervised and monitored banking transactions, is perhaps another interesting story. The famous Chinese, tongue-in-the cheek saying, "May you live in interesting times", appears to apply to more than one sector.

It is perhaps true that China's anxiety to join the WTO, was also driven by the fact that China, with its considerable achievements, in per acre production of food to eat, has to face continuous and growing insecurity, and resort to food imports for the foreseeable future, notwithstanding its double edged reversion to Capitalist farming incentives and processes and the giant irrigation potential of the 'Three Gorges Dam'. Growing food imports is not a happy prospect to think about, in the Chinese polity.

Perhaps, the biggest economic vulnerability that China continues to face, though it is hard to believe that it is unmindful of its growing dependence on Energy Imports. The attempt to build Oil and Gas pipelines, from the Caspian Sea Basin and Siberia is costly and will take years, and that will be mainly Gas, according to new prognostics (China's oil discoveries, and onshore, on Bohai Bay 2004 may relieve part of the huge consumption demand, by 2009-2010). In any case, Caspian Oil and Gas will likely be in the hands of US Oil Majors and under the control of the United States. West Asian Oil, including Iraqi Oil and Reserves, despite China building a minor Arms Supply relationship with the Arab Oil Sheikhdoms, is tenuous and subject to the US control (However, 'national' resistance movements are growing and may dispute this 'control' in the coming years). There is possibility of Venezuelan Oil for China, in the years ahead. China is out of West African Oil, destined exclusively for the US market, unless Dick Cheney has worked out some *quid pro quos* with the Chinese leadership on North Korea, Taiwan, the East Asia market, and above all collateral increase in China's imports from the United States, in goods and services, specially banking, insurance and investment services. At the time of writing there is news of China investing its Social Security (Pension) Funds in Western, read US banking and investment firms. China has also part under-written US Housing funds. China is helping the United States to resuscitate and thereby sustain its export market. Who is hostage to whom, especially for Food and Oil, is research material, for any number of Doctoral Thesis and academic papers! If it was only that we could rest! At stake is the entire Peace, Security and Development

Agenda of the world and the people. Which nation and people will be sacrificial lambs, at the alter of this Bilateral Relationship, which appears to enhance their mutual economic benefits, while simultaneously preparing for 'other options, other means'; this can happen if mutual accommodation suddenly fails. As Realists concerned with the interests and well being of our own 1,020 million, largely impoverished people, we have to simply work harder, to understand what is happening. Note, for instance, both China's and the US's record of the use of Veto, in the Security Council, for the last half century! China did, however line up with France, Germany and Russia, to vote against the aborted US Resolution, in the Security Council (withdrawn) to invade Iraq in 2003.

Few people, whether in the Government or outside, study, analyze or concede that foreign trade dependency, foreign investment and the operations of MNCs in the domestic economy, usually carry time bombs. China has generally handled the MNCs and FDIs well, using the latter for buying technology and setting up competition, right across the road, for its State Enterprises, with strict stipulations for the MNCs. Investment, Banking and Insurance firms, which are the creatures of Global Finance Capital, and the Wall Street (finally of the US Treasury), work hand-in-glove with the Intelligence Agencies and are quite another matter for a relatively inexperienced, 'learning curve' dominated, state apparatus which cannot possibly know all the 'tricks of the trade' and the innovative practices of the Business World. By the time they have caught up with what is 'new' in the bag of tricks, it is already old and replaced!

While China has perhaps the ability to hit a few US cities through its second Strike Ballistics Missile Submarine, capability this is limited, very limited! China was shopping with US$ 10 billion, in cash over the counter, for Russian Missile firing Nuclear Submarines, in 1998, (reportedly, the Russians did not oblige), which does not speak too highly of its nuclear submarine force which began slowly to join its fleet in the 1970s. Its Conventional Weapons Systems capability is also dependent on imports and licensed production from Russia. One does not know how much credibility is there in the leaked reports that the US Government had offered, or actually transferred to China laboratory equipment, for Simulation Testing of Micro-nukes and other warheads to China, in 1998-99, as a *quid pro quo* for China signing the aborted CTBT, so that the Nuclear Club preserved its exclusivity! China has wisely put in place, a major Optics Fibre National Telecom Network, with a second backbone for redundancy, and is concentrating on building its capability in the Electronic Warfare/Information Superiority, through Software and Radiation Warfare (Laser, Micro Wave, Particle Beam and Sub Sonic Wave Weapons). *'China Military Science'* and *'Liberation Army Daily'* are good sources for the prolific writings of military specialists, in the Chinese Military Academy and institutes. Almost invariably, they begin by invoking Mao Zedong and Deng Xiaoping's strategic thoughts and writings. Deng has often said, 'Combine fighting with negotiation'. Sun Tzu may still be an inspiration.

The big question is, to what purpose will China use its power, specially so, in relation to other peoples and nations, in the years ahead? There is not much in its past to indicate the future in this regard.

As stated earlier, can the Social Market Economy—resting on its showcase annual Party Congress, a magnificent spectacle, its spit and polish militia, its ceremonial Guard of Honor Contingent, its impressive resolve and medical skills to combat the recent SARS Invasion, and so on—survive the penetration by 'foreign' interests, of its State Apparatus, at various operative levels and the potential subversive role of 'big money', in the Market Economy, quite apart from serious Oil, food and unemployment (inequality) vulnerabilities, discussed above?

President Bush's National Security Strategy Document of September 20, 2002 is couched in diplomatic language and "welcomes the emergence of a strong, peaceful and prosperous China...adding that the Democratic development of China is crucial to that future... China has begun to take the road to political openness...yet remains committed to One-Party Rule by the Communist Party.....WTO's requirements for transparency and accountability will advance openness and the rule of law in

China, to help basic protections for commerce and for citizens. There are areas, however, where we have profound disagreements (Taiwan etc)". The interpretation or Judgment on the Democratic development of China, transparency, accountability...rule of law is reserved by the United States Administration! The NSSD of 16 March, 2006 is similarly nuanced.

'The PNAC, Rebuilding America's Defences, is more explicit and precise. It spells out absolute and unchallenged Military domination of the world and cyberspace. The NSSD is also explicit on 'not permitting this dominance to be surpassed or equalled by any other power.' The PNAC is again more precise and warns of pre-emptive Military action, against any power that attempts to challenge or even devotes resources to Research & Development, that may conceivably, in the future, surpass or equal the US Military capability. The US will adjudge such competing capability and take pre-emptive action to disarm and neutralize, by means at its disposal, including space platforms where it has declared US predominance, for all times to come.

The message is clear and it is addressed to China, a nation, that according to the assessment of global *pundits* is heading to be *Numero Uno,* as an Economic Power in 25 years time. Just in this period, the United States' Economy is on a steady decline, its savings, investments and debt problems are overtaking great creativity, adversely affecting its earlier innovativeness and scientific-technological lead. The message to China is, you can be another Japan, and nothing more.

What would be fascinating is, to get a glimpse of the Chinese response, their counter-strategy. China's perspective of how it is preparing to meet this oncoming challenge, how it assesses the penetration of the Chinese system, to what degree does it assess its people in the hierarchy who are subverted, bereft of a binding ideology, giving in to the 'good life', as it does appear on the surface. Is there a steel frame that will hold and stay the course? What lessons have been learnt to defend the interests of 1,200 million Chinese and the Middle Kingdom in the evolving new world order? Is China's 2005 multipolarity concept for real?

10

China's Military Power

An Eagle's Eye View

Historical Background

China's recent military past is dominated by the 'unexpected'. The final collapse and defeat of the KMT Regime and its Army, by the ill-equipped Peasant Force, led by the 'Long March' of People's Liberation Army (PLA) leadership in 1947-48, surprised many Western observers. The massing of the PLA on the Yalu River, during the Korean War, caused the US President to over-rule the US commander General Mc Arthur and recall him in a move, to de-escalate the War.

A few years earlier, two US Foreign Service Officers, who knew the Chinese Communist Party (CCP) and the PLA better and recommended that the US Administration should deal directly with them, were recalled and soon, thereafter, had to resign.

Apparently, the China of the 'Opium War' era, and the 'foreign concessions' from Shanghai, upto the Yangtze, which humiliated and brought shame upon China's rulers, were now a thing of the past.

Despite their differences in the Comintern, the Soviet Union chose to forget the past and made enormous sacrifices in the 1950s, soon after the devastation and destruction by the Nazi Fascist Armies, to transfer and transplant more than 80,000 industrial plants, to help 'reconstruct' a new China. This fifteen years' 'honeymoon' was short-lived, and 'ideological' (read 'nationalist') motivations brought China into a direct and open confrontation with its erstwhile 'brother', the USSR, beginning the early 1960s.

During the Korean War, the Chinese dismissed the US Nuclear Threat as a 'Paper Tiger', until 1964, when they themselves exploded a Nuclear device, preceding the NPT. It must be said to its great credit that China began its Nuclear Submarine Project, in the year 1958-59, soon after the US submarine, *Nautilus,* crossed under the North Pole. This programme was personally overseen by Prime Minister Zhou-en-lai, who signed the directives for the first series of sea-trials in 1968-70. This was China's Strategic Military Force to demonstrate to the world, the essence of 'survivability' of its Nuclear deterrent. While many 'teething' problems remained and still beset this 'second strike capability', it is there for all powers to reckon, as a 'factor of uncertainty'. How many US cities are targeted? San Francisco, Los Angeles, and San Diego or Washington DC, and New York, is a 'guess', but the 'guess' cannot be dismissed.

In 1949, China's Political and Military leadership, which was then one and the same, to the surprise of many 'China-watchers', declared the PLA (Navy) to be a 'Top-Priority' and 'Ship-building' as China's springboard to industrial development. Here was a nation with practically no maritime traditions and history (except one fleet sortie by a Chinese Admiral, in the 15th century, to India's Western Coast and the Gulf), embarking on an ambitious National Maritime Programme and the results are there, for all to see (India's Maritime assets are in the reverse gear with ports, shipyards, national shipping companies up for sale).

Modernization

After realizing the futility of using its huge Military Force against India, in 1962, and Vietnam, in 1978-79, China has wisely decided to concentrate on its 'Four Great Modernizations', of which the 'Military' is the last priority. This does not mean that China would place 'National Defence' a last, in the scheme of things. The institution of the 'Chinese Military Commission' ensures that China's defense and security issues receive the continuous attention of the Chinese leadership, at the highest level. No great significance is to be attached as to how many Generals are 'in' or 'out' of the Politbureau or whether a civilian politician may become the Defence Minister, one of these days.

The Military top rungs too, have had and continue to have problems with 'Chinese Characteristics'. Initially in 1950 and 1960s, and more recently, senior Chinese Military Officials have had to be retired or discharged, for running Military Supplies, logistics and Military businesses, for private profit. Many of them are closely related to the new ruling 'party-businessmen' elite, which drives the 'Socialist Market Economy'. In today's China in a lighter vein, power does not come from the 'Barrel of the Gun', but the 'Barrels of the Big Private Entrepreneurs', who happily accommodate the relations and friends of the Party and the Military, in the 'big, happy, prosperous' family, that increasingly determines 'national interest' viz. the common interest of the people, articulated in the past by Comrades Deng Xiaoping and Mao Tse Tung. Deng was a master of dialectics and overwrote the 'Red Book' in such catchy phrases, as, "Never mind the colour of the cat so long as it catches mice", and "It is glorious to be rich". However, personal wealth, riches and, greed are incompatible with the Military's professional integrity, and drive it towards ruination, no matter how much 'hi-tech' and 'Revolution & Military Affairs (RMA)' cosmetics are put on.

China and the US

Since 1964, when China happily permitted the US Electronic Spying Stations to be established, to monitor the USSR's Military radar and missile sites, China did not demur, or apparently has not demurred, being designated, unofficially, as the 'NATO' of the East. A little known or unmentioned fact is that, China's Military Specialists were training Afghan Mujahideen, in a camp, in the 'Wakhan Corridor', in the 1980s, to wage war against the Communist-led Afghan Government.

It is said that, China sees the world in a hundred years' perspective, and for it, a generation or two sacrificed in another country (like Indonesia for instance) so long as the 'Middle

Kingdom' benefits is 'passe'. So, has it been in the past 45 years, and one does not know the future.

China and the US are great friends and business partners, but also know that one can turn on the other. For the moment and for the next two decades, the dices are loaded against China, no matter how many compromises China makes. The Chinese 'Thinktanks' would have chewed upon PNAC (Project for New American Century) a thousand times, and debated on it, in their policy bodies/groups continuously, since the US NSSD 2002 in particular. Realists that they are, they would surely be working and thinking how to avoid their 'National Command Centres' from being blown up by the new 'Bunker Busters', field tested in Afghanistan's mountain caverns, to break into 16 ft. thickness of rocks and more. They know the effect of Depleted Uranium Munitions, the progress of Gene Warfare Projects, Microwave Weapons, the US declaration to monopolize 'Space', to target its missiles from space, at anytime, anywhere, against anyone?

It is true that Deng Xiaoping's views, reportedly quoted by Colonel Hong Baoxiu, make a wise assessment that, "the United States has become the only Superpower to dominate the world" (60 per cent of the Trans National Corporations (TNC) are US-based and global finance capital which far out-strips international trade, is based in Wall Street, New York).

Deng Xiaoping believed "World War can be postponed but accidental incidents and local circumstances are not entirely predictable." True, but as China's leadership knows only too well, that the PNAC has unleashed, with or without NATO support, war in more than one region of the world to price open national economies and/or take over strategic resources, wherever it chooses (West Asia, Central Asia, Western Africa or Latin America, Phillippines etc.).

In April 1998, India's brand new Defence Minister declared, "China is India's Enemy Number One'. He was not out of step. Prime Minister Vajpayee, in his May '1998 letter to President Bill Clinton said that, 'Pokhran II was aimed at China, not anyone else'. Jaswant Singh, the then Foreign Minister, later concurrently, the Defence Minister, then Finance Minister, author of the book *Defending India* believed that a US-India, Military alliance, against the Soviet Union and now China, is in India's best interests. Most members of India's, ruling elite and NRIs in the US, fondly believe that the US and India are 'natural allies' vis-a-vis China. The US has other priorities, interests and assessments. It has a well-defined policy on West Asia, Central Asia and the Indian Ocean-Malacca Straits 'Energy' Ocean Sea Lanes.

China does not view India as an equal, Politically or Militarily, and has used Pakistan as an effective proxy. The US has Japan as its proxy to checkmate China, should it adopt an overt, hostile, military posture. What agreements, compacts, secret clauses of treaties and agreements bind the US and China, will not be known. That both share many confidences with each other, is an open secret and there is enough evidence in the public domain, on that account.

China's Military purchases from Israel; the testing of new Chinese Nuclear Devices, while CTBT and FMCT negotiations were on, in 1998-99; the reported offer or transfer of US Nuclear Micro-testing and Simulation Laboratory Systems to China, the level of 'permissible' industrial espionage Chinese activities in the US (even as early as the 1960s, both the Chinese Space and Nuclear Scientists migrated to China, and effectively steered their strategic programmes. No great fuss was made by the US compared to the 1950s when the Rosenbergs were put on the 'Electric Chair' (Robert Oppenheimer was placed under surveillance, for alleged passing of Atomic Secrets to the Soviets). Except in the 1950s, China has since never faced the hostility that the Soviet Union attracted from the US Administration, despite these two latter nations being close military allies, in World War II.

China's leadership has managed the US's political-economic and military relationship (engagements) to its advantage; so it thinks! The US and China have enjoyed a love-hate relationship, over the past 100 years. Many 'bridges' between the two have been built.

Economic competition and rivalry over resources, has historically engineered conflicts. China's great vulnerability is its rapidly growing energy shortages and imports over long sea-lanes. The 'Socialist Market Economy' has provided all the ready made opportunities of 'vantage points' and positions, for China's 'new friends' and 'business partners', to monitor and penetrate China's 'Central Nervous Systems' and its 'Brain Centres'. These contradictions can hardly be avoided by the Chinese Political and Economic System and have become integrated with the process initiated with the 'Reforms', three decades ago. The brighter the Chinese economic miracle appears to be, the more 'open' it becomes for economic subversion. This is the 'dialectics' of a dangerous new operation.

China prepares for 'people's war, under modern conditions', and 'Active Defence' but this is not the War, China's adversaries are preparing for. Their War aims are for control of the Economy and Resources. Only if, there is a breaking point reached earlier or the Metropolitan centres enter a very deep, economic catastrophic crisis, suddenly, will Nuclear or Conventional war be resorted to 'Militarily destabilize China', since other instruments are already in place and fulfilling their intended purpose.

The Chinese leadership is too well informed about the US Economy and Global Finance Capital, not to appreciate that it is China's investments in the US Treasury Bonds and other market instruments that, along with Japan, are sustaining the US Economy, in general and its Military Industrial Complex, in particular. This has happened before in the 20th century, where industrial enterprises in Nazi Germany were part owned by corporations based in the US and UK, through 1939-45. The German enterprises produced weapons which brought to the battlefield, killed or mained American and British soldiers. China seeks peace, stability, development and prosperity, notwithstanding.

One can write about the comparison of Forces, Weapon Systems, and the Quality of Education of the Chinese soldiers to effectively use Hi-tech and Information Warfare tools, its Human Resources Development Programme, the obvious motivation of the PLA detachments, when they are engaged in the aid of Civil Power, in Natural Disaster situations, that occur from time to time in China. The PLA soldier is well-disciplined and motivated, eager to learn and improve, and is a symbol of State Power.

One may even speculate and ask that, if the 'Yuan' is not revalued upwards, will the imbalances in Sino-US trade be leveled by China, purchasing US Military Systems and Equipment on a large scale. If that happens, how will these be justified? Will they be intended for use in Defence of peace, viz. Japan, Korea, East Asian nations or to checkmate China's Northern, Western and Southern neighbours? Will then, a new sphere of influence be conceded to China, as a *'quid pro quo'*, for a balanced trade account? Or will China team up in a joint enterprise, for control of the new 'energy' locations? How long will Chinese Economic Diplomacy continue to be successful with new MFNs (Most Favoured Nations) as it has been, since the 1972 Shanghai Communiqué? So Far, Chinese leadership has proved itself to be agile, fleet-footed and balanced to advance its national interests.

11

Whither Self-Reliance

National Security in the contemporary context, has an altogether changed definition. The Armed Forces and Military Systems that are associated with it are just one dimension of national security. National strength or weakness is thus, comprised many strands, none less vital, than the other.

The country's demographic curve is such that, we will grow to be 1800 million people, in 2025, from the 1000 million that we are at present. If enough attention is paid to all that contributes to Population Stabilization, education of girls, economic security, employment and family earnings, individual and family security, health care, infant and mother mortality rates and nutrition security, we may just be able to stabilize at 2500 million, by the year 2050. This will depend on whether we steel ourselves, to tackle the challenges of the real, political economy or continue to feed illusions, like the 'feel-good' factor, for the elite.

Apart from the external concerns of Energy Security, the Military Capabilities of adversarial nations, near and far, we have, staring us in the face, Nutrition and Livelihood Security, Insecurity of Water of the neighborhood, our *mohallas* and our villages and cities, all fostered by growing Economic Insecurity of the vast majority of our people who are of course at the same time potentially our greatest human capital and resource, presently laid waste by illiteracy, ignorance, diseases, malnutrition, unemployment, or shelterless, feeding on superstition, rituals, and prejudices, instead of building on human solidarity. It was nearly a decade ago, that the US Government's East-West Centre at Hawaii, had initiated a project study, titled 'Conflicts Over Food and Water, in South Asia', not for nothing!

It is not that our national leaders have always lacked vision. It was in 1946, that Jawaharlal Nehru, after the Atomic Bombs at Hiroshima and Nagasaki in Japan had been dropped, concluded that, the 'world had changed and relations between nations would be altogether on a different plane, then onwards'. Our Representatives, Homi Bhabha and Krishna Menon, in 1954, at the IAEA said, on record, categorically that, "India and Indians cannot remain the hewers of wood and the drawers of water, for ever". In 1959, Prime Minister Jawaharlal Nehru, asked the Chairman of IAEA, looking at Homi Bhabha, whether "Bhabha can make it?" and the IAEA Chief, reportedly smiled and responded in the affirmative. What one is driving at is that, if a new Government took over on March 19, 1998, it did not perform any miracle that Pokhran II occurred on May 11, 1998. Infact, poor preparation for meeting the response of the United States and Pakistan, led to our compromising on the basic position on CTBT, and we announced readiness to sign it without building on a credible nuclear capability, agreeing to a 'Recessed Deterrance' regime, an American invention, to keep India impotent, forcing it to keep its Warheads and Delivery Vehicles in different locations, the former, with trusted scientists and the latter symbolically with the Armed Forces! To add to this confusion, we made equally untenable Policy Declarations of "No First Strike", which does not make sense when a Nuclear Weapons State lacks credible second-strike capability. Not only did we drive ourselves into a comer here but defacto, have compromised our position on Kashmir, on the suggestion that, it had become a Nuclear Flash-point and needed the US presence, and behind the scenes mediation/intervention, treating the 'Valley' as a problem, which needed a separate solution. Not a month passes when some 'team' or the other, does not descend on New Delhi and Srinagar, to talk with the APHC, who do not represent anyone in J&K!

Perhaps, equally revealing is the public statement by the Minister of Defence, in 2003, that we finally have a Command

& Control system, in place. The 'Support System' of a Nuclear Weapons System takes upto 30 to 50 per cent of the costs, if the surveillance, reconnaissance, command-control and the communications sub-systems, which constitute the 'central nervous system', are to have the requisite level of reliability and redundancy. And all this, while we were announcing, for public consumption, that we could destroy a neighbour if it dared attack us. We were deploying seven hundred thousand men and tanks of the Army in *Parakrama,* to drive in to avenge an amateur terrorist attack on the Parliament, when the conventional armour thrusts have, for all practical purposes, been stalemated. (The penalty for compromising our operational plans, by the Army and Navy in particular, and the attrition and losses suffered by all three Services, has been deliberately kept away from the Parliament). The fact, that we have exposed our weaknesses politically and in our overall national strategy, is a penalty to be paid the future. The weaker party, with less tanks and artillery, has declared that it will respond with a Nuclear Strike, if its territorial integrity is threatened, as it is Natural for it to do so, against an adversary with superiority in conventional arms. Was 'war-gaming' with the participation of the political decision-makers, ever done post 1998, or are well advertised visits to the 'Army War-Room' a substitute for 'ordering' a War, in a Nuclear scenario?

Even worse, has a National Intelligence Estimate been presented to the Cabinet Committee on Security, to enable it to take informed decisions from time to time? Sheets of papers or oral wafflings by the JIC or RAW Chief, in private or at the Committee, are not a substitute for NIEs, discussed in a scientific and disciplined framework. This is just one example to illustrate our disregard, for the core issues and the chase after prohibitively extravagant Conventional Weapon System acquisitions, from the West or Russia.

Since the days of criticism of the Planned Development Strategy, emphasizing at first the heavy industry infrastructure and agro-economy, by the 'Swantrata' Party types, and the self-proclaimed Nationalists, and soon afterwards, on allocating scarce national resources on Atomic Energy, Space and Electronics, just fifteen years after 1947, the National Policy Goal has been ' Self-Reliance'. We may not have made spectacular progress in Defence Self-reliance, and for that, the Nation deserves an answer from people like Dr. Abdul Kalam, who headed the DRDO for 10 years, but that the Ministry of Defence has laid so much store by Imports of Military equipment, of Rupees one lakh twenty thousand crores, in the period 2001-2015, to be largely deployed against a small neighbour, one-fifth our size, in every parameter, deserves answers, to the people. This is not the entire commitment to foreign suppliers. Maintenance Imports over average life-cycle costs will be atleast another one lakh twenty thousand crores, over the next twenty years. The climate of dependency, including the psychology of dependence, fostered in the Military has untold costs, not only on Defence capability but in any independent Foreign Policy, to defend and further the basic interests of our billion people and the next generation.

The climate for the media and the elite, was built up by wrong public declarations, that Armed Forces Modernization and Budgets had been down-graded in the preceding decade or more and now a 'Nationalist' Government was going to correct the dangerous gaps, by massive imports, no matter if the procedures have to be given the go by. There was really no reduction in Defence Budgets, despite financial difficulties. Only the accounting had been modified to exclude pensions, the Coast Guard and the Military segments, of the Space and Atomic Energy dual use programmes, properly embedded in the respective departments. The national leadership of the preceding years, never once winced or squeezed on any national priority Defence Programme, whether it related to Missile projects or other strategic projects, including major conventional, indigenous programmes like the LCA, ALH, the Arjun Tank, ship construction, and many others. Even in the indigenous Air Defence Ship, the programme was looked at positively, once the staff requirements and old military specifications were pared down, as the world-wide trends in Civil Military Integration confirm.

Our shipyards are functioning with 50 per cent or less capacity utilization, when their order books, at least with letters of intent, should be full for the next 10 years to enable them to modernize their production facilities, to achieve higher productivity. Despite our inefficiencies in management, decision-making and work ethics, our shipyards still turn out ships at less than half the cost, to the Navy, as compared to similar imported platforms, on a year-to-year and class-on-class of ship basis, despite some avoidable time delays, which have been largely caused by insecurity of receiving further orders from the Goverment. When we place orders abroad, instead of opting for the indigenous route, we deprive our workers of work, and subsidize foreign workers; we block the development of skills, and in some cases, are actually responsible for the country losing specialized design and production skills. We also demonstrate a lack of faith in our engineers, starve our main industries in which our nation has made investments in earlier years, strangle the growth of ancillary industries which support the major shipyards, aircraft or tank production facilities. In sum, by importing major systems, we are investing in the design and production facilities of overall growth of foreign countries, in preference to our own. In other words, we are giving aid to the Developed Countries who have squeezed us for the last 300 years!

How much is enough for Defence allocations? Debates have centred around 3.4 per cent or 4 per cent of the GDP, but hardly ever focused on Minimum Military Capability. The GDP is not under Government control, as it is the overall national product, so we should really be discussing the revenues of the Government, and its plan and non-plan expenditure. If it wants to spend more on Defence, it has to cut somewhere else, or raise more revenues through taxes. Since 1998, the Government decided that it wants to spend more, to build Military, Para-military and Police-dependent Security, than People's or Economic Security. Infact, it went one step ahead and reduced the tax-GDP ratio from 10.5 per cent to 8 per cent, lowered tariffs and duties on manufactures, capital goods and agricultural imports! The Defence Budget has nearly doubled from Rs. 34,000 crores in 1997-98 to Rs. 76,000 crores in 2003-04, (and to Rs 83000 crores in 2005-06) while the Budget for Rural Development and Agriculture has halved over the same period. Health and Education Allocations, similarly suffered heavy cuts.

To be fair, this Government knows exactly where it wants to take the country!

Let us look at all this from the 'Globalization-Liberalization-Privatization' perspective, and the Military-Industrial complex, and Arms Trade/Industry Players, the big Players! The profits in the Arms business are even higher than the ones enjoyed by the 'Oil Majors', while Arms manufacturers receive huge subsidies from the Pentagon and Defence Ministries in UK, France, Israel and Russia, to name a few. Public wealth is diverted to private accounts, in a largely unmonitored way. Even after this, to give just one example, the United States must export one Fighter Aircraft, for every Aircraft inducted into the US Air Force, and in France, three Fighter Aeroplanes must be exported, for every one Aircraft to be inducted into the French Air Force, to permit the economies of scale to operate. This is particularly relevant in Europe. For example, who will buy the Submarines, produced in UK, France, Germany, Holland, and Sweden, when Australia, Japan and South Korea, have set up their own production lines? France has invested nearly 20 billion dollars in the last decade, to upgrade its Submarine Manufacturing/Building facilities, but its main requirement is Nuclear Submarines, whereas the Agostas and the Scorpenes, the latter at Rs. 2,500 crores a piece, with a pea-shooter of a missile and torpedoes, is a seller's dream and a buyer's extravagant toy, an all singing, all dancing doll, to parade. There is no 'market' for Submarines in any European country, and so, markets have to be searched and they are easily found!

However, if this was all, one could rest and hope that better sense will prevail in the debt-ridden, pauperized Third World countries, with impoverished, unemployed or under-employed people.

The New World Order, the PNAC, NSSD 2002, 2003 and 2006; and Globalization, lay down the law in the Structural Adjustment Programmes and the conditionalities of the Structural Adjustment Loans, have been very kind to the Developing Countries, in the WTO regime! The New Global Regime of the WTO, sets enforceable rules for a nation; the important exception is, Article XXI of the GATT, which provides a freedom for Military Spending for any reason related to National Security.... to maintain order. The International financial institutions have also given a carte-blanche to Defence Budgets and do not exercise any scrutiny, in comparison to Welfare Budgets, and push for privatization of industries and services. This is because, the interests of 'Defense - Arms' Corporations are over-riding and have a clear precedence over those of the Nation-states. Military Spending is the basis of much of the 'New Economy'. To maintain order in the new and emerging markets, is a pre-requisite.

Sir Solly Zuckerman, the Scientific Adviser to the Ministry of Defence, UK, at the end of World War II, was often quoted, when New Weapons System Acquisition was being debated, as saying, "We are poor, and therefore, we must think". Perhaps, this advice does not apply to a country with nearly US$ 100 billion of foreign currency reserves, never mind they are largely of the 'hot-money' variety, or a US$ 100 billion Foreign Debt and a growing and not negligible adverse trade balance, factored by over 70 per cent of its energy requirements, dependent on overseas imports. Perhaps it does. Should we not also ask the growing millions of educated and hardly educated young people, who face the beatings and killings of the 'locals', when 2000 vacancies in the Western Railways, are to be filled, against six lakh applicants, to just recall one example, or the Army's Recruitment centres, where despite paying the '*dalals*' (middle-men), the future *'Jawan'* candidates suffocate or drown in the scuffles, to get ahead in the queue.

Hardly any informed citizen or official will deny that despite lethargic management decisions, faults and inefficiencies, we did make slow but steady progress, in our goal of achieving self-reliance, in Defence, especially in the Navy and the Army. The Navy, because of its early commitment, set up a Design Organization, which has to its credit, designed a modem Stealth Frigate and a capable submarine etc, is equipped with the up-to-date software to reduce design time and to produce detailed drawings and manufacturing drawings to compliment the computer-aided manufacture process. To this, the Navy has added a competent Weapons Systems Integration Establishment, which has successfully married or integrated indigenous, western and eastern systems, on the same Ship or Submarine platform. The close integration of the public sector shipyards and the Navy, has also helped this process.

The Army also in the past years, when the political leadership emphasized indigenous systems and self-reliance, has shown support for a larger part of its requirements, to be met indigenously. The shortcoming is attributable to two factors: overambitious staff requirements without an adequate appreciation of the cost and time penalties of on-the-ground R&D skills and the lack of sufficiently and closely integrated joint effort, with the Army Officers at various levels, participating and contributing to the effort.

The Air Force, as an organization, with some honourable individual exceptions, generally has a hands-off approach to indigenous projects. Providing Test-pilots is simply not enough. Modern or even older Air Force Systems have always required Design and Systems Integration Inputs from Air Force professionals at all stages, from conception to air staff, to design feasibility, to proto-type technology testing.

The overall approach of the Services and the Ministry is to overlook the deficiencies and limitations of foreign systems, during negotiations, and contract finalization stages, in comparison with our home-grown programme. The contracts have so many lacunae, weak or legally unenforceable clauses, that they result in the suppliers' calling the shots and the buyers having to become poorer and vulnerable for the life-cycle of the imported system. And who facilitates all this, are 'Middle Men' or 'Agents', who work for the supplier firms, the Governments of the countries of origin of that equipment/system, inflate prices for raking off and sharing it with all participants. These Agents and Middle Men are compromised in the very process of this business and while they may consider themselves very smart, the Intelligence Agencies consider them as 'assets' and run them on short leash, to do their dirty work and subvert both the system and individuals, placed in key posts.

Bold public announcements are made, that the ultimate intended purpose of these prohibitively expensive Imported Systems,.each approximating Rs. ten thousand crores, and some, in excess of Rs. fifteen thousand crores per Cabinet approval, is 'progressing' *Swadeshi'*. It starts by imports of tens and hundreds of T-90 tanks, armoured fighting vehicles, artillery pieces, SU 30 MKIs, Hawk Jet trainers, Submarines being imported and the rest of the requirements being progressively indigenized/produced under license, mechano set fashion; the first stage from assemblies, then from sub-assemblies, which are of the highest value, components ..., and lastly, from raw materials. By the time we reach the' Swadeshi , the Supplier has lost interest, the Ministry and the General Staff are already looking for New Systems, and the Tank, Submarine or Aircraft has been superseded as obsolete or obsolescent, no longer good enough for us, to defend the country with. Since in 'License -Manufacture' 'know-how' to assemble or manufacture is parted with by the Arms Company, and not the 'know-why' of the design, we are invariably back to the start-line!

Let us take the Hawk Trainer; it is more than a 30-years old design. The manufacturing facility, which had closed down, is now being revived. All of us know that assurances of License Manufacture, perhaps even re-export to Third Countries, are included, but who will seriously consider that spares will be available, upto year 2030, when the basic Aircraft System will be 60 years old. All Air Manuals, recommend a 60:40 or at least 50:50 Simulator Type to Aircraft Type flying. Simulation of the Aircraft Type and its Missile Combat Profile, have to be continuously gamed in the' Advanced Distribution Simulation' facilities, with outstanding virtual reality environments, created by advanced computer systems support, to enhance Air Fighting Standards. Investments in these are not talked about or are not a budget priority, because in comparison, though absolutely vital to the purpose, they are low-ticket, non-glamorous items.

When are we manufacturing the SU 30 MKI here in HAL, as a genuine Indian/*swadeshi* product? When will the Submarines be made here, when like the MTCR, a Submarine Technology Control Regime is hanging over our heads, and for critical sub-systems like the low-noise propeller and certain other sub-systems are already in place? Whistle-blowers are not required. Like the London Club 'Trigger' list, all on line networks in the Western Alliance System will simultaneously give alarms and stop processing, when such a proscribed item is on the import list of a designated country. That is why, the Navy, in collaboration with our industry and labs, developed some of these sub-systems as common in different projects. The Aircraft Carrier design was also modified to cut costs, through the Civil-Military Integration approach, which is today a Governing Principle in the US military systems design, requirements and manufacture. What this means is that for example, civilian electronic, micro-processor or even propulsion systems offer such a high level of reliability and maintainability, that an exclusive Military standard/specification or design is not considered essential or vital and, therefore, not desirable. Quality Standards in industry, since the days of Admiral Rickover's insistence, and new technologies have made Dual-use Technologies, the norm, rather than the exception.

Leaving these arguments aside for a moment, one is entitled to ask, in the public interest, that if the Naval Staff placed a Letter of Intent, through an understanding Defence Secretary, for let us say about 50 ALH Navy version, in 1994, completed the most exacting Small Ship (frigate) Sea Trials, established the Air Envelope as satisfactory to Naval Air-staff requirements, in the spring of 1997, with Naval Test Pilots, then why is it now being publicly stated that ALH Manufacture Programme is facing a budget squeeze? Take the Feasibility Study for the Navy version of the LCA. The files were sent round robbin, for almost five years, before a paltry sum of five crores or even less, received the President's pleasure. To sanction a billion dollars, for the MIG-29K version, for Admiral Gorshkov, which has of course never operated from a Gorshkov size platform, with or without limitation, no one has really counted the costs or the 'change'.

The Raksha Mantri (Defence Minister) has also named the LCA and the Arjun Tank as the Programmes, which may face money constraints. There is no constraint of money in the import of big-ticket items, which are all whizzing past the CCS though. I recall a particular afternoon, as Deputy Chief, with Defence Secretary, K. A. Nambiar. We were having serious problems with the Sea Harrier Engines and a particular British Aerospace Weapon, for the Harrier. The Air Force too, had its problems with British Aerospace. The Chairman, British Aerospace, had been summoned and told at the Government level, that they had faulted several times on their contract obligations, and that this state of play was not acceptable to the GOI. After offering a whole set of excuses, British Aerospace promised to make good in the future. The Defence Secretary then sounded the Chairman, if under the overall Defence Cooperation Agreement; British Aerospace will consider marketing and world-wide servicing support to the LCA, on commercial considerations. I recall his serious yet wry comment, "The LCA is on the drip, maybe if and when the tooling for production facilities are in place and the GOI have made budgetary provision for a minimum 400 Aircraft run, British Aerospace will surely consider the offer".

However, in big-ticket items import, no money constraints come in the way. Yet, in all such deliberations, the rupees ten thousand crore mega, and sub-mega projects, the *swadeshi* goal is dutifully articulated. The catch is that those who do so, will not be there ten years, hence. There is a dictum that, in dreaming the military dream, the "Best is the Enemy of the Good". If even after 56 years, our General Staff and the Government are still looking for Imported Systems, implying a long term commitment to dependency, then neither can we claim the pursuit of an Independent policy in the interest of the vast majority of our people's basic interests and well-being, nor can this approach contribute to 'building India's Defences'. Above all, we may be in the danger of falling into a dependency syndrome, which infects our very thought process.

In conclusion, it may be appropriate to quote from the lessons of our history, as so well expressed by Lawrence Lifschultz in the 'Introduction' of his book, *'The unfinished war in Bangladesh'.* He writes "Just over two centuries ago a contingent of over 800 irregular Soldiers faced an Army of nearly 50,000 Troops, from the *Nawab* of Bengal's standing Forces. Not only was there numerical superiority, on the Bengal side, but in this instance Artillery and Technical supremacy were also against the European Force. Nevertheless, in the most miserable skirmish ever to be called a decisive battle, the Europeans walked off with a victory, which would change the world history. That was the 'Battle of Palassey'. The date was 23rd June, 1757".

All sorts of racial, national and historical myths, developed out of this event, but the story of the 'conquest of Bengal' was no mystery. In the modern parlance, 'what happened' of the Western Intelligence community, was a classic 'covert' operation, carried through with great clandestine success. There never was a Military Defeat of the *Nawab* of Bengal's Army. The method of victory was much more simple: the Commander of the *Nawab's* Armed Forces, had secretly been bought off by the British, before either side had reached the mango groves around Plassey.

Through an astute and subtle understanding of the political factions, within the Bengali leadership and ruling classes, by carefully distinguishing the patriotic from the corrupt...and through the unabashed capacity to buy and sell comprador loyalty from those who deal in their ambitions for power, the small British expeditionary Force under Robert Clive, secured its Military triumph, by a neat gamble, on prior political arrangement. From the incident at Plassey onwards, 'the British waged a more or less continuous War, against the Indian people, consolidating their 'power' in India, and the conquest of other regions, breaking up the old system of self-sufficient and self-perpetuating villages, and supporting an elite whose self-interest would harmonize with the British rule.

Over the next century an entire world was remade and reshaped, under the global expansion of the British Empire. In Bengal, a precapitalist mode of production was totally transformed. Indigo, Jute, Tea, Opium, private property in land, *Zamindari*, landlordism, land tax, and the right to buy and sell a peasant's property to extract debt from him, were all introduced. And from its staging post in South Asia, the new European based epoch of commerce and modern industry, broke open markets throughout Asia, with the rumble of War and the 'right' to an open door".

12

Kashmir

The Kernel of Our National Security

Historical memories are sometimes deliberately assumed to be short-lived. Nevertheless, the documents and records in the Ministry of External Affairs are in good order; at least they were until, March 1998. The Archives and records in the UK and US are kept even more securely and backed up by the Presidential Libraries and the archives of the Intelligence Agencies.

In those tumultuous months in 1946-47, preceding our Independence, the groups and individuals who had either played no role in the Freedom Movement or worse, collaborated with the British in endorsing the Two Nation Theory, since the 1920s and 1930s, began to play a treacherous and manipulative role in the politics of the day, trying to emerge as leaders. (It was the great struggle for India's freedom, as a consequence of which Pakistan emerged as an independent entity, the creation of the Secessionist Conspiracy plotted in White Hall).

Some of these 'freshly emerged politicians' went about advising the Princely States; as far apart as Travancore-Cochin to J&K, to declare themselves Independent. Even though everyone was aware that under the Indian Independence Act 1947, passed by the British Parliament, India, not Pakistan, was the Successor State. In J&K, a 'Rajput' body and members of the *Jan Sangh / Hindu Mahasabha*, advised Maharaja Hari Singh to declare 'independence' and not join the Indian Union despite the known position of the National Conference, led by Sheikh Abdullah, which was a People's Movement, and also led struggles for land reforms, called *'Naya Kashmir'.* The invasion of the Valley, by so-called tribesmen, led by Pakistani regulars and officers, reaching Muzaffarabad on October 24, 1947; and pillaging, burning and raping co-religionists in the Valley, in Baramulla, to name just one, got delayed enroute in their March to capture Srinagar. (There are documents on record, to prove that J&K was invaded by Pakistan Army units, as early as October 28, 1947. These were contained in a telegram, signed by the British Commander-in-Chief of the Pakistan Army, for the Governor General M. A. Jinnah).

The Ruler of J&K State was compelled by the National Conference to sign the Instrument of Accession, on October 26, 1947. This legal and binding document was countersigned as accepted, by the Governor General of India, Lord Mountbatten on October 27, 1947 ("I do hereby accept this Instrument of Accession"). "That cannot be undone. The Right of Accession does not exist in our Federation and (more importantly), in our Constitution. The Constituent Assembly of Jammu and Kashmir, in adopting the Constitution of the State, resolved ... We the people of the State of Jammu and Kashmir, having solemnly resolved of the Accession of this State to India...on the 17th day of November, 1956, do hereby adopt, enact and give to ourselves, this Constitution."

The US Supreme Court said: "When Texas became one of the United States, it entered into an indissoluble relation."

A company of troops was flown in (after the Accession), first to defend the Srinagar Airfield; which done, the real defenders of the Valley, the people, and the J&K Militia, joined our advance detachment, to repulse the invaders who had spearheaded the invasion, to capture Kashmir through Armed Force. The Kashmiri people fought them as an enemy. On the Indian Army side, Lt Col. Rai, Brigadier Usman, Major Somnath Sharma, later Air Commodore Mehar Singh, emerged heroes, even as countless Kashmiris, unknown, unsung stood to repulse the Pakistani regulars and irregulars. (A similar drama was to be repeated between March and December 1971, in East Pakistan when the Pakistan Army butchered millions of co-religionists, in order to deny them the results of an All Pakistan Election. The *Mukti Bahini* and its riverine wing, the *Jal Bahini*, helped liberate and give birth to Bangladesh in December 1971. Without these brave men and women, there was no way, the Indian Army would have reached Dhaka, on the 11th day, to effect the surrender of some 94,000 Pakistani Army personnel).

The people of Kashmir — with layers of Buddhist, Advait, Sufi philosophies and Central Asian Islamic teachings/influences — are Kashmiris, above everything else. They have had a recorded history, since Emperor Asoka's times, and a way of life, which has embraced brotherhood and tolerance, distinct from sectarian designs and bigotry. (Some alienation and foreign infiltration into their environment, which periodically erupts as violence, is caused by administrative neglect and foreign-funded Proxy Operations, post the *Mujahideen* activities in Afghanistan and Pakistan.)

As it happened, India being the victim of aggression, went to the UN Security Council, in the first instance, with a complaint under the UN Charter, about the situation created by this aggression.

There was no dispute about territory, as endorsed by the Security Council Resolution of January and August 1948 (The Security Council at no time, challenged either the Sovereign choice of the State of J&K, or the validity of the Accession, and as Krishna Menon argued in 1957, that is the only thing that stays). "We sought redress, under the UN Charter. The idea of Sovereignty of the State is indivisible, its parts cannot be taken by invasion ...."

The Accession of J&K to the Union of India was final and irrevocable and cannot be reversed. It has been endorsed by the Parliament, as the Apex Sovereign Body.

No one else, no nation, not the UN, least of all a Military Dictatorship, which is a partner in a Military Alliance System, since 1954, and is jointly operating in Afghanistan, with NATO and the US, has any locus, whatsoever. All its propaganda to 'ascertain' the wishes of the people of Kashmir, rings hollow, when J&K has elected members to the State Legislature and the Central Parliament, several times over several years; while the people of Pakistan, Pakistan Occupied Kashmir, Chitral, Gilgit and the Hunza Central Agency (India had considerable trade through these areas into the Central Asian Region, the lower provinces of the USSR, China and Tibet) have never been allowed to have their say. Pakistan self-dismembered in 1971, for this very reason. A Military-theocratic State is incompatible with Democracy.

Just to recapitulate a bit of history—Jawaharlal Nehru was well advised to prefer Gurdaspur in Punjab, despite some pressures from the Punjabi business lobbies to opt for Lahore, in the discussions prior to the Radcliffe Award, dileanating the International Boundary between India and Pakistan. Since 1947, Pakistan has launched an aggression in 1965 and 1971 and recently, in 1999, in Kargil. That hardly fits in with the UN Charter and the Shimla Agreement 1972, (the joint decision to solve all disputes through exclusively bilateral means), where we magnanimously released 94,000 POWs without pre-condition, on the pleading of the then Prime Minister of Pakistan Z. A. Bhutto.

It was unfortunate for this country that we had a Government in power which not only patronized such projects as the Kashmir Study Group Report, December 1998, but which made Major State sponsored diversions to mirror-image itself on Pakistan, towards driving India to a Theocratic State Agenda, with a Fascist vision. It deliberately neglected and jeopardized national security, resulting in Kargil 1999. To get out of this it tried what it thought was a smart and clever move to request the President of the United States to 'compel' Pakistan to withdraw from the posts and heights, in the Kargil sector, in time for the October 1999 General Elections, and thereby, effectively 'Internationalize' Kashmir, away from the Bilateralism that was binding on Pakistan, since the Shimla Agreement. Thereafter, it made itself prisoner to the US Regional Strategy, for becoming the arbiter and the hegemon, in the Central/West/South Asian region, and compromised India's Sovereignty, across the full spectrum — economic, political and military.

Embracing Globalization, Privatization and Liberalization as in East Europe, Yugoslavia and the former Soviet Union, resulted in Balkanization/dismemberment and prior to that, in unmitigated misery, unemployment, impoverishment ...all this is well documented and needs no elaboration here.

The news article by Seema Mustafa, in the *Asian Age* of October 16, 2004, needs the engaging attention of all Indian citizens, as it has far reaching consequences for the future of our nation. The article says: after the top level meeting between the President of Pakistan and the Indian Prime Minister, 'the back channels are active' between Tariq Aziz and J. N. Dixit, the two designated interlocutors. 'The options appear to be to going along with one or more of the following: 1) Keep Kashmir aside for active discussion but get the other Peace CBMs on the ground; 2) Start the Muzaffarbad -Srinagar bus, let the people of Kashmir meet, and let a solution flow from there; 3) Let the entire Kashmir unite, be One Autonomous Region with a joint administration, if required; 4) Andorra, Chenab and the Kashmir Study Group are three reports, cited as possible basis for further discussions.' The Kashmir Study Group effectively recommends the trifurcation of the State of J & K on communal grounds, and was blessed by the BJP-NDA Government's Prime Minister in December 1998. (TV and newspaper reports of 25th/26th October 2004 quote President Musharraf talk on the '7 Regions' in J&K, which could be considered for 'Autonomy/Independence' together or separately, to reach a resolution to the dispute (his words). He also graciously concedes that 'Plebiscite is no longer a practical solution'.

The then Leader of the Opposition, Sonia Gandhi, placed on record, a nine-point chargesheet, in the Parliament, in October 2003. She stated, and it is on record: "First, I charge this government (NDA) with jeopardizing the country's Defences; Second, I charge this Government with weakening national security..." Where does this leave us if the writer of the article, above cited, says, in the very first paragraph ... "on the plane of options for a Resolution of Jammu & Kashmir that India has recognized as a dispute".

We have been reading denials at various levels of the US State Department, including from the Secretary of State, Colin Powell, that 'the US has no interest in playing the Mediator in the Kashmir dispute, though it remains a Nuclear Flash-point and is, in the world's crisis arc, from Kosovo to Kashmir'. British Ministers faithfully follow this line.

The question arises that if the US and UK are not compelling us, who else is?

A restatement of our position on Kashmir becomes imperative at this point, to refresh faded memories.

For the sake of authenticity, of our country's stand and brevity, I quote in extenso from the statements on record in the United Nations Security Council debates in two sessions in 1957 and one session in 1962.

The narrower problem became a more general exposition of India's policy from 1947 onwards, after the division of the country. The refusal to accept the Two Nation Theory, (as Krishna Menon said for India, ..."We are not a Theocracy; we are a modern Secular State governed on Democratic principles, where the Right of Citizenship is based upon residence, upon domicile, and upon loyalty to the Constitution. Therefore, we totally disregard the argument with regard to the Muslim majorities and Hindu minorities...)". The accession of Kashmir to the Indian Union, as an expression of the will of the people of Kashmir was predicated on a Secular India. Where as, post the late 1990s, India weakened and secular fabric it provided 'extremists and terrorists' fertile ground to challenge the premises of the Accession.

During the eight years, since 1949, the Baghdad Pact and the SEATO, encouraged Pakistan to a belligerent position. In the UN, it is the US and UK which played an activist role in the discussions, correct and friendly towards India but unquestionably on the side of Pakistan, on matters of substance (the Western powers had, in fact, become rather hostile to India after India's performance on Colonialism etc. at the 1946 Session of the General Assembly, and later, according to A. K.

Damodaran, a distinguished Indian Diplomat). This was a logical follow up of the British policy on the subcontinent, pre and post 1947, and on their advice of the Dixon Agenda after the ceasefire in J&K. Ambassador Jarring's Report did not reject the basic Indian contention of the need for the vacation of aggression, before further steps leading to a Plebiscite, could even be discussed (for details, see Resolution of January 5, 1949 of the UN Commission for India and Pakistan (UNCIP), which stated in its note, "before India's acceptance of the Resolution of 13th August, 1948"... that the "Responsibility for the security of the State rests with India...The Sovereignty of Jammu and Kashmir, over the entire territory of the State, shall not be brought into question...the territory occupied by Pakistan is not to be consolidated. ('It is part of Pakistan, according to their Constitution') ...and the UNCIP Resolution stated, "there shall be no recognition of the so-called 'Azad Kashmir Government...'). But Jarring had a series of proposals which had the advantage from the UN point of view, of keeping the question very much alive, in the Security Council framework. The Indian position was and remains that, we accept the Security Council Resolution of January 17, 1948. India refused any subsequent attempts to accept the equal treatment to "the aggressor" and "the aggressed". In simple terms, this would mean, first the evacuation of the territories occupied by Pakistan and thus, the elimination of the aggression. It would mean, the total acknowledgement of India's Sovereignty, as a result of the perfectly legal and Constitutional act of Accession.

B.N. Rau and Krishna Menon, representing India, made it plain time and again that, there was no problem of Kashmir; except that the law had taken a long time to do justice. India's stand has since 1949, been that 'we will negotiate, if by negotiations it is meant—exchange of views, 'composite dialogue' *et al* and furtherance of good neighbourly relations ...but, there cannot be negotiations on the substance of Sovereignty'. 'India remains the Successor State ... Pakistan was carved out of parts of India...aggression eats into our vitals, it is something that affects our national integrity, to put it mildly, it is something that sits on our economic development; it is something that contributes to the unsettlement of our continent, which has been our basic stand.'

The people of India and Pakistan, strongly desire to live in peace and concentrate on getting rid of the oppressive and exploitative impoverishment, that has made them miserable and brought into question their very existence and future. Kashmir is orchestrated as a 'dispute' by external powers and by the feudal oligarchy that rules Pakistan, whether in uniform of the Military or the self-ordained order of the *Mullahs,* which is prohibited by Islam (no one is permitted to come between the people and their Creator/*Allah* in Islam).

Perhaps the wisest and most perceptive comment on Pakistan's ruling, feudal oligarchy was made by Sheikh Abdullah, to the State's Constituent Assembly (S/PV.762/ Add.1, annex VI). He said, "The most powerful argument which can be advanced in its (Pakistan's) favour is that, Pakistan is a Muslim State, and, a big majority of our people, being Muslims, the State must accede to Pakistan. This claim of being a Muslim State is of course only a camouflage. It is a screen to dupe the common man, so that he may not see clearly that Pakistan is a Feudal State, in which a clique is trying by these methods to maintain itself in power..."

...Continuing, Sheikh Abdullah stated, "Naturally, if we Accede to India, there is no danger of a revival of Feudalism and autocracy. Moreover, during the last four years, the Government of India has never tried to interfere in our internal autonomy....This experience has strengthened our confidence in them, as a Democratic State (Indian Constitution Article 370).

..."The real character of a State is revealed in its Constitution. The Indian constitution has set before the country, the goal of a Secular Democracy, based upon justice, freedom and equality for all, without distinction. This is the bedrock of modern democracy. This should meet the argument that the Muslims of Kashmir cannot have security in India, where the large majority of the population are Hindus. Any unnatural cleavage between religious groups, is the legacy of Imperialism (and its new coinage,

'Globalization') and no modern State can afford to encourage artificial divisions, if it is to achieve progress and prosperity. The Indian Constitution has amply and finally repudiated the concept of a Religious State, which is a throw-back to Medievalism, by guaranteeing the rights of all citizens irrespective of their religion, colour, caste and class."

"The national movement in our State, naturally gravitates towards these principles of Secular Democracy. The people will never accept a principle which seeks to favour the interests of one religion or social group, against the other. This affinity in political principles, as well as in past associations, and our common path of suffering, in the cause of freedom (Azadi), must be weighed properly while deciding the future of the State...We are intimately concerned with the economic well-being of the people of this State. As I said before, while referring to the Constitution-building, political ideals of the State are often meaningless, unless linked with economic plans ...As you know, and as I have detailed before, we have been able to put through our 'land to the tiller' legislation ... and the artisans and their arts and crafts...minerals in the State ... efficient supply of such basic necessities, that the standard of living of the man-on-the street depends"... Sheikh Abdullah did warn of "certain tendencies...of communal organizations.... The continued Accession of Kashmir to India should, however, help in defeating this tendency...From my experience in the last four years, it is my considered judgement that the presence of Kashmir, in the Union of India, has been the major factor in stabilizing relations between (sections of Partition affected people, etc). Hindus and Muslims of India".... Gandhiji said ... before his assassination, which paraphrased reads: 'I lift up mine eyes unto the hills, from whence cometh my help'... Right thinking men would point out that Pakistan is not an organic unity of all the Muslims in this subcontinent...it has on the contrary, caused the dispersion of the Indian Muslims, for whose benefit it was claimed to be created..."

Pakistan was, it is a historical fact, created by the British to continue their Imperialist Agenda. This purpose is being well-served, not only by Pakistan but their counterparts in the rest of the subcontinent, as a furtherance of the globalized, imperialist enterprise.

To conclude, for the moment intrigues, back channels, secret behind-the-scenes dialogues carried out at the directions of the 'great powers' have been the order of the day. And all this behind-the-back of Parliament,. and therefore, the Democratic will. At least one Indian Army Commander, some years ago, had the courage to stand up to such intrigue, 'a thin end of the wedge operation in Kashmir', and send in his Letter of Resignation, notwithstanding the fact that he was to be the next Chief of the Army Staff. Destiny robbed this great nation of such a patriot from assumption of that high office. What followed, is there for all of us to see.

13

Oil Resources

Strategy and Defence Policies

During a TV panel discussion, the Union Petroleum Minister Shri Ram Naik in April 2004, turned down the suggestion of a member of the panel that except as a theoretical analysis, he (and his Ministry), were not aware if there was any connection between Oil resources in the Caspian Sea Region and Iraq, and the launch of the operations in Afghanistan, in October 2001, and Iraq, in March 2003. The former Minister added that he had visited Iraq, as India had friendly relations with Iraq and sourced part of its Oil imports from that country. Since 1990, the proportion of domestic production to Imports of Oil, had reversed from one-third of imported oil to two-third, for meeting its requirements in 2003, and the trend was continuing to grow more adverse, as the Oil Import Bill remained the main reason for our large Annual Trade Deficit, with no relief in sight.

That China's Oil Imports were increasing by an approximate 10 per cent annually, was no consolation. China seemed somewhat unmindful of this growing dependence and a long, vulnerable supply line, across the seas, originating from a potentially and politically, unstable region. It had perhaps factored this into its Foreign and Security Policies, and compromised its National Policies to the extent that was bearable in its calculus. China had however, been energetically pursuing Bilateral and Multilateral Pipeline Projects from the Central Asian Region.

However, these were costly and long gestation projects which needed review, as the estimates of recoverable reserves, particularly Oil, had been scaled down in the last 24 months, from 233 GB to 13 GB, in the Caspian Basin. (China has, in November 2004, disclosed a huge on-sure and off-shore Oil Discovery in Bohai Bay).

China apart, since the time the British Empire's world-wide 'Coaling' stations became part of history, when the British Fleet and industry switched over to the much more easily handled Oil; Oil flow and control/access of Cheap Oil became a central and driving concern of the national strategic enterprise of the Western/industrialized Corporate world. To recap briefly, while the First World War was launched to settle the question of colonial possessions and their agricultural and mineral raw materials, by force, the Second World War was more openly declared to capture the Oil Fields in the Caucasus and Baku, by Nazi Germany; and in the East, by Japan, to assert possession of Oil Resources in Jawa / Indonesia / East Indies, and monopoly trade in East Asia / South-East Asia, called the Great Co-prosperity Sphere, without which, Japan's imperial and corporate interests could not compete with the United States.

Germany's drive to Baku was halted at Stalingrad. Japan was blockaded and starved by the US Submarine Ring, around her major islands in 1942-43, so that, by the time of the Argonaut Conference in Washington DC, in December 1943, it was recorded that Japanese industry and transportation had been grounded to a halt. The Great War was over for Japan, for all practical purposes, except isolated Army Posts in the near Pacific and Kamikaze fighters. On the US side, General MacArthur's island hopping, Iwo Jima and Okinawa were dramatic camera opportunities for the historical record and heroics. They did little to contribute to the US strategy and victory in the Pacific.

Britain, her legendary 'Lawrence of Arabia', the first Military campaign into Iraq, in the 1920s to dislodge/replace the power vacuum left by the Ottoman Empire, the Anglo-German rivalry to build railway lines in Iraq, the finding of a 'Royal' to establish the Pehlavi dynasty in Iran, later to establish the Anglo-Iranian

Oil Company, with the Royal (British) Navy's insistence that the RN hold shares in the AIOC, were all a series of manoeuvres to take over the prognosticated oil reserves, established by British, the Anglo-Dutch and US Oil Companies which gradually installed their preferred kingdoms and Sheikhs, executed regime changes by covert and overt means, and minor military campaigns. Indian workers were the backbone of these Oil Companies, doing all the donkey's work, in the desert!

After the Great Power Yalta Agreement, which formalized the post-War 'spheres of influence', the US actually threatened the Soviet Union with atomic weapons, if it did not give up its alleged ambitions in Iranian Azerbaijan. Obviously, the Oil 'prize'/ franchises in Iran, were considered sufficient reason to threaten a greatly acclaimed war ally, so soon after Yalta!

In the post-World War II era, Oil and Oil Politics is a big game. The comparatively small chessboard of the Middle-East, grew into Zbigniew Brzezinski's 'Grand Chessboard'. Global policies of the G-5 are more sharply defined by the new and updated 'Resource' Maps. Global Military deployment and 'readiness' to intervene are determined by the 'Energy Assessment' of the 'Oil Majors', be it in West Asia, East Europe, Georgia, Azerbaijan, Caspian Sea Region, West Africa (Angola, Gulf of Guinea, Equatorial Guinea, Congo, Nigeria, Sahara) or Venezuela, Bolivia, Mexico or Indonesia, offshore and onshore Bangladesh and India. Shell Companies with indigenous/local firms and front partners, with private Military companies as back up, are the order of the day, specially in Africa, West Asia and Central Asia. Global Military presence/pre-positioned facilities, prepared logistic and operational launch bases, avoid the difficulties of on-site Military presence, which can be a political embarrassment/tension to host Oil (Gas)-rich nations.

In this context, it is a matter of some concern that policy-makers, security experts and specialists in New Delhi, with adequate funding support, appear not to have sufficiently advised the erstwhile NDA Government Ministers concerned or the Cabinet, on Global Energy policies of the Big Powers and the 'Oil Majors', in particular. There has perhaps not been a single

News article in any of the major national, large circulation dailies, or even on the *India Today* and *Pravasi Diwas* associated Seminars or thinktanks, devoted only to discuss India's national concerns, that otherwise receive such wide media coverage, that appear to have devoted a few minutes to the 'Report of the US National Energy Policy Development Group (NEPDG)', appointed by President George W. Bush, headed by Vice President Dick Cheney (a former US Defence Secretary, and Halliburton CEO), also known as the 'Cheney Energy Report' of May 17, 2001.

The basic goal of the Cheney Plan is to find additional resources of Oil for the US. Earlier, on March 19, 2001, US Energy Secretary, Spencer Abraham, told a National Energy Symposium, "The failure to meet this challenge will threaten our nation's economic prosperity, compromise on our national security and literally alter the way we lead our lives."

Though the Cheney Report is guarded about the foreign oil that will be required, it gives enough figures to extrapolate. It notes that domestic oil production will decline from 8.5 million barrels, per day (mbd) in 2002, to 7.0 mbd in 2020, fifteen years hence. Imports, according to the New Energy Policy (NEP), are aimed at providing 7.5 mbd increment to the present imports, equivalent to the total consumption of China and India.

Implementing the Cheney (NEP) Plan has major implications for the US Security and Military policy. In brief, US Military plans are integral to the NEP on a global scale, and Oil Fields form the landscape, around which future conflicts are predicted to take place (for example, around 20 per cent of US Oil Imports already come from the Middle East). The US Military has a huge stockpile of oil in Saudi Arabia, for any War. More importantly, the handling of Oil Exports from the Middle-East/West Asia is done under the auspices of US Oil Majors, which gives the US unparalleled leverage in global power and international relations. The future holds even more promise, as Saudi Arabia has 25 per cent, Iraq 11 per cent and Kuwait 10 per cent of the proven world's Reserves, not counting UAE, Qatar, Omani reserves and Iran, which may at some stage in the years ahead, on present trends, revert to a pre-1979 Oil relationship with the US.

It was already in early spring 2002, that the US policy-makers had concluded that containment through sanctions of Iraq/Saddam Hussein was not working in eliminating Iraq's perceived threat to the US (Oil) interests in the Gulf. Hence, the follow up soon, thereafter.

Incidently, the Africa Opportunity Plan, focused on in 2003 by a US Presidential visit to the African States, was complimentary to the accelerated Oil interests of US Oil Majors, in Angola, Gulf of Guinea (Equatorial Guinea), Nigeria and other Oil/strategic raw mineral-rich States, as an alternative to the unstable West Asian countries and regions as a whole. West Africa is producing 10 per cent of the world's Oil, and has forecasted to meet upto 25 per cent of the world's Oil requirements, by 2020.

The Caspian Sea Region, once prognosticated as blessed with the second largest Oil and Gas Reserves in the world has been undergoing a review. The Gas Reserves remain, but the Oil Reserves are down from the original forecasts of the US Geological Survey. The Caspian Sea Basin Reserves were estimated to be 33 billion barrels, at 90 per cent probability, and 233 billion barrels, at 50 per cent probability. Thus, the original Oil Reserves of 200 GBs of Oil, has been reduced to an estimated 9 to 13 GBs, about the same, as the US potential today. However, the Gas Reserves of the Caspian Basin remain the largest in the world, to date.

Venezuela and Mexico in the Western hemisphere remain important US suppliers, though Bolivia has recently rescinded to export Gas to the US, due to domestic pressures from the people of Bolivia. Mexico Oil Reserves are 25 per cent larger than the US oil reserves.

In India, the domestic demand and imports of oil have trebled in the last decade. It would, therefore, be in our vital national interests to keep a hawk eye on the global oil scenario, specially as several prima facie, credible reports of North Sea and Saudi Oil 'peaking' around 2007, have been presented in the last two years, including by C.J. Campbell, a respected Oil Energy specialist, to the House of Commons—All Party Committee, as early as on July 19, 1999. What stops our

Parliamentary Committees at least from listening to such people, specially when we are all 'ears' for not so reputable global advisers, on disinvestment of our *'Oil Navaratnas'.* (An Indian Agriculture and Food trade Policy expert, Devinder Sharma, was invited by the House of Commons All Party Committee, to give evidence on GM foods, as recently as March 22, 2004).

If, our decision-makers had read or been briefed about the corporate plans of UNOCOL, CENTGAS and ENRON, for the transportation of Caspian Basin gas through Afghanistan, their failed negotiations, financial deals that did not fructify with the Taliban/Northern Alliance Governments in the period July 2001, India's responses to the US attack and invasion of Afghanistan, may have been more balanced and our diplomatic, economic, trade and Military assessment and projections been more firmly rooted, to advance our national interests. The widespread use of Radioactive Depleted Munitions which are Nuclear Warheads in cruise missiles, bunker busters, cluster bombs, tank and small-arms, not only turned Afghanistan into a grave-yard of DU fall out in the dust, water systems and direct ingestion into lungs, affecting human, animal and plant life, but its 'down wind effects' which cover upto a thousand mile /1600 kilometres radius from Kabul, have the potentiality of causing Cancer, AIDS epidemic in Northern and Western India. Our Health Budgets simply cannot cope with these after-effects which will start surfacing three years from now, about 2007-08.

In all the noise, thunder and hand-clapping that the media partook, in regard to the Afghanistan Operations, Radioactive DU anti-tank and small arms bullets found their way to the Pakistan arsenal, which have the same effect on human physiology as Nuclear Weapons inflicting slow and silent genocide, over a longer term. Now with the most important Non-NATO Ally, MINNA status, one of the major supplies to our western neighbour will be, 'Depleted Munitions', as the *Indian Express* correctly highlighted on the top of its front page, but the Ministries of Defence, External Affairs, Home and Health, and the Cabinet Committee on Security, have simply ignored and turned their gaze away. Afghanistan is our neighbour hardly 500 kilometres away from Western Rajasthan, about the distance from Delhi to Amritsar. The Gulf and Saudi Arabia are just 1,000 kilometres distance away by sea, less than the distance by land, from Mumbai to Delhi (1,400 kilometres). For how long can we ignore the presence of NATO in Afghanistan?

Why did the Iraq invasion also take our Government by surprise or did it? Why did the Indian Leadership fumble? If it had read or had been briefed about the Cheney Report and its concluding recommendations in the last chapter, India would have been spared of the many learned commentaries and exhortations, that our learned Foreign and Defense Affairs specialists made, on the TV channels! More importantly, the National Security Advisory Board, which serves the CCS and its intelligence, supported by RAW and other high budget agencies, would have prepared 'National Intelligence Estimates', on the developing scenarios, periodically on the Pakistan-Afghanistan-Caspian Basin and Central Asian Region, all neighbours to India, almost touching Kashmir. All is still not lost. If we read 'The Grand Chessboard' of Zbigniew Brzezinski and the 'National Security Strategy Document' of September 20, 2002, endorsed by President Bush, its backgrounder, the Project for the New American Century: 'Rebuilding America's Defenses: Strategy, Forces, Resources for the New Century' write out its implications for India's thousand million people and their minimum well-being, it may help future Governments to better prepare for the 'Great Storm', that this region, described as the 'one with the greatest potential for conflict' (and instability) must face.

It is possible that faced with the situation, as we are facing, it may serve India's national interests to not go for the obvious, increase the Defence Budget but to strictly implement an earlier decision to diversify our foreign exchange holdings in a 'basket of currencies', and try our best to get at least part of our Oil-in-Barter terms, make a determined effort to de-link the economy and our project loans from the World Bank and the IMF. This may just give the autonomy in decision-making that our economic security so sorely needs, at this moment.

13

Corporate Globalization, Its Militarization and Possible Response of a United People

The Contemporary Scenario

We share a common historical experience in Asia, Latin America and Africa, though the evolution of the colonial structures in the Latin Nations has been somewhat different. Therefore, when we speak of a region or 'project', it has a whole lot of real linkages with each other. The battle-lines in Palestine, Iraq, Colombia, Sierra Lone, or the Philippines, are common, they are shared battle-lines and overlapping.

Prof. Michel Chussodovsky, in the Case Studies of several countries, in his book, *'Globalization of Poverty'*, has attributed conditions in these countries, to the contemporary 'Project for the New American Century' (Empire), with inevitable fratricide, economic genocide and the political *Balkanization* of nations. True, that the Oil and Gas-Rich Nations, enjoy a higher precedence as target. This, in the US assessment, justifies pre-emptive War. However, in a PNAC, based on the concept of an unending War on Terror, and unending Wars, it is universal in its application, though the time-lines of the phases are varying. As Bush says, "Who can tell where one begins, and where the other ends."

Pursuit of the Military Strategic Doctrine of Imperial Globalization, in contemporary time (new Imperial Grand

Strategy), is of similar genre as the barbaric terror, unleashed on nations and continents, colonised and plundered, on the indigenous people of South America, the Red Indians, the Africans, Indians and Asians, in the last four hundred years. The methodologies, ideological underpinnings, deception and deceit, are fundamentally the same. Only the daisy-cutters are aimed from high above, the targets are the same. (The revised plans of the US Space Command, go beyond control of space, for Military purposes, to "Ownership of Space", which is to be 'permanent', according to the NSS, September 17, 2002 Document. The Pentagon Planning Document, partially leaked, has no historical parallel, to attack any target, anywhere from space).

As High Visibility Wars are being progressed, a whole host of agendas, with their Action Plans, are being simultaneously operationalized. Nations are divided into ethnic mind-sets; hate and identity politics are fuelled, leaderships and Governments are subverted, and growth of a comprador elite is encouraged. The institutions of the 'Republic' are broken up by the very same people, now rented out, whose job it is to uphold them; the Diplomatic, Military, Police, and Intelligence Agencies of the nation are staffed through a system of 'Certification' or pre-clearance, rendered subservient to the Imperial Interest. Simultaneously, local terrorist outfits and anti-State actors (people) are operationalized through receipts from thriving businesses in narcotics, gun-running, dirty-money transfers and Mafiosi, selling pseudo-religious rituals and symbolisms of hate. This is the internalisation of the Terrorist armoury, while Corporate globalization simultaneously drives the politics and economics of unprecedented accumulation of surpluses and global finance, and defrauds the nations, without paying taxes. The Imperial State says that, it is there to save the Victim States, by its pretense at 'drug enforcement', for example, while actually subverting and recruiting Military and Police Officials, extending its 'extra-territoriality' of laws and enforcement tools, to also subdue the people. A majority of narco-outfits receive external material, Intelligence and operational support. Afghanistan, is, but one example of the consequences of narco-Terrorism, giving birth to the *Taliban, Al-Qaeda,* and other actors, for a pre-determined purpose, that is, for the control of an entire geographical regions. The US of course, now says, *Al-Qaeda* and its associates are spread over more than 60 countries, all on the US hit-list. One needs to recall *'Operation Phoenix'* in Vietnam, as one more in the series of examples. *Al-Qaeda's* patron saint is none other than the US.

Prof. Chussodovsky may kindly permit me the indulgence of summarizing from his 'Yugoslavia Case-Study'. The sequence is relevant to so many of our nations, and to Anti-Imperialist Movements. We ought to have a historical memory, but 'greed' apparently causes total amnesia in those, who govern us. Only months ago, former Malaysian Prime Minister Mohammad Mahathir stated, "The Rich Nations fuelled Terrorism and Poverty in the Third World, and certainly did everything to turn a country against itself". Speaking to the UN General Assembly, on September 24, 2003, he focussed on 'Imperialist Europe'.

The Yugoslavia Case-Study is entirely relevant to South Asia, as shown below:

1. IMF-WB-US Department of Treasury, imposed runaway Import Liberalization, that devastated the Yugoslav industry.
2. The Central Government was directed to suspend payments, due to the Federated Republics and regions which fuelled the process of *Balkanization* and Secession, resulting in the De-facto Secession by Croatia and Slovenia, in June 1991, egged on by NATO.
3. Massive Privatization of all socially-owned, or State Sector Enterprises, and sale to Western Corporates, was insisted on, at nominal book value, as part of the Restructuring Programme.
4. Supporting Legislation, drawn by Western Financial Consultants and Lawyers, to safeguard the 'Rights of Foreign Creditors', and unrestricted entry, permitted to foreigners, not only in Industry, but in Banking, Insurance, and Service Sectors.
5. The entire Nationalized Banking Sector was dismantled.
6. Practically one-half of the work-force, or more, was laid off due to Privatization.

7. Ethnic Strife and Ethnic Cleansing, with the strategic objective of the break-up of Yugoslavia, by funding and supporting of violent Secessionist groups, by the Western Intelligence Agencies, and the ISI, and the Private Military Companies (PMCs) in US and UK (details of the world-wide operations of the PMCs are available in www.icij.org), hiring Mercenaries of Arab/Afghan fighters, trained in the killing-fields of Afghanistan, the Kosovo Liberation Army and its *Al-Qaeda* arm, financed through Drug Trafficking, White Slave Traffic, and supplied with unlimited arms, first initiated in Croatia.
8. The 'November 1995, Dayton Accord', initiated by the US and EU, installed a full-fledged colonial administration *(a la* DFID) in the State of Andhra Pradesh, and being progressed in Kerala, by the ADB) *'Politics of Reform: the ADB in Kerala,'* by K. Ravi Raman of the Centre of Development Studies, Thiruvananthapuram), in Bosnia, with expatriates. Article VII of the 'Dayton Accord', stipulated that, the first Governor of the Bosnia Central Bank, will be appointed by the IMF, and will not be a citizen of Bosnia or Herzegovinia. (In South Asian countries, the Governor has to be 'certified' by the IMF).
9. The entire inflated, so-called 'Peace-Keeping Expenses', were paid for by the new Autonomous Republics, and the foreign debt was divided proportionately between them. Oil Exploration in Bosnia was commenced, thereafter by the American Oil Company, AMOCO, in much the same pattern as in Iraq, and the West African countries.

The Iraq Invasion is being referred to as a 'Corporate Oil Invasion', and it is so. The PMCs are fanning out in the region. The Corporate Media, including the BBC, are feeding the US public and listeners, with deception and disinformation, as 'partners of the Imperial Enterprise'. The proliferation of Terrorist organizations has been a direct consequence of the Globalization project, its other half, deliberately diversionary.

The growing economic empire, as James Petras, in his book, *'Globalisation Unmasked'* emphasizes, was matched even earlier to Iraq II, by the growing willingness to use force in Central Europe, Asia, Africa and Latin America, to increase the US Military Budget and to appoint Hard-line Presidential Intelligence and Security Advisers, to direct the covert and overt Military interventions. Washington is prepared "to defend its newly re-gained economic ascendancy, by 'Free' Trade, if possible, by Military Force, if necessary".

The new global regime of the WTO, sets enforceable rules for Nation States, the important exception is, Article XXI of the GATT, which provides a freedom for Military Spending, for any reason related to national security...to maintain order. The International Financial Institutions have also given a *carte-blanche* to Defence Budgets, and do not exercise any scrutiny, in comparison with Welfare Budget, and push for Privatization of Industries and Services. The interests of 'Defence-Military' Corporations are over-riding, and have a clear precedence over those on the society. Military Spending is the basis of much of the 'New Economy'.

Project for the New American Century and Fascism

The key elements of the PNAC Project, in South Asia, bought out elites and compromised leaders, collaborating in the subversion of the most vital institutions of the Republics, including the Criminal Justice System. The Judiciary, the Military, Civil Servants, and the Intelligence Agencies, are all beholden and increasingly obligated to the US Administration. This vast region, South of the Hindu-kush and the Himalayas, and stretching into the lap of the Indian Ocean, is literally a stones-throw away from our Arab, Central Asian and South-East Asian brothers. With the rich Oil and Gas finds in Central Asia, we thank to the strategic concerns of the US Project, and the Oil Corporates (Major Oil Arteries are only a few hours sailing distance, and the projected Trans-Afghanistan Energy Pipeline, right there), in the strategic reckoning of the US, vide the September, 17, 2002, National Security Strategy Document. China is an additional factor, in the US calculus.

Perhaps, it needs to be reiterated that, the 'War on Terror' is an Imperial War, to secure US Global and Strategic domination and economic interests. Force is integral to the process of Globalization of the Empire, to ensure uninhibited access to markets, energy supplies and strategic resources. Even in the earlier era, Colonial Armies and Police were available to the Imperial States, both for security and expansion in the Non-European world, and for Inter-State competition and all-out War in Europe. The 'hidden hand' of the market, needs the 'hidden fist' for back-up. That is what Kosovo was about. That is what is halted, thanks to the Iraqi and Palestinian resistance. Tony Blair is right, "the (Imperial) War against Terrorists is a wider War, for a New World Order".

The South Asian market is of 1,500 million people, never mind the 800 millions who are desperately poor, and the 400 millions who are eking out a miserable living, deprived of their livelihoods, thanks to the SAP/SALs of the IMF, Free-Trade, TRIPS, MAI regimes of the WTO, the US, and the TNCs. Nevertheless, the Corporates can offer their goods to an estimated 300 million consumers. Not only the goods, but the siphoning off of surpluses, via the unrestricted use of Private Banking, Hawala Channels and OCBs. The new champions of religion are beating their drums in crescendo, to create diversions from this uninterrupted loot. Behind these, are the Criminal Political Mafias, in and out of Government, their hidden face, carrying on the 'Great Business' of Drugs Arms, Dirty Money Laundering, Child and Women Trafficking, and above all, impoverishing people, depriving them of their livelihoods, aiding Privatization, or stealing publicly created wealth, by 'looting public money' in banks and public FIs, by non-payment of huge loans, manipulating the stock markets, defrauding pension and provident funds, all in the name of Liberalization. Some say that, this is Capitalism, essentially, it is Barbarism. The substantive issue is the Militarization of Globalization, both on a world-scale and the regional context. The big increases in Public Spending, on Military, Para-Military and Police Forces, is the other issue. The push of the Arms Industry in the US, its all pervasive influence, the push of the 'Star War' Programme (keys to US Military effectiveness, permitting instant engagement anywhere in the world), the R&D, devoted to the new Nuclear Weapon System, protecting property, killing people, the RNEPs or the Deep Penetration Nuclear Devices, the new Micro-nukes, the galloping pursuit of Chemical and Biological Weapons of the race-specific genes variety, for example, are to induce fear and terrorise the Non-Western world. The US has a million troops, located in five continents, Carrier Battle Groups, deployed in all the Oceans, and Military Bases of different types, specially in and around Energy and Mineral Resource regions. All this shapes the minds of the Power Elite, to "Have, will use" thinking.

In South Asia, we have a dangerous mixture of Military Power, and the strenuously pursued project of the Militarization of Society, essentially, the Militarization of the majority communities. This is proceeding apace, in several insidious ways, covert and overt, in India, Pakistan, Sri Lanka, and Bangladesh, and has the potential to tear them apart into shreds, as an inevitable consequence of 'Globalization' which shorn of its rhetoric, is Corporate Fascism. The Globalization Project, for example, needs the 'Hindu Militias" and the 'Internal Enemy,' as an absolute must. Mussolini was candid to define Fascism as Corporatism, "When State Power merges with Corporate Power". Because we are face-to-face with Fascism, let me elaborate a little. "It is impossible to conceive the *Nazi (Fascist) Movement, without War: German martial glory was its Father, its first musketeer is its Leader; the War's hardy spirit, its Soul"*. (Herst Von Mesch's book, *'Kreig als Saat War as Seed,* published in Breslam,1943). There is enough evidence in the Public domain, that this is well underway. An indigenous version, inspired by the original Fascists, linked with Global Fascism. It is not just cheaper and cheaper labour, Informalisation and Contract Labour, or steadily depressing wages, imposed by Corporate Fascism, in fact, Slave Labour in sweat shops, depriving the people of health-care, minimum nutrition, hospitals, and education for their children, water — via privatization, taking away of hard earned rights of collective bargaining, over a century of sacrifices and struggle. Will there be a revolt of the slaves? How is it to be waged? Perhaps, the seeds of destruction lie within. Their much vaulted strength has vulnerabilities that the organized resistance in little Cuba, Palestine and Iraq, appear to have exposed.

Briefly, in South Asia, "Terrorism has been used as a matter of State Policy, in particular, after the Vietnam War; when the costs in terms of direct deployment of troops, in a Declared War Counter-Insurgency, were found to be financially, and in terms of human lives, no longer acceptable to domestic public opinion (therefore, the resort to PMCs and Para Military infiltration, as in Northern Ireland). Countries unwilling to abandon the path of Independent Political and Economic Development, are primary targets of Terrorism, used as an alternative means of warfare; the ground was laid by more than one Intelligence Agency; executed through various Mercenary Leaders and groups, financed in many cases by the Drug Trade. The training of Mercenary Terrorists and their deployment was, and is, a crime, in violation of International Law and Charter of the UN. Civilians, State Force, Head of State, Development Projects, Schools, Hospitals, are all targets... (Niloufer Bhagwat, in *"Islam, the New Enemy of Imperialism"*. Published in the 'International Review of Contemporary Law' 2002). Economic Terrorism, imposed by the PNAC, invariably leads to Economic *Balkanization* and complements the fragmentation of hitherto peaceful societies and nations.

A steeply rising curve of violence in society, coincident to the fuelling of hate and identity politics, appears to be the direct consequence of initiation of the Globalization (Privatization and Liberalization) Process in South Asia, tearing apart the age-long cohesion of societies.

Sri Lanka

Sri Lanka, by the seventies, had achieved remarkable success in Nutritional Levels, thanks to 'A Rupee-a-Kilo Rice' programme, Literacy Levels, School Mid-day Meal programmes and a reasonable Employment satisfaction. In 1980s, the then President, Jayawardane, desired to make Sri Lanka another Singapore, by opening the economy. But first, the Tamil Minority was to make way for the Majority community in jobs, public services, and the school system. Privatization, foreign take-overs, FDI at any cost, became the order-of-the-day. Steady Socio and Economic progress was abandoned, in the pursuit of Capitalist development. Ethnic strife sprouted, with the foreign-sponsored and financed LTTE, with overseas Headquaters in London and Belgium, to initiate a Fratricidal War, another minority group, supported by the Saudis, fronting for their masters in Sri Lanka South-east with no end in sight. Drugs and Gun Running operations, in collusion with the Burmese, Indian, Thai and later, the Pakistani Mafiosi, became the LTTE's mainstay. In the Israeli Training Camps, separated by just a kilometre or two, were the LTTE, the Sri Lankans and a host of Asian detachments, known to be Pro-Arab! That was real International Cooperation! Sri Lanka was truly stopped in its tracks. Norwegians, fronting for the US, broker peace, notwithstanding.

Bangladesh

Bangladesh, as a consequence of Imperial vivisection of South Asia, into two States of India and Pakistan, was for many years, at first, a politico-economic colony of West Pakistan, and later, became Independent, in 1971. Thereafter, within four years, a *Military Junta* took over, in a CIA-supported assassination of its then President, Sheikh Mujib-ur Rahman, in an Army Coup. Military Rule continued for a long while, supported by the Saudis, who bank-rolled the clergy and others, and in fact, continue to do so, as directed. The poor here, are desperately poor, and share a language and culture with the Indian Bengal. However, the Minorities and the poor, are constantly pushed out to Tripura, Assam and West Bengal, to keep the pot boiling. Bangladesh Intelligence even supports Insurgency in Tripura, and North-East India. Though there have been recent finds of Oil and Gas, off-shore and on-shore, there is enough explosive mixture in Indo-Bangla Relations, to make the External Forces happy, while the desperately poor, fight over the crumbs, thrown by such Multi-nationals, as Reebok and Disney Garments, at between five cents to fifteen cents-a-day, in competition with the Mexican, the Indonesian, and the Chinese poor.

Myanmar

The *Military Junta* in power, is willing to deal in an all manner of things, behind the curtains. Myanmar is well located, for this kind of trade with South-East Asian countries. The UNOCAL Company, as documented by the National Lawyers' Guild (US), and other organizations in the US, in a Memorandum to the Attorney General of California, against the activities of this Company in the US, and other Companies, has complained that, this US Company used Slave Labour, supplied by the Military Government, in areas of Myanmar.

The Sub-continent

For Narcotics and Gun-running, Myanmar is part of South Asia. More in North-East India, located near the Border, is the centre of the trade. Many figures in the Government of India (1998-2004) are involved and this is an open secret! The area is a second home to a few of them, ostensibly because, they love the Nagas, Manipuris, Zomis and others! Narco Trade is the soul of Democracy, keeping the Indian Army and the Para-military tied up in knots. One of the reasons an Indian Navy Chief was removed was that, he acceeded to General Roy Chowdhry the Army Chief's request for intercepting Arms and Narco Shipments from Thai offshore, via the Andaman Islands, to the North-East. This hurt the then Minister of Defense and his friend, the Arakanese Foreign Minister. The North-East has one of the largest Criminal Mafia operations in the sub-continent, and these Terrorist outfits are well-connected to other Terrorist groups in India, including Nepal, Pakistan, Sri Lanka, Afghanistan, Kashmir and our *Khalistan Liberation Army (KLA)*. Narcotics, Gun-running and Dirty Money operations are interlocked, and have a common 'God Father' in the Foreign Banking Systems, and India's own Private Sector, '*Hawala*' System, an informal, but highly efficient Money Transfer Operation. All the Terrorist groups are closely connected to Right Wing groups, who claim monopoly of 'Nationalism' and give certificates to other citizens, on their patriotic commitment. A large number of Places of Worship are useds as hubs for 'business' coperation. They are inter-connected by extensive networks with Foreign Agencies and organizations, across South Asia and beyond, globally.

The LTTE has bases in London and Benelux cities, the Sikh Separatists in the US (earlier in Canada), the 'Freedom Fighters' of Kashmir in London and New York, the Naga and Mizo Fronts meet the Government's Negotiators in Amsterdam and Switzerland, and Pakistan-based Terrorist brigades have been sponsored by the CIA and Saudi Intelligence. The *Taliban,* until two months prior to 9/11, was paid for by the US. The 'Other Commanders' are also paid in bags, by the US. Why has the question not risen, to the fore that, host training bases, for all Terrorist organizations, operating in South Asia, are in Western countries, while they loudly proclaim pre-emptive action against those who harbour terrorists? The Pakistani establishment was subverted, as early as in the 1950s, when Military Rule and Membership of the CENTO, carried huge rewards and continue to do so. They are, in President Bush's words, "allies", while we have been vying to replace them. A Progressive regime, which took over in Afghanistan in 1978, brought In land Reforms, schooling for girls and women, *purdah,* reduced the power of the Clerics and the War (drug) Lords. The rest is history. As Ahmed Rashid's book, graphically describes, it became the training-cum-breeding ground for the erstwhile '*Mujahideen*', now Terrorists, to the US. Now, we also have Guest Freedom Fighters who murder, rape and loot women, children, and fellow Muslims, in the Kashmir Valley, while turning the Minorities into Refugees; the State and Centre have done little to help the people with development and job opportunities, as befits a Constitutional, Secular, Democracy, on which the Kashmiri people's Accession to India was predicated. With a Fundamentalist 'Hindu' Central Government in power in 1998-2004, fully backed by the US Administration, things are going the classical Fascist way, and the institutions of the State, including the Constitution, stand subverted, and Rule of Law, already a casualty.

I would not like make any elaborate comments on Pakistan, except that, one land and its people were divided into three countries, in South Asia, in 1947, as a matter of a deliberate policy by the British Imperialists, who longed to return to the entire South Asia. They have, in one sense, seceded elites, have always been part of the Imperialist project, though India is a complex nation with its diversity, yet, the people share a common bond and a common destiny.

In India, the largest country in South Asia, the subject of the 'Internal Enemy', needs attention, as it is at the core of Militarization of Globalization, in South Asia. The Fascist Party, the BJP, also known as the *Sangh Parivar* (Sangh family), has its organizational, cultural and inspirational roots in Mussolini's *Black Shirts (Marzai)* and Hitler's *Nazi Party Swastika,* the Fuerher, the Aryan race, the final solution for the Minorities, the Internal Enemy. Allied with it, are a large number of Corporates, our own indigenous versions of the Krupps, IG Farbens, Siemens, Funks and their international partners in the US and UK, the Duponts, the Fords, the ICI, and so on...We have almost all the Big Business, in a joint operation with Politicians and Bureaucrats, to loot from the Public Sector Banks, Public Financial Institutions, in the privatization of the hugely profit-making Public Sector Enterprises, on the same pattern, as in Latin America, Mexico, Russia, and EE. Like there, here too, it is a *quid pro quo,* you don't have to pay Income Tax, Corporate Tax, Excise, Customs Duty, and Sales Tax, as long as you pass on and share the loot. Money laundering, official tax amnesty schemes, and more and more exemptions for those who make super profits, are the order of the day. 'Privatization is Briberization', says Stiglitz, and Privatization is the biggest fraud, since our Independence, bigger than even the exhorbitant Arms Imports, with the heftiest commissions. This is the stuff that Militarization of the South-Asian societies are made of.

It is the Hate and Identity Politics of certain political formations, flush with unlimited funds, that is militarizing societies at the grassroots. The biggest achievement, says the BJP, is its fight against 'Terrorism'. Not a day passes when a large number of citizens, with names that denote a denomination, are arrested, and their homes and localities raided, under the Prevention of Terrorism Act 2002, (POTA), the indigenous equivalent of the Patriot Act, since violence, both State-Sponsored and its counter, has increased. All this suits Corporate Globalization to the 'tee'. It is the best diversion that could be conceived and operationalised. There is only 'one mother' of all issues, a Temple for a Deity, who already has millions of Temples built for Him, while His billion devotees don't have a roof over their heads! The Fascists live by the 'Big Lie', and the media faithfully repeats these lies in every edition. Aggressive Religious Identity and agenda are pursued by both sides.

In Policy terms, the Logic of the 'Internal Enemy' was publicly announced a few months ago, that true Democracies such as the US, Israel and India, can effectively fight Terrorism, because they are themselves 'prime target' and therefore, must form an Alliance. According to India's then National Security Adviser, there is no need to define Terrorism, or discuss its causes...it is apparently enough to decide that all Terrorists come from a particular source. The then Deputy Prime Minister, LK Advani, in another statement in Los Angeles, had once said, "Post the 9/11 attack in US, and the December 13 (2001), abortive Terrorist attacks on the Indian Parliament building, both attacks have one common source, and that, the 'common source' has described the US, Israel, and India, as its three Main Enemies." Both the then National Security Adviser and the then Deputy PM, held the view that, there is not much time to waste in discussing the possible causes... "In other words, political solutions are a waste of time. Both these Policy Statements came, when these persons were in the US, one, speaking at the American-Jewish Society, in Washington. Both were authorized statements, and the Indian Ambassador in the US, was duly present. Both promised their hosts that 17,000 Indian troops would be sent to Iraq, soon!

Even in the Parliamentary Election Meetings, in 1999, the then Prime Minister of India, casting aside the Constitution, declared that, his Party did not need the "votes of a particular community". This is not a Pre-Fascist stage, as some Progressives would like to describe. It was Fascism, Indian style, slow and steady, following a carefully calibrated programme, keeping the shell of Democracy intact, subverting the Constitution and the institutions of the Republic, every hour, with the initiative firmly in their hands. The 'Opposition' was kept off-balance.

Kashmir Valley issue is sought to be handed over to the United States (Kashmir Study Group Report, December 1998, published from New York, and blessed by the then Prime Minister, Atal Behari Vajpayee). The Report recommends the trifurcation of the State, on communal basis. US technicians are already there, ostensibly to supervise ground sensors, purchased from US firms, for Border Surveillance. Israeli Advisers are also in place in New Delhi and Kashmir, on how to tackle Insurgency! Police Stations, manned by the British Police, are also a feature, allegedly to investigate crimes, committed in Britain by Kashmiris. Separately, the US pursues an Agenda to build and share Military Bases in India. The FBI, CIA and the DEA, operate in Delhi and other cities, keeping safe the Government from its own people.

There are Reports, not without foundation, that British Agencies used well trained UK Immigrants, to help the Killer Squads, in Ahmedabad, the capital of Gujarat, in March 2002, during the State-Sponsored Programme. This was yet another instance of the evolving relationship between our Fascists and the US-UK Empire. The 'Funding Hate' program ex the US has been widely reported in the last few years.

The most vicious and diabolical programme underway, in India, is Militarization of the minds of the people, using the Media to brainwash the people, and use of age-old festivals of the land, to distort the idea behind each one of them, to prepare them for an indigenous 'final solution', having identified the 'Internal Enemy'. Counterparts of *'Balilla'* institutions of Fascists, Italy, have been nurtured from 1940s, and now, have the direct support of the State's administrative and financial resources. The idea was first conceived by Mussolini, for Italy. We are witnessing the Military Re-Generation of the *'Hindutva'*, a Fascist concept, the ideology of those who line up with the RSS/BJP. Their objective has for long been the Military re-organisation of the Hindu society, all in favour of organized violence, in the form of Militarism. Globalization or Corporate Fascism needs them and supports them financially. Mussolini and Hitler used to say, "Our desire for peace and collaboration with Europe is based on millions of steel bayonets."

Mussolini is the original inspiration for the Indian Fascist Party. In his doctrine of Fascism, he says, "I absolutely disbelieve in perpetual peace, which is detrimental and negative to the fundamental virtues of man...War alone brings up to its highest tension, all human energy, and puts the stamp of nobility upon the people...Fascism believes neither in the possibility, nor in the utility of perpetual peace. It thus, repudiates the doctrine of Fascism. (The RSS, our native Fascists, say further, "As a consequence, there will no longer be any distinction between the Citizen and the Soldier, between the Civilian and the Military man, in uniform". (Marzia Casolari: *'Hindutva's Tie-up in the 1930s—Archival Evidence'*).

Nepal

Nepal has formally never been under any foreign rule, though de-facto, it was a British protectorate. The Nepalese are very poor, struggling between a Feudel oligarchy, Monarchial and Democratic dispensations. They have been, in the past, the British Empire's soldiery and now, also serve the Indian Army, on account of historical and cultural ties. The rulers have not delivered, so there is a rising tide of Peasants' Struggle. The Cadres of the Movement are said to control most of the countryside. Their recent successes have been the pretext for stationing US Advisers and Military assistance to Nepal, as also, the signing of an US-Nepal Anti-Terrorism Pact. China is reportedly not happy. How the future will unfold, is anyone's guess. Separately, the US has publicly stated that, the Left Front Government in West Bengal is Anti-Democratic, even though it has been Democratically elected, in centrally supervised Elections, for the last nearly three decades. Is this a portent of a 'Regime Change' Solution for India, should Election results not be agreeable to the PNAC?

Afghanistan

Much has been documented on Afghanistan and its hapless people, that it is not perhaps necessary to summarize here, the main course of events and the role of the Afghan persona and organizations. Ahmad Rashid has faithfully recorded, what we need to remember. The Narco trade flourishes in a joint venture. NATO has come right to our doorstep, uninvited in its new Imperial role, discussed and decided in its councils, ten years ago. That is the central reality with which South Asia must live. NATO in the Balkans has already dismembered countries and effected 'Regime Changes'.

It will adjudicate on 'Failed States' and act upon to establish Benign Empires, administered through non-residents, of the likes of *Karzai* and *Chalabi* or *Allawi,* where and when it decides.

Alternatives

No one is ready to concede a pre-determination of the inevitability of the victory of the New Imperialist Project. Imperialism has its own vulnerabilities: political, in its economics, culturally, and indeed in its seeming possession of overwhelming Military Power. Just as the US is internally becoming 'two nations', countries and people in the South, are already split into two unequal halves. The ruling elites are busy facilitating the transfer abroad of national resources. The perceived sense of injustice of the Majority, is potentially a political, revolutionary force in the making, provided of course, it can be welded into local and national level organizations, connected globally.

'The Call for Arab Unity,' issued through *Al-Awda*, by *Muzna Shihabi*, is a purposeful document, relevant to all of us. As a document to inform us of the plunder, pillage and destruction of Iraq, Rania Masri's, *"Constructing or De-Constructing Iraq"?* is a comprehensive Reference Paper. The ANSWER coalition in the US is on the streets, leading a coalition of people and organizations, representing an estimated one-third of the American people, despite the incessant propaganda of the Corporate Media, with the 'Big Lie', which Hitler would have applauded. ANSWER is organizing the Anti-War, Anti PNAC Movement, uniting the American people and the people of different countries, against US Imperialism, Corporate Globalization, which manipulates the slogan of 'War on Terror', as a diversion to carry out the Socio transfer of wealth, from the bottom to the top within the US, and accumulation globally. ANSWER has a common perspective on 'Pre-emptive, Unending War', the use of US troops and Military, as private security detachments of Corporate America's plunder of Iraq's Oil riches, acceleration of the programme of Micro-nukes, for use against the poor of the world, and the growing Fascist Programme of Militarization at home, in the US. The Jakarta Peace Consensus, in which Delegates from 24 countries participated, in May 21-24, 2004 also deserves note. A few, including the *New York*

Times, have called the growing People's Consciouness as the 'Other Superpower'.

The theoretical framework is already apparent in such works, as those of Michel Chussodovsky and Prof. James Petras and Prof. Veltmeyer, among other creative thinkers. The immediate frontlines in Iraq, Palestine and Cuba, are an inspiration. We have some idea of the others who are targets of the Neo-Imperial Power, who have been identified as the 'Axis of Evil'. Global solidarity is a duty, because humanity is the victim on every front.

The adversary has some key vulnerabilities. Movements in Vietnam, now in Iraq, and also in Cuba, Palestine, Venezuela and other such movements have demonstrated this. The precision guided weapons used in Iraq were in some cases nowhere near precise, the cruise missiles launched in such great numbers did not achieve their advertised kill probabilites, their logistics train was so thin and stretched, that it could have been cut into pieces. It did take more than five days to take over the small Port of Umm Qasr. The Military Victory came after the use of *Napalm, Daisy Cutter, Bunker Busters*, perhaps the most intensive Aerial Bombing in the History of Warfare, against the starved and sick people. Importantly, the 'Arab Street' appears to be changing. The Arab people may have begun to realize that their rulers have been betraying them, to the Imperial Masters in the US. The real change will be when the Arab people will think for themselves and organize resistance to this betrayal.

The then President Saddam Hussain had switched over the Oil Accounts to the Euro, as a small step that sent shock-waves to Wall Street. Iran, and perhaps Russia, may do the same. Saudi Arabia, Kuwait, and UAE, will not do it, except for token amounts. Recall that, it was Saudi Arabia that had secretly signed the Agreement on Petro-Dollar Accounts, in US banks, and the Dollars and the denominated International Oil Trade Pact, which is the key to the Dollars and therefore, the perceived strength of the US Economy, and the 'Green-Bank's, Exchange Value, as the World's Reserve Currency. While freely selling their Oil to all countries, just the act of accepting payments in their national currencies could disturb the balance of forces in the world. PNAC could be vanquished on just this one act!

The US is not Militarily invincible. Politically, the Bush Administration has lost credibility at home and abroad, and the US Economy and the Corporates, except the Oil and Defence Industry corporates, are operating at the margins. If the people, who oppose US hegemony and corporate globalization, stop buying products that these MNCs market, the major coporations will be in the queue for Chapter 11 Bankruptcy Proceedings. This notwithstanding, the succeses of the Oil Majors, backed by the US Military, in obtaining the control of New Energy Resources in Central-Asia, East-Europe and West Africa, by deceit, Military occupation of countries, and the fake War against Terror, have to be reckoned with.

The cost of drilling one barrel of Oil in Iraq is approximately one-sixth, and that ın Saudi Arabia, one-third the cost of extracting a barrel of Oil, in mainland United States. There is almost nothing, except some medicines, surgical equipment and software, that we do not produce or are not available from alternative sources. If we do not buy their product, we are by individual acts, opposing their empire at its grass-roots. If we do not use their banks, insurance companies, investment, brokerage and consulting firms to defraud our own people, that empire will be on the run. Then the chances are that, it may run out of gas! Even the British Empire ran out of gas at the end of World War II. Mahatma Gandhi's Non-Cooperation Movement — emulated by the Civil Rights Movement in the United States, and Boycott of Foreign Goods, may be relevant in some situations.

The poor farming communites in the 'South' are beginning to understand the consequences of GM foods and seeds being dumped on them, as demonstrated so visibly by Kenya, Botswana, and Nigeria, at Cancun, that subsidised agriculture, exported by heavily subsidised US food exporting MNCs, destroy their livelihoods. A Movement to return to Organic Farming is beginning to gather momentum, replacing profiteering in Chemical Fertilizers and Pesticides, which have poisoned indigenous soil and water resources. People have started understanding, how their own Governments have sold them out, colluding in the theft of the invaluable genetic resources, plant and animal wealth, their Human Rights through TRIPs, and the WTO Regime, fronting for the US TNCs in particular. The inducements by WB and IMF to turn from Food and Edible Oils' sufficiency, to Food Dependency, by the false allurements of turning to Cash-crops, to pay back debts incurred by their elites to import luxury goods. This is the stuff that revolutionary consciousness is made of, when it reaches a threshold. People are waking upto the 'Water Barons,' as far away as Bolivia and the Philippines. Water, which belongs to all, is being privatized, to enable profits for the few. When this is opposed, Police and Military Force is used, to crush the opposition, sometimes with US Advisers, who raise the familiar cry of Terrorism and Terrorists. This is yet another dimension of the Common Resistance Agenda, against Globalization.

There is no alternative to organizational unity and purpose, of people learning to run Parallel Administrations, or even Governments, exemplifying real Democracy. They can meet all the basic needs of the people, from food, water, health, education, housing, and employment, though to start off, they will do so at minimum subsistence levels. The Movement of the Zapatistas and the Chapias in Mexico, parts of Bolivia and Colombia, in Brazil by the MST, in the freed lands, turning largely from the Military to the Political mode, is a lesson that small, impoverished communities can establish Self-Governments, demonstrating independence from and defiance of a Central Government, that has, by its illegal acts, made itself illegitimate, by betraying the interests of the people (notwithstanding the experience of the December 2001 popular uprising in Argentina, which regressed thereafter, in the absence of a Revolutionary Leadership and Party).

In waging a counter to the Economic Warfare, imposed by the Corporate Empire, led by Wall Street, supported by the US Treasury, WB, IMF, WTO and the TNCs, with the support of the Bank of International Settlements, BIS, which coordinates the G-7 Agenda, several thinking Economists, including Kavaljit Singh, have been suggesting a package of measures, to rein the ravages of the speculators and currency raiders:

i Introduction of the Tobin Tax, to be administered by a new UN authority.

ii A new Bretton Woods to review the IMF and WB, as also the BIS, to bring them back to their original purpose. To transform them from their role as the World's Biggest Money Lenders, enticing elites to sleep-walk into Debt-Traps, or in other words, to re-structure and 'Reform' the World's Financial Architecture. Till then, the SAPs, SALs, and the 'Reform' Programmes, 'Good Governance' etc., could be put on hold. There is enough on the record to hold these institutions to account, for deception and fraud.

iii Prime Minister Mohammad Mahathir's suggestion to adopt and reintroduce the 'Islamic Golden Dinar', as the Currency of Exchange for Oil Producing countries, and other Islamic countries, is worthy of consideration, when the overvalued dollar is in reality, a 'paper', which buys goods and services for the US.

In a situation where, after 30 years of a unilateral decision, taken by the US, of delinking the US Dollar from the Gold Standard, we have a Dollar along with the USA, skating on thin-ice. We have a further dangerous, unreal world of financial instruments, derivatives, all paper, underwritten by several types of banks, dealing in investments, brokerage, forward trading, (new terminologies are coming into such quick circulation, that ordinary mortals can hardly keep up). We have OFCs, OCBs, i.e. Offshore Financial Centres and Offshore Corporate Bodies the Mauritius Route, providing free financial space, with unregulated financial players, such as Trust companies, Shell Companies, Hedge Funds, Brokerage Houses, not to forget Junk Funds, the savings and loans and the KPMG Scandals, all ultimately to be compensated and rescued by the common folk, after emptying their pockets, again and again.

The brokerage, investment, and insurance functions have been combined as 'Super Bank', scantified, or to be scantified by the Basle Convention. Casino Capitalism is disguised as the New Saviour.

These are all challenges to People's Movements, as the War alternates between the Battle-field and the Board-rooms. It is countries like China, Japan, South Korea, Taiwan,

Singapore and EU, that invest hundreds of billions of dollars every year, to keep the US which needs nearly a trillion dollars, annually.

Kavaljit Singh, the Economist says "People's Movements need a quantum leap from Washington to Wall Street". We need to build alternative strategies to the operations of Global Finance Capital and build up public pressure for stringent regulatory mechanisms and disclosure standards. Mergers and Acquisitions, Multilateral Agreements on Investments, and Capital Account Liberalization have to be scrutinized by the people. Social Control over Global Financial Flows, by People's Movements and elected bodies to counter the Globalization Project, are essential.

Ultimately, the Militarization of Globalization is a Transnational Companies' Board-Room Agenda (despite its Military sting), for which Military, PMCs and Government structures are hired, bought, and sold.

Quoting Dr. Fidel Castro, "When you ask, why all this threatening, to use force against 80 countries... it is becasue, what they are really afraid of is not actual Terrorism...what they fear more than that, is the rebellion of the poeple...what they fear are the Movements that build awareness and mobilize public opinion...making it impossible for G-7 and WTO to meet... that is why, they react with such fury and arrogance, with the idea of using their formidable, brutal, blind and seemingly invincible power, to sow panic and terror, amongst all the people of the world".

"The consequence of this will be an even greater resistance, an even greater opposition, an even greater protest, and an even greater discontent, on the part of the species, threatened not only by the worst form of slavery and colonialism ever known, but also endangered by its very survival".

"It is this awareness, that has mobilized people from the middle classes, in the industrialized countries, who have gained greater knowledge of the dangers, looming in the environment and over their very lives and the lives of their children and grandchildren".

15

Silent WMDs—Effects of Depleted Uranium Munitions on Asian Peoples & Their Future

Heat not a furnace, for your foe so hot ...that it do singe yourself.

- William Shakespeare

There has been a Silent War, waged on the people of Afghanistan and Iraq, since 1991, and it has been hidden by the mass media, as a deliberate policy. The fateful and disastrous consequences of the indiscriminate use of depleted and non DU munitions, on the people of the West, Central and South Asian regions; women, children, men, animals, plants and animal life, now and in the future, is in gross violation of international law, the Hague Convention and Domestic US Military law.

The WHO 2001 'report on the Effects of DU on Health', was classified 'Secret' and not released to the public, according to Dr. Keith Barestock, Senior Radiation Specialist to WHO, who rendered the 'Report'. Official Gamma Ray damage, caused US studies, have been deficient in ignoring the consequences, in a number of respects...internal contamination, internal dose to individual cells, ommissions of diseases, other than cancer, mutagenic, long term degeneration, ontogenesis, of the effects of the killer isotopes in particular. The Case Studies for the years 1945-50, were simply omitted. A recent European

Parliament Report, ECRR 2003 (European Committee on Radiation Risk) has concluded that, 'A' Bomb Studies, under estimate the radiation risk by more than 1000 times and fail to consider the internal exposure and diseases, caused by 'Alfa' and 'Beta' Rays. They did not consider the Manhattan Project classified memo that, in case the Project objective of producing Plutonium Fission and the 'A' Bomb did not succeed, 'Depleted Uranium' munitions would be deployed towards the attainment of the same objective.

DU Weapons emit 'Alfa' particle dose to a single cell from U-238, which is 50 times the annual dose level. Cancer is initiated with one Alfa particle. Its daughter isotopes effect generations as the isotope bio-concentrate in plants and animals travels up the food-chain. It is a Nuclear Weapon because the energy is derived from the nucleus of the atom. They enter the body through the lungs, the digestive system or breaks in the skin. One gram of DU releases more than 12,000 particles, per second. The radiation slowly kills the cells making life possible. The Gulf War Syndrome of 1991, did just that (reported by Dr. Asaf Durakovic, Prof. of Medicine, Georgetown University, and discoverer of the 'Gulf War Syndrome').

We are well aware of the 'Radiation Fall-out Map, 'Under the Cloud: Decades of Nuclear Testing'. This has demonstrated the effects of 1,200 Nuclear Weapon Tests, conducted at the Nevada Test Site; and the US Government admitted in November 2002, that every living person in the US, between 1958-63, was exposed to this fall-out — resulting in cancer, gene mutation, heart disease, autism, diabetes, Parkinson's, ALS, asthma, chronic fatigue syndrome, hypothyroidism in newborns, obesity and learning disabilities. One out of twelve children, in the US, is disabled. The fall-out did not stop at the US Borders. It travelled around the world, as atmospheric dust, and remains in the biosphere/ sub-orbital space, even today. High breast cancer rates have been co-located in the proximity of Nuclear Power plants in the west, and more so, in the east coast areas of the US (The Breast Cancer Map from 'The Enemy Within: 'The High Cost of Living Near Nuclear Reactors', quotes US Government Disease Control Centres).

The Radiation & Public Health Report (RPHP), rendered by a group of independent scientists, collected 4,000 baby's teeth and by measuring Strontium 90 levels in the baby teeth (a built -in dose-metre) they have been able to co-relate with Radiation related diseases, in children living near the Nuclear Power Plants; the main pathways being dairy products and drinking water.

The induction of DU Weapons in 1991 in Iraq, the Radioactive Trash from Nuclear Plants, broke a 46-years taboo. This *Trojan Horse* of Nuclear War, an Homicidal Weapon has since then continued to be used more and more. DU remains Radioactive longer, than the age of the earth (estimated at 2.5 billion years.)

The long-term effects from over a decade of DU Exposure are emerging in Southern Iraq. They are devastating. The increased quantities of Radio-active material, including non-depleted Uranium, used in Afghanistan are 3 to 5 times greater than Iraq in 1991. In Iraq, 2003, they are already estimated to be 6 to 10 times as that in 1991, and will travel through a larger area and affect many more people, babies and the unborn. Countries within a 1,000-mile Radius of Baghdad and Kabul, are being affected by radiation poisoning, that includes the Indian capital, New Delhi, where the ruling elite lives. The reported coming of an AIDS Epidemic, last year, in India, may have a relationship to DU Bombing in Afghanistan. If we think that cancer is a problem, now wait until more DU is released in Wars against Terror and for 'regime change', on 'mistaken' Intelligence reports.

More than 500 tons of DU Munitions have been dispensed in Afghanistan. Professor Yagasaki calculated that, 800 tons of DU is the Atomicity, equivalent to 83,000 Nagasaki Bombs, in a paper presented at the 'World Uranium Weapons Conference' in Hamburg, in October 2003. The amount of DU, used in Iraq, in 2003, is equivalent to nearly 250,000 Nagasaki Bombs (Busby and Leuren Moret have calculated that ,1,900 tons of DU, is equivalent to 60 TBq of Alfa and Beta particulate activity).

We need not enumerate all the DU Munition types, used in Iraq, 1991, Kosovo 1999, Afghanistan 2001-04 and Iraq 2003-06. F-15E 'Strike Eagle' and the A-lO 'Warthog' are two of the primary delivery vehicles, with their weapon loads of GBU24, GBU-28/37B, and a variety of shells/bullets. They have been dispensed by nearly all Air/Ground and Sea based Weapon Systems, on innocent civilians. DU burns intensely and is very hard. It releases Uranium Oxide. The aerosol contains particles of 0.5-5 microns in size. Once they are in the air or dust, they are inhaled or ingested, including from contaminated soil. Once in the lungs, one such particle is equivalent to having one X- Ray per hour, for life. Because it is impossible to remove, and the victim is gradually irradiated. Still births, birth defects, leukemia, damaged central nervous systems and other cancers, have been common in children born since 1991. Child Leukemia has risen 600 per cent, in areas of Iraq, as reported by the Netherland Visie Foundation. Beyond just the health consequences, DU Munitions are in fact, Weapons of 'Silent' Mass Destruction, in so far as the consequences of their usage vast, indiscriminate and violate all Human Rights Conventions. Tora Bora, Kabul, Paktia, Karises or underwater supply tunnels, have been contaminated forever. All this has been documented in a comprehensive paper, *Uranium Wars : The Pentagon Steps up Its Use of Radio-active Munitions,"* by Marc W. Herold.

In another Paper, Dr. Mohammed Daud Miraki, Director, Afghan DU Recovery Fund, quotes George W. Bush, "we will smoke them out", condemning the unborn, the living and the future generations of Afghans and the neighbouring people, to a pre-determined, death sentence. "After the destruction of our village, I realized that the Americans had sentenced us all to death. When I saw my deformed grandson, I realized my hopes for the future have vanished. This time, we are part of the invisible genocide, brought on by America... a silent death, from which we will not escape (Jooma Khan of Laghman Province...March, 2003). Similar stories are repeated from Paktia Province of 'Jelly Babies'. Pregnant women are afraid of giving birth... DU is cheap for the US, utilizing Nuclear Waste, cheaper than Titanium and Tungsten, not for the 'liberated'(non-DU is still cheaper, as it is the Uranium feedstock, pre-enrichment).

The Uranium Medical Research Center (UMRC), Washington DC, and the Bulletin of Atomic Scientists (l991) Steve Fetter and Frank Von Hippel, have reported on extensive research by 'Field' Teams of the UMRC in Afghanistan. Testimonies of fathers' mothers are horrifying—"What else do the Americans want? They killed us, they turned our newborns into horrific deformations, and they turned our farmlands into graveyards, and destroyed our homes. On top of all this, their planes fly over and spray us with bullets...we have nothing to lose... we will fight them, the same way we fought the previous invaders ...(Sayed Gharib, at Tora Bora)"

Radiological Dispensing Devices or Warfare is the latest of the weapons of the new millennium, but it singes even those who use it, as shown in the after-effects of the tests at the home ground in the US, where evidence of cognitive damage, during early infancy, have been compiled. In Eurasia, Pakistan, and India, we have a new Health Epidemic, to drain our scarce resources.

As World Citizens, we need to focus on a new scourge, The Reality of the PNAC — Rebuilding America's Defences, Strategy, Forces, and Resources for a New Century.

The Report notes that, "Much has been written in recent years about the need to transform the conventional Armed Forces of the United States to take advantage of the 'Revolution in Military Affairs'... Our Military requires a dramatic transformation, lest we lose our ability to fight the future's unconventional Wars... some may be fought in cyberspace, others under water, or in outer space. And some, even within our bodies."

Paul Wolfowitz, William Kristol and others are some of the men, representing contemporary 'power centres', who define the US Policy. History indicates that, the men who define US Military Policy, from the shadows, are worthy of our attention.

Genetic Bombs

When creating genetic-bombs or weapons, to target specific groups, genetic profiles are subtler and more accurate than the coarse pseudo category, called Race. The group with ADHD (the Edison Gene), uniquely shares common inherited variations in their dopamine regulating genes, regardless of race, geography or ethnicity. Thus, anybody who is part of a group with a shared genetic profile, may be at risk in the future.

A virus or bacteria may attack only a particular type of person, killing, disabling or sterilizing only those of a particular gene profile. Threatening a particular type, would be sufficient political blackmail.

Wolfowitz, Kristol and their colleagues suggested that, the Pentagon should be thinking about not just Germ Warfare, of which they have plenty of capabilities, but Gene Warfare.

Genetic Terra-forming could replace diplomacy, or it could change the face of politics, if an organism got loose, that killed all the people of a particular Minority community, who tend to vote for a particular political party.

According to the PNAC, "Genetically Targeted Weapons could change World Politics forever, and the report notes, advanced forms of Biological Warfare, that can target specific geno-types, may transform Biological Warfare from the realm of terror to a politically useful tool."

To conclude, fourth Generation Micro-nukes, with their Warhead composition, were deliberated upon and decided, at the US Air Force Strategic Command Headquarters at the Offutt Air Force Base, Nebraska, between the top Corporates / Weapon Manufacturers and the US Military Brass. They not only have prior knowledge of numbers and all types of Nuclear Weapons, but also the Corporates and the locations of the planned and approved targets, globally.

This meeting took place on 'Hiroshima Day', August 6, 2003, and to reiterate, the aim was to define a New Generation of Nuclear Weapons to be used on a pre-emptive basis, against rogue enemies and terrorist organizations. (Mini-nukes have an explosive capacity between one-third and six times a Hiroshima Bomb).

In this Strangelovian logic, Nuclear Weapons are now viewed as a means to ensuring peace and security, against non-existent WMDs.

A Few Eye-Openers:

1. In the 2003 War, the Iraqis were subjected to the Pentagon's Radio-active Arsenal, mainly in the urban centres, unlike in the desert, in 1991. The aggregate effects of illnesses and long-term disabilities and genetic birth defects will be apparent only from 2008 onwards.
2. By now, half of all the 697,000 US soldiers, involved in the 1991 war, have reported serious illnesses. According to the American Gulf War Veterans' Association, more than 30 per cent of these soldiers are chronically ill, and receiving disability benefits from the Veterans' Administration.
3. The number of disabled veterans, is shockingly high. They are in their mid-thirties and should have been in the prime of health.
4. Near the Republican Palace, where US troops stood guard, and over 1,000 employees walked in and out, the Radiation readings were the 'hottest' in Iraq, at nearly 1,900 times background radiation levels.
5. At a roadside stand, selling fresh bunches of parsley, mint, and onions, children played on a burnt out Iraqi Tank, just outside Baghdad, the Geiger counter-registered 1,000 times normal background radiation.
6. "The Pentagon and the United Nations estimate that the US and Britain used 1,100 to 2,200 tons of Armor Piercing Shells, made of DU, during attacks in March-April 2003, far more than the 1991 Gulf War (this does not include air dispensed DU Munitions and Missiles)," wrote the *Post Intelligencer.*
7. An otherwise useless by-product of the Uranium enrichment process, DU is attractive to Military Contractors, because it is so cheap, and often, offered for free, by the Government.
8. The long term effects, as Dr. Asaf Durakoviç elaborates, after the early neurological symptoms are cancer, related radiation illnesses such as, chronic fatigue syndrome,

joint and muscle pain, neurological and/or nerve damage, mood disturbances, auto-immuno deficiencies, lungs and kidney damage, vision problems, skin rupture, increase in miscarriages, maternal mortality and genetic birth defects/deformation.

9. For years, the US Government described the Gulf War Syndrome as a post traumatic stress disorder. It was labeled as a psychological problem, or simply as, mysterious unrelated ailment, much in the same way as health problems of the Vietnam veterans, suffering from Agent Orange Poisoning.

(With acknowledgements to Sara Flounders, Coordinator of the DU Education Programme).

16

The Intelligence Business

Had 'Operation Iraqi Freedom" not gone sour, had the Oil begun to flow to the expectations of the 'Oil Majors' and had Afghanistan not been in disarray and near anarchy, it is doubtful if the kind of uncomfortable and noisy debate that is reflected in the media, would emerge in the US. Not finding WMDs is being termed an Intelligence Failure — a Presidential Commission has been appointed to report its findings by March 2005 in the US. In the UK a post-script is being played out by a committee, announced by the Prime Minister, to submit its Report by mid-year.

WMDs, or rather the absence of WMDs, would hardly matter to the Executive Branch, in normal circumstances. It is the politics of the decision to invade Iraq and execute a Regime Change, through use of Military Force, that needs to be justified, to the growing number of critics, gathering into a storm, that has to be cooled. After all the indiscriminate and disastrous use of 'Depleted Uranium Munitions', the 'Silent WMDs' in Afghanistan and Iraq (earlier in Kosovo), have not yet evoked the opposition, that its use deserves.

The appearance of George Tenet, Director, Central Intelligence, first at the UN Security Council at Georgetown University, televised live by the CNN, BBC and other networks in 'defence' of the CIA, is as astonishing as it is unprecedented. The CIA of course, has an excellent group of experienced analysts, who help prepare the draft 'National Intelligence Estimates', which are processed through the National Security Council's second tier, as a sound staff vetting, before the NSC's proper scrutiny, before they, with the assent of the President, become formalized. The NIEs are usually prepared, country-wise. However, they could also be region-wise or subject-wise. This has been a sound practice, as it demands accountability from the US$ 40 billion CIA budget, and more importantly, that its priorities are strictly in accord with its 'tasking', by the President/NSC. However, the CIA's over-riding purpose is, 'Operations, covert and overt', where its energies are directed. Its Intelligence gathering is facilitated by a host of organizations/ institutions, with global reach, including the media, financial institutions, and 'technological means'. The US Intelligence apparatus is supported by the willing participation of the Western Alliance systems, the G-7, their myriad fronts and associate business, social, cultural and media fronts. The technical means, include the giant 'US National Security Agency (bigger than the CIA), The National Mapping and Imagery Agency, now designated, the national Geospatial Agency; the Defence Intelligence Agency (both under the Pentagon), GCHQ Cheltenham, UK, the North West Cape, Australia facility and a host of others hosted, like the US Military Bases and facilities in a hundred countries. The pointer to US Intelligence is only because, it is probably the best example of a sound and successful Intelligence set up.

Intelligence Agencies, no matter what their track-record and excellence, ultimately deliver only when, after the 'national tasking' by the political executive, have a healthy tradition of professionalism, and enjoy autonomy of functioning. If they begin to look over their shoulders, to take cues from the political masters, they are compromising their integrity, and therefore, their ability to serve the national interest or even the interest of a particular Government. That is one reason why the CIA was legitimized by the National Security Act, 1947. Sometimes in the past, Heads of the CIA, MI-5/6 have been perceived as 'independent' of the Chief Executive, and even had a British Prime Minister, like Harold Wilson, under surveillance because the Intelligence establishment thought that he had been too close to the Soviets! Certainly, people close to the Political Executive are meant to be under the watchful eyes of counter-intelligence, and State Security requires this.

The point that is sought to be made is that National Intelligence organizations are necessarily committed to the national vision and goals. They are its Strategic Arm. While following annual tasking by the Executive Arm of the Government, they should not become subservient to its political manipulation or partisan viewpoint. In our own case, in the late 1950s and 1960s, the Intelligence Bureau appeared to be suborned to an External Intelligence Agency's manipulation, contributing to a national debacle. Later, it had to be rescued, split, and a separate External Intelligence Agency created, which made a substantive contribution to several national enterprises including the victory in 1971. This agency, the RAW was weakened in 1977-80 and again started to get manipulated thereafter, permitting its own subversion; leading to the assassination of two Prime Ministers in 1984 and 1991; followed by a string of fiascos like the LTTE, Sri Lanka and Afghanistan, to name just a few. The Report of the erstwhile JIC Chairman, Khandelwal in 1987, hardly set matters right and was neatly filed. Kargil was the result of both the MOD, the General Staff, being lulled by the magic of Lahore. President Reagan's wise words, in the US-Soviet dialogue, "Trust but verify", have been forgotten on home-ground. The maxim for the armed forces had always been that, apparently successful diplomacy does not permit lowering of the guard.

A sound and solid political vision and economic strength, is a pre-requisite to Successful Intelligence Operations, contributing to enhancing the national interest. When the 'correlation of forces' is more or less evenly matched, good intelligence can, and does make the difference, but like politics, it is also dependent on the stakes that the majority of the people have in the system. Apathy and disenchantment may make it very difficult for the Agencies to perform, even though Intelligence Organizations, which have been subverted, often use this very environment to turn people away from Democracy to Fascism.

In the last century, there were a number of inflexion waypoints, that changed events beyond the control of ordinary institutions: the October 1917 Soviet Revolution, Gandhiji's Non-Violent Freedom Movement, the aftermath of the Second World War, and the creation of the Bretton Woods International Financial Institutions, concurrent with the Hiroshima-Nagasaki Bombs, to terrorize and play on people's fears and insecurity; the steady rise of 'Finance Capital', after 1975, the steady decline of the Socialist World, through masterful subversion of its key institutions, including the Politbureaus, so well described by Yuri Andropov, the Head of the KGB, and the weakening of its ideology. The Capitalist system too, has been in decline since 1980, except for its illusory peak in the mid 1990s.

1997 was just the opportune moment for Brzezinski's, 'The Grand Chessboard', a game-plan for the domination of Eurasia by the sole Superpower. Fukiyama's boastful *'The End of History'*, and Huntington's *'Clash of Civilization'* were the philosophical underpinnings of the draft of the *'Project for the New American Century'*, Rebuilding America's Defences: Strategy, Forces, *Resources for the new Century*. The 'Grand Chessboard' and the PNAC (made public in September 2002) are a quest for world hegemony, not necessarily through the control of territory, except for temporary periods, but resources and markets, through the agency of the MNCs , WTO, WB-IMF, navigated by the Department of the Treasury and ultimately, by the Wall Street (Investment Banks). The prizes are Oil, Gas, Strategic and High Value Minerals, Drug Money and Laundered Money, and the means of accumulation of surplus, deregulation, liberalization, free trade, and privatization are the buzz words. Brzezinski prognosticates that, the control of Eurasia is central to this new Imperialist Enterprise, which the Britain's thinktanks have already justified, in several postulations (Prime Minister of UK, Tony Blair 's Chief Foreign Policy Adviser, Robert Cooper in a written Paper, in a pamphlet, with Blair's Foreword, published by the Foreign Policy Centre,

London, called for a 'New Defensive Imperialism', in respect of Afghanistan, and such other States , which Cooper reiterated at a Conference on Afghanistan, held in Germany, in April/ May 2000). But Brzezinski, with his deep perceptions, also argued the conclusion that, the Central and West Asian region, specially the CAR, will be the next major region of conflict, starting from Pakistan and north-westwards to Khazakistan, which will be an anchor for the new enterprise (see map). The 'War on Terror' is just a punctuation in the new century of 'Unending Wars'.

At this inflexion point, where the '500 Billionaires Club' has more wealth than the less worthy 2.6 billion people of the world, Brzezinski philosophizes that, 'Democracies are inimical to Imperialist Mobilization'. Before we revert to the efficiencies or the productivity of the Intelligence organizations, which must necessarily have their networks and co-opted institutions/groups/individuals spread world-wide, especially in the targeted resources (not necessarily territories), let us look at some of the more favourable opportunities and fundamentals, which facilitate their operations.

Brzezinski underlines that the "American Global System emphasizes the technique of co-optation to a much greater extent than the earlier empires did. It likewise relies heavily, on the indirect (perhaps direct too) exercise of influence on dependent foreign elites, while drawing much benefit from the appeal of its democracy and institutions (albeit eroded, after Iraq, and the current domestic Patriot Act etc). All of the foregoings are reinforced by the domination of Global Communications, Popular Entertainment, and Mass Culture, and by the potentially tangible (felt) clout of American Technological Edge and Global Military Reach (and presence)."

America has become a Mecca for those seeking advanced education, with approximately half a million students flocking to the US, with many of the ablest, never returning home. Graduates from American Universities are to be found in almost every Cabinet, in every continent. (And in every Civil, Military, Intelligence and Financial institution of the State).

Brzezinski elaborates, "Special security arrangements in the Persian Gulf, specially after the brief punitive mission in 1991, against Iraq, have made that economically vital region into an American Military Preserve. Even the former Soviet space is permeated by various American sponsored arrangements, for closer co-operation with NATO". EU, Finance Capital, Oil Majors and naturally, the Intelligence Agencies, stretching from East Europe, Georgia, Ukraine Azerbaijan to Kazakstan, are all hungry to control Energy Reserves in the CAR. Afghanistan, Pakistan and Kashmir are part of the game plan, a friendly co-opted regime in India is a valued asset.

Brzezinski continues in the Grand Chessboard, "... One must consider, as part of the American system the Global Web of specialized organizations, specially the 'international' financial institutions. The IMF, the WE (and BIS) can be said to represent 'Global' interests (Global finance capital, added). In reality however, they are heavily, American dominated and their origins are traceable to American initiative...Bretton Woods 1944.' (and added Basel Convention 2000)... ' Rather America stands at the center of the interlocking Universe and the consensus/dialogue (Washington Consensus), that power originates from a single source, Washington DC."

Brzezinski may well have said, "Wall Street", for that is where it really belongs. So, most of the Directors, Deputy Directors and third echelon hierarchy, is drawn from Wall Street lawyers and bankers, who have actually been reorganizing the CIA set up, from time to time, to serve their interests. Political Scientist, G.John Ikenberry using political sophistry, adds, 'Europeans...and the Japanese, were able to reconstruct their societies and economies in ways that were congenial with American Hegemony, but also with room to experiment their own autonomous and semi-independent political systems."

Huntington also asserts that a world "without US primacy will be a world with more violence and disorder and less Democracy and economic growth, than a world where the US continues to have more influence than any other country, in shaping global affairs."

Brzezinski concedes that, "while America's Global Hegemony is admittedly great, but its depth is shallow, limited by both domestic (and one may add declining, economic power) and external restraints. The dynamics and potential of Eurasia, places a premium on geo-strategic skill, on the careful, selective and very deliberate deployment of America's resources, on the huge Eurasian chessboard." Here perhaps, lies the root of the failure of US Policies in West Asia and Afghanistan, where the resistance of the Palestinian and Iraqi people was discounted by the US Government, and then the Military men in uniform, and the Intelligence community in the US and UK, have been left to hold the baby, and to face domestic public opinion, as scape-goats. The principle was, in part applicable to the Indian Intelligence Agencies, in the case of Kargil.

The three grand imperatives of Imperial Geo-Strategy, writes Zbigniew Brzezinski, "are to prevent collusion and maintain Security Dependence among the vassals, to keep the tributaries pliant and protected, and to keep the barbarians from coming together.' A more apt description of the State of play, in West Asia and the Central/South Asian region, would be difficult to find.

Now the CIA, Mossad and the co-opted Western Alliance Intelligence Agencies have their job cut out; and they have been so hugely successful in the past, in securing the precious resources for the Imperial Centre, be it from Latin America, South Africa, Congo, Zaire, Sierre Lone, Guinea, Nigeria, Saudi Arabia, Kuwait, UAE, Iran (pre-1979), Indonesia, South Korea, Phillipines, East Europe, Ukraine and Russia, to name only a few, replete with a history of assassinations and regime changes, that it would appear that, nothing would stop them from delivering on their further tasks. Apparently, there is some difficulty in this 'New World Order.' Maybe, it is Imperial over-stretch, or, an over-drive in Imperial/Corporate ambitions, for control. and profits.

Enron was not simply an 'Energy trading' company. It had over 300 subsidiaries in the Cayman islands. It navigated, perhaps, the biggest Drug Money Laundering Operations in the world, that being the shortest cut to raise the market value of company stock, on the NYSE and NASDAQ. The lawyers, investment bankers and the accounting firms, all were party to it. One domino fell and the others too rolled. (The estimated flow of Drug Money is US $ 700 million, annually. The United Nations estimates of 'Criminal' Money is US$ 1.7 trillion, per year). That gives unlimited opportunities for the Big Intelligence Agencies to compromise and blackmail top officials, prominent members of the local ruling establishment, political parties and groups in countries, connected with these activities, including the big names that initiate 'flight of capital' and recycling of official aids/grants to Dollar Accounts abroad, as has been the widespread practice, in Latin America and Africa in particular, in the past.

In Afghanistan the abominable *Taliban*, bank-rolled by the US Government Agencies, destroyed the Opium Crop planted in November 2001, and therefore, indirectly assaulted the liquidity of the big banks, and accidentally dropped a big Economic Bomb, where it hurt.

The big Intelligence Agencies have a massive job to do. The Veteran Intelligence Professional for Sanity, VIPs, Ambassador Joseph Wilson and Scott Ritter, Head, UN Weapons Inspection Team, Iraq (1991-98), have raised their voices. So have the serving and retired top-notchers in the UK (Brian Jones, MOD's top WMD Analyst is quoted as saying that Intelligence Experts of the UK Defence Intelligence Staff, over-ruled — Pages 6-16 of *Secret Intelligence Service (MI6) Report,* released on February 2, 2003, by British Prime Minister, Tony Blair, entitled: "Iraq: Its infrastructure of Concealment, Deception and Intimidation", was directly copied from an article in September 2002 *'Middle East Review of International Affairs',* entitled *Iraq's Security & Intelligence Network: A Guide and Analysis,* by Ibrahim al-Marashi, a post-graduate student, at the Monterey Institute of International Studies — a plagiarism without acknowledgements. This MI6 report was praised by Tony Blair in the House of Commons, on February 3, 2003), Israel, Germany and Australia. Vincent Cannstaro, former Head of CIA, Counter-Intelligence, says, "Basically cooked information is working into high-level pronouncements." The Commission, set up by President Bush may well end up reshaping the Intelligence Institutions, in the image of the a right (*a la* Pentagon's Office of Special Plans, created recently by Defence Secretary, Rumsfeld), 'to offer a more alarming picture of the Iraq Threat, than the Intelligence professionals were willing to provide, 'writes Paul Krugman, in the *New York Times.* The Senate Intelligence Committee, has since departed from the standards, earlier set by Senator Church. Professional Intelligence Officers are standing up in the West, to resist politicization of National Intelligence Institutions.

Another challenge faced by the big Intelligence Agencies is that, while they have, over the years, built up valueable 'assets' and 'sleepers' in target areas and countries, there appears to be a new 'fly in the ointment'. Margaret D. Tutwiler, US State Department in charge of Public Diplomacy, in her very recent testimony before a Congressional Sub-committee, acknowledged that, America's image abroad had deteriorated to such an extent, that "it will take us many years of hard, focussed work", to restore it. "Unfortunately, our country has a problem in far too many parts of the world, ..a problem that we have gotten into, many years through both Democrat and Republican administrations, and a problem that does not lend itself to a quick fix or a single solution or a simple plan." That makes the operational working environment, a little difficult, but not impossible for the 'Department of Dirty Tricks' of Intelligence Outfits. It may also have the effect of making them more aggressive and desperate.

Our Intelligence Agencies need to focus particular attention towards the Financial Warriors, waging Economic Warfare against the nation, speculators, currency traders, the invisible faces that manipulate the 'participatory notes', and the levers of 'future trading', mergers and acquisitions, the ones who control and exploit the 'Mauritius Route', and those that are pirating the surpluses, generated by the hardworking people of India, and the rest of the 'Third World', to the 'First World' (classic case of Reverse Transfer of Wealth). Follow the Money trail, is a time tested maxim.

For us, in the Developing Countries, the object lesson is that, when political establishments get suborned, Intelligence Agencies usually follow in the wake. It is hard then, to find gentlemen, who having sworn to defend and protect the Constitution and the national interest, stand up and say: "Not in my Watch!"

17

Signing Away Vital National Interests

Even as the world is made smaller by instant communication technologies, information networks, and more efficient transportation, the wise and far-seeing nations are focused on advancing their vital national interests, in favour of their ruling oligarchies, or in a few cases, those of the majority of their people.

Foreign and Defence Policies of the US have been articulated in terms of 'National Security Strategy Doctrines' (NSSDs) and Presidential Doctrines, usually suffixed by the year of promulgation. These are supplemented by 'country' specific plans/programs/projects/doctrines, furthering the interests of the US, primarily Economic and Commercial, where necessary, Military. They truly demonstrate that Foreign and Defence Policies are two sides of the same coin. Lest it be perceived that the US (and UK) Foreign Policy Projects are just grand Diplomatic Eloquence, implemented by Diplomats in striped suits, out to influence leaders, bureaucrats and businessmen of the countries where they are assigned, the Embassies are mandated to execute time-bound moves on the global chessboard, usually translateable into profit and loss figures on the balance-sheets. More than the Generals and Diplomats, US vital interests ride on chariots of the giant Energy, Mineral, Agri, Chemicals and Finance (Investment Banking-Insurance) Corporations, whose interests are convergent with US vital interests. Where the Military option has perforce to be exercised, it is in truly Clauswitzian terms...the continuation of policy by other means.

Few nations or people have withstood or retained their autonomy of decision-making, in charting and implementing their own path of development: Vietnam until 1980, Cuba, Venezuela and Iraq — 2003 onwards, stand out. The relatively well-endowed and powerful nations have melted away, succumbed, or worse, have permitted the subversion of their systems and key officials, much less preserve their independence and freedom. Some examples may be useful to quote. China resisted until 1964-65, and India until 1984. The ultimate subversion of the second great Superpower, USSR, began in 1982, and was completed by 1990. Tanks, Aeroplanes, Missiles and Warships, stationed just a few hundred miles away, were mute observers and onlookers.

Charles de Gaulle's *'Force de Frappe'* and Non-Military NATO-status, did however permit France to carry on with its Colonial projects in Francophone Africa, as long as it remained aligned with Global Finance Capital. Belgium in particular, furthered its mining interests in Africa, under the benign umbrella of the NATO in Brussels. Germany, a great Economic Power House, post-1950s, hosted US and NATO Nuclear Arsenals, and was integrated into the Nuclear Trip-Wire Strategy, without some Chancellors of the FRG, realizing that the German people and nation, had in fact, signed into a full scale Nuclear Holocaust/ war 'should it happen', by a few Soviet Tanks-columns crossing the 'Red Line'; 'ostopolitik' notwithstanding.

China's sophistry in defining National Interests, lies in the articulation of leaders like Deng Xiaoping and Ziang Zemin, in particular. Deng Xiaoping noted the exceptional importance of national interests, in strategic policy decisions, on conducting State Affairs, amplifying, "Our National Interests are the common interests of all the Chinese people". "Our National Interests embody and outweigh the interests of classes, nationality and social groups"..."When dealing with State-to-State Relations, the differences in social systems and ideologies should be subordinated to the National Interest. We should maintain friendly exchanges with other countries, regardless of their social systems or ideologies. On the other hand, we should uphold the National Interest as the highest criterion, when dealing with State-to-State Relations. Under no circumstances should the National Interest be sacrificed." As a big country", Deng Xiaoping continues, "we should have our own dignity and our principle to abide by. We should rely on ourselves to safeguard our National Interest, and never rely on alliances, or depend on a foreign country to pursue our National Interest". (Deng Xiaoping: *"Theory of War and Peace"*, as quoted by Colonel Hong Baoxiu). Deng Xiaoping also holds the view that, "Though the United States has become the only Superpower, it lacks the Economic Power to dominate the world". In his assessment "the world's multipolar process has created a situation, where various forces are balancing each other".

The paradox is that, successive Indian Governments, until 1984, and for a few brief moments in 1988-89 and 1996, stood up, unfazed by the might of Military or Economic Power, when India has just begun to Re-Industrialize after 1947, was suffering from Food Shortage until the end of 1960s, forced to Devalue its Currency in 1966 consequently more than doubling its Foreign Debt and Import Costs. Struggling to establish Self-Reliance in Defence through indigenous capabilities, where necessary under License Production from diverse sources, and quietly building her Space, Electronics and Nuclear strengths. ISRO specially became a byword for low-cost, high-efficiency enterprise, much admired for its achievements in Space Technology.

In May 11, 1998, the much trumpeted *Pokhran-II* also marks the U-turn to surrender India's sovereignty. Spin doctors have used millions of clever buzz words, turn of phrases and foreign paeans, to white-wash and camouflage the signing away of India's Foreign and Defence Policies, and the series of surrenders of Sovereign Space, over the last six years, from May to May, at the cost of our impoverished millions, whose livelihoods have simply vanished or are gravely endangered.

As early as 1997 the East-West Center, in Honolulu (US), had commissioned a major study on 'Likely Conflicts over Food and Water in South Asia'. This is just one of the Scenario

Building Studies, like the ones' commissioned by RAND, Heritage Foundation, IISS, and the Foreign Policy Center (London), which excel in gaming, using inputs from expatriates of South-Asian origin for feeding the Pentagon, State Departments, NSC and the Foreign and War Office (London).

Pokhran-II was a 'push-button' affair for the BJP led NDA Government, which took office six weeks earlier. It represented the effort of our AEC and BARC, over the past 24 years, since *Pokhran-I.* It should have added to national strength, self-confidence and acceleration of all round national capability, through self-reliance. In fact, it led to a series of surrenders in every sector of the National Polity, Economy and Science & Technology (S&T); and most importantly, to a culture and mindset of dependency. No matter what the 'establishment spin-doctors' tried to show, the entire spectrum of the decision-making establishments from seeds to arms, patents to TRIPS, bottled water to indigenous electrical power generation plants, AIDS to Malaria, primary schools to banks and insurance bio-diversity and gene banks to rice research, roads to airports, employment generation to land alienation, were suborned to just the desire to be amongst the 14 invitees, to a G-7 Dinner in Moscow, and to be able to buy luxury goods in our 'Shopping Malls' and drive a *Merc* or a *Toyota.*

The slow and steady progress to a sustainable, self-reliant economy, was given up for 'spectacular shows' of all kinds, which have cumulatively "opened all doors" to Economic Insecurity, the very opposite of what the 'Reforms' (and 'conditionalities') had promised.

In reviewing the Foreign and Defense Policy decisions, 1998-2004, we need specially to focus on those that adversely affected our National Interest and specially the ones that have impacted negatively on the country's Political-Military-Economic and Social Security, affecting the lives and livelihoods of millions of our people.

- June 1998—Unilateral Moratorium on Nuclear Tests, post-*Pokhran-II,* without completing the minimum

Testings, as per the international norms, to appease those powers who had imposed 'Technology Export' sanctions on us.

- September 1998—Public Announcement of Readiness to Sign the CTBT, by the PM, abandoning the three decades old national position on the NPT, and the principle of Universal, Non-Discriminatory Nuclear Weapons Disarmament, 'the great principle on which our then Prime Minister Rajiv Gandhi struck his neck out.'
- Public Policy Announcement in October 1998 to sign the 'Fissile Material Control Treaty' (FMCT), which vitally compromised India's Nuclear Weapons' status in the future.
- September 1998 onwards, the very private Strobe Talbot-Jaswant Singh Talks, to work out a lifting of sanctions, progressed behind the back of the Parliament, with no White Paper on the deal or deals, made to date.
- December 16, 1998—The Agreement on Agriculture, signed with the US Department of Agriculture, on Liberalizing Agri Imports, including advancing the lifting of 'Quantitative Restrictions' on 2700 items within two years. The Parliament informed only in February 1999, after much public criticism of the AoA.
- The Kashmir Study Group, prepared by a mix of US based thinktanks/individuals like a New York based Furniture Maker, a Kashmiri Expatriate — Farooq Katwari, Former Foreign Secretary — S.K. Singh, and Vice Chief of Naval Staff — Vice Admiral K.K. Nayyar, presented to the then Prime Minister Vajpayee, on December 20, 1998, and blessed by him. One of the Recommendations in the Report was the Trifurcation of J&K, on communal basis; the Kashmir Valley was to be steered to a Special Neutral Status of the types experimented in European Diplomatic History.
- The Lahore Talks, in February 1999, following suggestions to India and Pakistan to sit across the table. As per records, Pakistani Prime Minister, Nawaz Sharif, and the

then Army Chief of Pakistan Gen. Musharraf, had jointly visited PoK sites across the LoC, opposite Kargil, in December 1998. The famous Reagan Maxim with the Soviets, "Trust but Verify", was forgotten (Earlier in September' 98, Chief of Army Staff in India was told by the PM, not to match big calibre Artillery firings across the LoC in J&K). Finally the Kargil intrusions were reported to the local Army Command by a Shepherd (Gadaria) who had seen Pakistani soldiers and posts on our side of the LoC in April 1999.

- The Government used Back Channel Diplomacy and directly sought the then US President, Clinton's intervention to get Pakistan to withdraw its Forces and Posts, to hurry up and claim laurels. The media was used to full effect to gain a *Khaki Shine* for the September Elections (having been voted out of office by Parliament in April 1999, over its unjustified action in respect to a Service Chief on December 30, 1998).
- The intervention sought by the Government to help withdrawal of Pakistani Forces, led to the (Internationalization of Kashmir), de-facto, negating the 'Shimla Agreement'—1972. A number of powers now emphasize the 'Disputed Territory' status of Kashmir.
- The increased intensity of Cross-Border Terrorism and Proxy War, elicited a level of lip sympathy from the US Administration, greatly increased frequency of official visits, securing FBI Presence in New Delhi, Foreign Presence in J&K, under various pretences and guises, Military Exchange, and exercise including the Military Intelligence, visits of the then Deputy Prime Minister and his 'team' to CIA Langley and Tel Aviv (Mossad), increasing dependence on Foreign Intelligence Agencies for Internal Security Planning/Operations.
- By 2000-01, an Arms Import Plan, with an outlay of Rs.1,20,000 crores (approx. US$ 28 billion) was unthinkingly and hurriedly concurred with, by the Scientific Advisor in the Ministry of Defence and

approved by the Defence Minister and the then Government, causing a huge setback to the entire National Defence Production base, including the shipyards, weakening the Civil-Military integration process, and putting India amongst the top two or three Importers of Arms, to become a happy hunting ground for Arms Merchants and Foreign Economies, which are Arms-Export-Dependent. India's Foreign and Defence Policies, thus became even more amenable to pulls and pressures.

- Exposure of our Intelligence personnel to foreign inputs and influences became endemic.
- Army-Air Force Exercises in sensitive areas of J&K and North-East, were the order of the day, based on perceptions that, there was "Strategic Convergence" and we were "natural allies".
- The knee-jerk reaction of the Cabinet Committee on Security, after 9/11, was to offer Awantipur (J&K), Adampur(Punjab) and Bhuj(Kutch) as Air bases to the United States, for the planned reprisals on Afghanistan. This informal offer was politely declined, in favour of logistically and politically more convenient environment of the Pakistan Military bases.
- The supply of Depleted Uranium (DU) Munitions to Pakistan Army in 2002, and much earlier to it even being designated as the "Most Important Non-NATO Ally", were accepted by our the then Government, without even a protest. (Public Opinion in India, in 2003, later prevented the embarrassment an possible repercussions of the deployment of and Indian Army Division in Iraq).
- The deployment of NATO Forces and thus, extention of NATO's jurisdictions in Afghanistan, just 300 to 400 miles or less from the J&K, Punjab and Rajasthan Borders, neither analyzed, nor did it evoke a suitable political response from the foreign and national security establishments presumably clouded by our self-conceived "natural ally" status. An example of touching faith.

- Widespread use of DU munitions in Afghanistan, poisoning that country's Water Systems, rivers, flora and fauna, turning its habitats to graveyards, and subjecting its newly borns and unborns to slow death, were apparently, of little interest to the Government of India, in the face of well documented studies by the US Uranium Medical Research Centre, European Parliament Report — October 2003, and scientific evidence, presented by Japanese scientists, all of them describe the Radiation affects, upto a circle of a thousand miles radius, from Kabul (and Baghdad), which have already initiated Cancer (all forms) and aggravates the AIDS epidemic, covering Delhi, Mumbai, Rajasthan, Punjab, J&K etc. with grave consequences to people's health and well-being, for several generations to come.
- Naval Exercises and attempts to impose a Maritime Security Arrangement in Malacca Straits, without prior consultation and concurrence, has evoked a strong protest from Malayasia.
- Large presence of Foreign Military Contingents and build-up of operating bases in the Caspian Sea Region, and Central Asia, and its possible implications on India's Security and Energy interests, appear to have been brushed under the carpet. This region has been assessed by Brzezinski, a former US National Security Advisor, as the most likely region of future conflict, for Energy Resource Wars.
- The largest ever mobilization and deployment of the Armed Forces, without a political objective, after the Terrorist Attack on Indian Parliament, on December 13, 2002, is perhaps a classic example of its own type; described later by the Spin Doctors, as the success of "Coercive Diplomacy". On being ordered to deploy the Armed Forces, the then Chief of Army Staff, Gen. S. Padmanabhan had asked the then Prime Minister, "What does the Government expect from the War?" The PM's reply was *"Woh baad mein batayenge"* (that we will tell

later), as quoted in the book *"Operation Parakrama: The War"*, by Lt. Gen. V. K. Sood, and Pravin Sawhney, who adds..."Neither were the political objectives defined, nor did the Military Leadership press too hard to find them". The 10-month deployment was just as suddenly terminated, without assigning any plausible rationale. India's main armour (Tank Strike) thrust axis, and to a degree, the 'Electronic Order of Battle' stood compromised. Heavy attrition was caused to equipment, by sand, dust and heat, being exposed in the open. The then Navy's Concept of Operations were announced to the media by the Navy Chief, in competition with the Army and the Air Force.

- Equally sudden and surprising was the transformation from *"Aar Par"* (decisive or final battle) posture, to the 'Peace Offensive', initiated within days of the termination of 'eyeball to eyeball' confrontation, in Operation *Parakrama*; presumably to facilitate the deployment of the Pakistan Army, for Afghan Operations, also called the "Spring (2004) Offensive". All this hardly speaks well of the staff support, given by the National Security Advisory Board (NSAB) and the National Security Advisor, to the Cabinet Committee, on Security. Perhaps the National Security Advisor, was too pre-occupied in fine-tuning the Indo-US-Israeli axis, for the joint 'War on Terror', announced by him and the Deputy PM, while on a visit to Washington DC, in 2003.
- Creating an "Internal Enemy" appeared to be a pre-condition for prosecuting a War on Terrorists, as perceived by the NDA Government at home, no matter that it was destructive towards National Unity and cohesion, and weakened the 'rear' of our Armed Forces, in Peace and War.
- Liberalized Food Imports, Edible Oil, Cotton, Soya, began cutting into the 5 to 10 per cent margins, at which our small farmers survived. Weakening the ICAR, and allocating research on new variety of Rice to Canada,

acceding to the WTO Patent Regime, on drugs for Leukaemia, permitting giant, highly subsidized Global Agri-Businesses and Seed/GM Food Companies like *Monsanto* and *Cargill* to implement their strategies in India, sale of Tea and Coffee plantations to foreign companies, encouragement to corporates and Contract Farming, handing over Water Resources / Supply Systems to the Water Barons, Scrapping the Indian Patents Act 1970, TRIPS all bode ill for our people's Nutrition Security. As recently as March, two months ago, Robert Zoellick, the US Trade Administrator/negotiator, stated quite bluntly in New Delhi that India must liberalize further, its Agricultural Imports, if it wants a reciprocal arrangement in Software/IT Services, Exports and Business Process Outsourcing (BPO). That is the bottom-line for US Vital Interests. Is there a similar position that informs our Foreign Policy which must primarily serve the economic interests and strengthen the Economic Security of 1100 million Indians.

- A criminalized Political Economy has been exemplified by the unchecked flow of "dirty money", and drained our country's Internal Vitality.

The former External Affairs Minister, K. Natwar Singh, in his first Public Statement on May 23, 2005, rightly focused on our Foreign Policy, serving India's vital national interests. It is a long and difficult road ahead, to go "back to the future".

Then Chief Justice of India, V.N. Khare's observation to the effect, in the Supreme Court, regarding the Gujrat Victims Case, that "Inciting and supporting Sectarian violence, is worse (for the country) than the acts of a Terrorist or an alien enemy", is all too timely.

18

Design to Cost Approach in Military Systems

In late 1996, the Naval Staff was confronted with a challenge, which was likely to affect its Force Architecture in the opening decades of the 21st century. The indigenous Aircraft Carrier, also designated the 'Air Defense Ship' (ADS), for tactical reasons, and to allay the apprehensions of some Indian Ocean nations, was not getting on to the Building Dock, from the Design Board, inspite of ministerial support, due to a veritable array of pen-pushers, who kept repeating the queries on cost of the platform, forgetting the versatality and survivability of a Carrier. We then got down to a second stage exercise of reviewing the design of our ADS. We had an example of the HMS Tiger, an amphibious Assault Ship, which was to carry large Transport, Combat Support, Airborne Early Warning (AEW) and Rotary Wing Helicopters. The US Navy was also experimenting then with, the Tilt Rotor V-22 Carrier borne version aircraft. Even with their big budgets, the high cost of the Carrier was a criticism they had also to contend with, and satisfy the financial bureaucracies. So we put our heads together, the Navy's Design Bureau, the Naval Staff, the Naval Air Staff, and the Ship Builders, who were on line with industry. The Naval Staff basically re-did the Vital, Essential, Desireable (VED) analysis again, and recategorized those systems and equipment, and later, the compartments that were vital, and where Military standards and specifications (milspecs) brooked no compromise and risked mission effectiveness criteria.

The result after this scientific-technological and cost trade-offs was an ADS where the budgetary projections of approximately Rs. 1,800 crores, were brought down to around Rs. 1,165 crores. The very next year, *INS Delhi,* a modern 7000 Tonne Guided Missile Destroyer was commissioned, and the bills totalled to about Rs. 750 crores. So, here was an ADS which was only 1.5 times the cost of a Destroyer, in 1997 (and now, prospectively less than 60 per cent of the cost of an SKD/CKD, Scorpene Class Diesel Powered Submarine, with a 50, kms. range missile!) This case is quoted to illustrate a 'Design to Cost' approach, which incorporates 'Civilian Off The Shelf' (COTS), civil-military integration, advances in civilian technologies at lesser cost, and are more versatility and superior to a gold-plated or exclusive 'military' R&D products. In the choice of technologies too, there are several relevant and growth optimal factors and parameters, that could save on obsolescence, and costs, while providing options to replace/modernize through the life cycle, without necessarily waiting for half-life 'Modernization', or the 'Capital Repairs/Refit/'opportunity window, to occur (a 10 per cent reserve of compartment and superstructure space is also kept for future add-ons.) If Modular Systems are selected, they could be replaced at opportunity costs, without laying off the platform for long periods, so that the integrity of 'Force-levels' is maintained. This is applicable to propulsion, power generation and weapon/electronic systems, as also to hundreds of ancillary systems, which go to make a modern warship.

Mass consumption and economies of scale have helped civilian technologies, with greater R&D financial inputs, production tooling and quality competition, to bring new, more reliable, and maintainable products, on line. Even with the growing Defence Budgets, nations or a group of nations, like the EU, are unable to match the sectoral R&D and 'Laboratory to Manufacturing Plant' time-frames of civilian products. This is specially so, in the fields of Micro-Processors, Micro-Electronics, Nano-Technologies, and MEMS, which now dominate contemporary Technology applications. It, therefore, becomes far more advantageous to the Military Staffs, to adopt/adapt and incorporate, what is already a product, or about to enter the market, rather than 're-invent' the wheel. Thanks to Admiral Hyman G Rickover, Father of the US Nuclear Submarine Project, in the 1950s, who got the US industry to come to uncompromisingly high Naval Standards that he set for the Special program that he led; US industry has hardly looked back, except where the Japanese stole a march, specially in Robotics and Electronics. The US remains ahead in software applications, though the Japanese do have superior, high-speed Computation Hardware.

The point that is being emphasized is that, Civilian and Military products and production processes are compelled to converge, and the smoother this is, the better it is for all. Flexible and lean manufacturing, innovated in the Civil sector, is an added advantage. Cross-sector applications have increased, because of advanced materials and composites. Instead of parroting 'Privatization' one wishes there were Civil and Military Decision-Makers, focused on these aspects and emphasized the 'national sector', than articulating their Private-versus-Public sector ideological predelictions. This is specially so, when Technology denial by the Developed Nations, to maintain their dominance in the hierarchical structure of the international system acts to our detriment (never mind the public relations statements in the media). The fine print of the PNAC is explicit on this 'pre-condition' by the US. If our ISRO can do it, so can the other sectors.

A Design to Cost approach is inclusive of a number of concepts and applications in Technology, which enhance a Military platform's cost, and Military effectiveness, many of which are Civilian Industry innovations. Commonality in the 'software simulation' of the Rafale Fighter Aircraft, and the Boeing 777, is a good example. Virtual Prototyping and Computer Aided Manufacturing, first adopted by the Civilian Industry, soon became commonplace in Defence Industry too. *Advanced Distributed Simulation*, a joint development between Civilian and Military R&D, provides the means to design, train, disseminate, and put into practice advanced combat philosophies.

Whatever be the equipment and systems we plan to induct in future, Modularization through a Building Block Concept, engineered to produce the end product, would seem to be a sound approach. This is particularly so, because of the exponential rise in the cost of the Systems; replacement of Complete Systems is not an affordable option. Enhancement of the System, through replacement of System Modules, and the latest Software Processing Programmes, is on the other hand feasible within the financial allocations. The Modular Hardware and Software Approach, would not only reduce the time required to field a proven system, but also help overcome the problem of viable volumes required by the Production Agencies.

The enormous Unit Cost of new major Systems, compels us to examine other Technological options like Virtual Reality Prototypes, and thereafter, decide on the mix and types of Sub-systems, that suits our budget, providing for alternatives and upgrades in the future life-cycle. The industry, of course, has to provide for 'Surge' capacity, or reserves, to meet a future national emergency.

A part of the 'Design to Cost' or 'Design to Budget' approach, is a radically new approach, called *'Cooperative Engagement Capability' (CEC)* in providing the means for Air Defence. This allows Systems to share unfiltered Sensor Measurements Data, with a very small time delay, retaining its precision, enabling the Units of a Battle Group, Task-Force or Fleet, to operate as one entity. What this means, in effect is that, a fleet, whose combatants are dispersed in an area, over thousands of square miles, is enabled with Sensor Synergy. Each combatant, and Aerial/Space Platform, has one or more Sensors, and each will observe a somewhat different 'picture' of the situation, due to its unique characteristics and the platform's vantage point and horizon. Amidst this variation in pictures from one unit to another, are efforts to co-relate Target Tracks and identifications via satellite linked data-link aided Command-Control Systems, and to coordinate a number of Missile Launchers, and a comparable number of Interceptors of Aircrafts. Such concepts were a part of the architecture named 'System of Systems', and were driven by both Cost and Military effectiveness criteria, enabled by near real Time Networking Digital Data Technologies.

Yet another mini revolution is under way in the Design, Production and Installation of Command, Control, Communications, Computers, Intelligence-vision and Architecture, which is reducing Costs, and dramatically improving Battlefield Responses. Commonsense, and a closer Naval Staff-Design Interface, are enabling the Design-development of the *'Shipboard Modular Arrangement Reconfiguration Technology' (SMART)* systems, referred to earlier above. Smart is a methodology, for installing Equipment in Shipboard Spaces, that provides the Fleet with enhanced mission flexibility, while helping its reserves and redundancy. At the heart of this is a Track Rail System, which enables equipment to be bolted to the deck, bulkhead or deckhead, meeting the shipboard's Shock and Vibration requirements. Designated spaces can be reconfigured, to receive New Systems, install equipment upgrades, position cross-decked systems with minimal industrial re-work. Such new Technology Insertions can enable rapid deployment of state-of-art Technologies much faster, than the old standard method of extensive fabrication and hotwork. The SMART system includes a Foundation Track System, Modular Containerized Power, and lighting and modular work-stations. SMART enables Navies to meet the need for modified capabilities, to support new mission/roles. Additionally, a SMART system will enable the latest equipment technologies to be installed "later" in ship construction schedule, at a substantive cost saving.

Progress and advances in Technology, since the 1980s, in Micro-Processors and their support sub-systems, have led to improvements, in shorter time-cycles, of Device Technologies, Internal Architecture for Data and Control Flow, Configurations for scaling the size and complexity, and Data Bus for connectivity and communications. This has enabled *'Open Systems Interconnect' (OSI)* Architecture, and this concept has made the design of very complex Computer Embedded Applications realizable. The advent of *'Reduced Instruction Set Computer' (RISC)* Architecture, and the consequent emergence of work-stations and *'Computer Aided Software Engineering' (CASE)* tools, has made it possible to develop software applications, at a faster rate. This trend has maintained its upswing, whereby there is an order of magnitude enhancement, every 4 to 6 months. The combination of Hardware and Software Development Cycle, is having a profound effect on fructification of large, complex and capable Electronic Systems, at much lesser effort and expense. The advent of better and better Computer Aided Design (CAD), Computer Aided Manufacturing (CAM), Computer Aided Engineering, Knowledge Engineering Environment (KEE), Concurrent Engineering Environment (CEE), have given rise to excellent Development Processes, for highly sophisticated Software Embedded Systems. With powerful 'Virtual Reality' Engines, and 'Walk-through' Software, it is now possible for the Service Chiefs and his Staff, the doubting Bureaucrats and a positive, forward looking Minister of Defence and Finance, to view not only the 'Design-to-Cost' Warship or Submarine, Aircraft or Helicopter, or other Combat Vehicles, but their simulation in the battle environment, and the adversary's responses; and take informed decisions, not only through the dull, prosaic notings on the files which are usually 'Merry-go-Rounds', depending on the Babudom's moods, proclivities, and preferences.

Here lies the possibility, if these tools are used wisely and honestly, to not only evaluate the single Service Force Architecture, but as a first stage exercise, for the political leadership, advised by the Service Chiefs, to get a Joint-Services Perspective of the War Fighting Capabilities of the nation, and to spend our scarce resources, in an informed, competent manner, bearing in mind the other competing priorities of the Government, as indicated by the Common Minimum Programmme, and the Prime Minister's Address to the Nation, on 24th June, 2004.

19

Decision Making
Force Architecture &
National Defence Capability

1987 was in a sense, a Golden Year for our nation, as the unity and singleness of purpose amongst the three Chiefs of Staffs, the Army, Navy and Air Force, was near absolute. This was demonstrated by stand taken by COSC, their straightforward, free and frank discussions on all important matters with the then Defence Minister and the then Prime Minister, the 'Gentleman's Agreement between Admiral Tahiliani, General Sunderji, and Air Chief Marshal La Fontaine, on sharing of the Defence Budget Allocations in the next five years. The Navy's Budget would increase from 12 per cent to 18 per cent, and the Air force from about 21 per cent to 24 per cent, and this was at the cost of the percentage hitherto spent by the Army. (The Allocations made for National Strategic Systems were not to be counted/included for this purpose. General Sunderji's concepts on this were published in several of his articles, as long ago as 1980, when he was Commandant of the College of Combat). The third substantive agreement, related to a strategic matter, where a one-page note, hand written, was given to the then P.M. Rajiv Gandhi, for the "Prime Minister's Eyes Only". All this provoked a former Cabinet and later Principal Secretary to remark, in January 1999, 'that the Chiefs, at least some Chiefs, had been going directly to the Prime Minister', a well established convention in our system since 1947, and had perhaps, become too big for their boots, this needed to be set right, he opined. Just a month before this remark, a former Foreign Secretary and a former Defence Secretary, opined in signed articles in the *Indian Express,* much the same line, even recalling the 'ghosts' of General McArthur.

There have been exceptions like Sushital Banerji, K.A. Nambiar, Krishna Rao Sahib, Satish Chandran, and a few others, who drew the fine balance of administrative prudence and advice rendered, to the Political Executive, and the large majority who ascended and arrogated authority in the name of the Minister, to 'Divide and Rule' the defence services, mostly by extending behind-the-scenes patronage to ambitious officers, and have the final say in the Financial Service Budget Allocations and Priorities. As said by Appleby, 'The Civil Servant may or may not make Policies, but he makes the implementation of policies possible or impossible'.

When the new Administration came to power in 1998, its major refrain was that the previous Governments had never given priority to the Defence and the major Acquisition Programmes of the Services. The BJP manifesto specially referred to the Nuclear Submarine/ATV Programme in the Party's Election Manifesto of January 1998 and said that it would see to its speedy fruition. Exactly a year later, its Defence Minister stated in a *Doordarshan-T.V.* interview on January 1, 1999, that **he could not sleep because the Nation's (best known) top-secret had been disclosed** to the newspapers (by an unnamed Chief, as his detection work had revealed!). Subsequently of course, a spate of articles at regular intervals have quoted the highest Defence Ministry and Naval sources, to write news-stories about this top-secret project, the latest by Rahul Bedi, *Jane's* Defence Correspondent in New Delhi, in a recent issue of the *Frontline.* One of the reasons for the delay in the project, ascribed by Bedi is, financial constraints. Nothing can be further than the truth. Perhaps, it may be appropriate to ask six years down the line from March 1998, what the BJP Government did, to expedite the 'Nuclear Submarine Project'. Why was this vital National Defence item, missed out in the BJP-NDA's Election Manifesto (and Vision Document) of April 2004! If six years of BJP rule is not enough to deliver on this high budget, high priority project begun in the 1980s, what is it that they promised in the Manifesto-1998, and delivered? This is merely to illustrate the games that have been played in the Defence Ministry, *a la* the 'Washington leaks' which are a regular feature of its political play.

Nothing can be farther from the truth, about 'inadequate Defence allocations', by the Parliament, than the assertion repeated by the BJP and its Ministers, that 'Defence' was neglected by previous Governments, as regards the money approved by the Parliament. Some percentages have been quoted, even by Defence Analysts and commentators, who should know better. A number of heads of expenditure were moved out of the Defence Budget, as early as 1998 for good reason, namely Defence Services Pensions, which are now approaching Rupees ten thousand crores, per annum, for the Coast Guard and some other Heads and Sub-heads. Allocations to ISRO or to the AEC which in time may have had Defence applications, were also not counted. Special projects had separate allocations. The last Government knew all this. After all, their MPs had been Members of the Defence Ministry's Consultative Committee, and the Public Accounts Committee, and they had the benefit of a sizeable number of Uniformed and out of Uniform Defence Experts, as Advisers, even prior to March 1998. The question they should honestly introspect on *(Chintan)* is, how, after all they knew, Budget Allocations passed by Parliament, year after year, remained unspent uptill March 31, even after all the restrictions on "Middlemen and Agents", who were now officially 'persona-grata' (and it is reported that they were given access to all required official papers from the Defence Ministry and Services Headquarters files and documents but they still could not move things on schedule; not even the Kargil purchases, which are the subject matter of a C&AG Special Report). Most of these arrived, the following year *Kargil,* and many of them, particularly the ammunition and shells/rockets had shelf-life expired or unacceptable to the Army! The Defence Budget was indeed doubled from that in 1998 to the Allocations in 2003! Mostly slated for some of the biggest deals of the world's Arms Market, all in billions of dollars. A *'Swadeshi'* Budget for *'Videshi'* companies (Native Budget for foreign companies). Apparently, money was not lacking. In 1998, in meetings after meetings, the Army Chief was pleading with the then Defence Minister, for canvas shoes, boots, bullet-proof vests, and intercept radio equipment, which his formations lacked in Kashmir, and the North-East. In the year 2000-2001, after retirement, the same former Army Chief, now a part of the Reliance Foundation and REL has been criticizing the inability to spend the allocations, due to the Bureaucracy, which the 'Best Defence Minister'of India, in an interview on T.V. by Karan Thapar, said, was "rubbish". When Ministers' describe as "rubbish", what their own Army Chiefs state in public, in articles, and interviews, this situation must lead us to find, exactly where the "rubbish" lies?

The former Honorable Defence Minister was referring to his announcements in 2000, about the formation of the Defence Procurement Board, which was set up to expedite Defence Procurement decision-making. What the busy Defence Minister possibly did not pay attention to is, the veto in the last paragraph of the Ministry Order, setting up the Board, that "all recommendations of the Board, made from to time, will be subject to scrutiny and vetting on the relevant Service Headquarters/MOD File, as hither to before, and will stand approved only after due sanction/approvals by the Ministry of Defence (Finance), and or the Ministry of Finance, as hereto before" or words to that effect. Now the Defence Procurement Board is a talking shop! It is true that, some limited Delegation of Financial Powers have occurred, beginning 1996, first in the Navy, and then in the other two Services, but, these relate mainly to civil works, spares from indigenous sources and motor transport.

The substantive issue is not even this. Civil Servants, whether they be from the IAS, Posts and Telegraphs, Indian Forest Service, Audits & Accounts Service or the Indian Defence Accounts Service (originally attached as cashiers to Battalions and Regiments deployed in the field in Iraq in 1920 etc), do not wish to comprehend the need for change of the ' Force-mix' architecture (also described by the term 'Recapitalization' in the US Armed Forces, when, what is in Service, is not necessarily replaced by the same), compelled by technology and the 'Revolution in Military Affairs' (RMA), or rethinking on Doctrine and Strategy which is the primary responsibility of the General Staff, Naval & Air Staffs. Bureaucracy is happiest with the simplicities of Replacement of equipment, one for one, on becoming obsolescent (at one point of time in the 1970s, they agreed to a life of 12.5 years for Electronic Equipment on the recommendations of the Electronics Commission). This was a revolution of sorts, but the catch was, it had to be a successor of the same basic item/type.

Now, what all this lands us in is to Defence Plans 'frozen in time', as one Editor of a national daily is fond of describing, what he does not like. If the Army has 7000 tanks, then it can hope to replace them one day, after number of years, to be argued in a file battle over some two or three Chiefs' tenures. The same goes for Artillery Guns or AFVs or Tank Transporters, variety of Vehicles, Fighter Aircraft, Frigates, Patrol Vessels, what ever was in the inventory or the 'War establishment/Peace establishment'. It is all as per scales. If artillery shells had a hit year, probability of one in a hundred, and today's Technology enables a probability of one in ten, then we have a problem with the Bureaucracy. A Missile with a kill probability of 0.2, to be superceded by a Missile System with ECCM, a Multi-Sensor Detection Head, and a kill probability of 0.8, is a bigger problem, unless it is part of the outfit of a big-ticket Military System, then it could go through like a bolt. In other words, upgrades or modernizations are generally up-hill, while Billion Dollar Systems, if the environment is congenial, will go through give or take for a few years. What the Forces need, is also Mini-force Multipliers but they are very hard to get through.

That is, when it was suggested that we need to review our Force-Mix and the Budget Allocations within, and on an inter-disciplinary basis between all the three Services, after *Pokhran-II,* the Minister either did not want to hear or had some other dream projects in mind. Like in other National Defence Systems Assessment, post a major happening like Nuclearisation, or new threats on the horizon, Force-Mix and Architecture, comes in for major change/reviews. Here, as I said, even a common sense recommendation at the Defence Minister's Committee, in June 1998, that we raise /build a new/restructure our Force capabilities, for Unconventional/Special Operations Forces (joint) and reduce Allocations to the Conventional Mix of Tanks and Armoured Vehicles, or Frigates /Destroyers etc., which have lesser survival indexes in contemporary Electronic and Space Surveillance environment, increase numbers of both smaller and bigger submarines, was answered by a blank look (fortunately, it did get recorded in the Minutes). This was not an off the cuff recommendation but the result of staff work, and thinking. December 13, 2001 was not too far off. A few amateur Terrorists transgress a lax outer security cordon of the Parliament House, a shoot out follows, fortunately, these 'guys' are killed. This is followed by an emergency Cabinet Committee on Security Meeting. Only General Padmanabhan and his colleagues from Navy, Air force know a part of the truth. He asks the then Prime Minister, "What is the (political) objective of the ordered mobilization for the War *(Aar Par ki Larayi)*?" He is told "*Woh Baad Mein Batayenge*". Nearly eight lakh troops with supporting armour, artillery, field ammunition depots, Air Force, fully on alert, and re-deployed, the Navy on forward deployment with the Navy Chief and his Operations Staff declaring the intent to blockade Karachi, all a part of 'hugely successful coercive diplomacy', first time ever, declared by New Delhi's Defence and Foreign Policy Experts, on all channels and the national print media. All because, instead of a well assessed, selective (surgical incision) strike, with the limited purpose of a stern warning, in action, for which we had neither planned, nor exercised, nor had the wherewithal with night, precision manoeuvre; we fumbled along an unthought of Nuclear Confrontation. The Army Chief was brought into broadcasting a Nuclear Warning, through a Press Conference. Even the American or Israeli Generals don't do that, not now, not during the Cold War, when Europe was on a trip-wire!

What were the damages, one may be permitted to ask? There are various assessments, Rs. 8,000 crores (US$ 2 billion) or more, costs to replace the damage, attrition, cost to overhaul and replace, and a bonanza for the Arms Merchants. Electronic Order of battle, formation deployments, and armour thrust axis, compromised (as desert geography and canal, anti-tank defences, narrow operational courses of action/options). More importantly the effects on National Morale, the Forces Morale and confidence, intervention/scrutiny in the Nuclear Preparations/security of Nuclear Command, and control structures by the Superpower, though this will not be officially conceded by the then Government; successful 'persuasive and friendly' Diplomatic pressure from the US to India to withdraw and sit for peace talks, monitored by them, with the US objective to enlist Pakistani Army, for the Spring Offensive 2003.

In so far as decision-making at the Bureaucratic levels,. with parallel files being maintained in the Defence Ministry and Defence (Finance), to state it plainly, it is not for the first time, there is too much authority, without responsibility, and accountability. This was stated in the First Report on Defence Matters (by Chairperson, Sharda Mukherjee, later, Governor of Maharashtra), of the Administrative Reforms Commission in 1968, subtly superceded and sidelined by a more ambiguous Second Report, a typical Bureaucratic sleight of the hand. This is a defect, which has multifarious consequences, right down to every level of War fighting readiness and military capability. Yet, there has been a healthy tradition of Ministerial accountability since Independence, until the major departures from it during March 1998-April 2004. Shri Lal Bahadur Shastri, the then Railway Minister, resigned over a train accident, T.T. Krishnamachari, over an LIC-Mundhra matter, presumed by the Honorable Judge, on the enquiry to be influenced by the Minister's Office, and K.D. Malaviya, the Father of India's Oil Onshore and Offshore Wealth, over Rs. ten thousand only, paid by a Calcutta firm to the Party treasurer. We now have *Kargil*, big-ticket-deals, C&AG and CVC, the Coffin scam, where we paid inflated prices for unusable coffins, for which the Minister disowns constructive responsibility and blames his Defence Secretary, whose CRs he writes, and who is elevated to Cabinet Secretary, the latter does not say a word on the issue, even after retirement!

These may be considered relatively minor matters, when we consider the fractured and faulty decision-making, that has inflicted wounds and injuries on our Sovereignty, Independence and Integrity, in the past six years, and whose repercussions and consequences, the body politic and the people have yet to assess and gird themselves, to restore India, as was. Compromises in Economic Sovereignty apart, what of the internationalization of Kashmir, and the layers and layers of secret-deals, handled by Messrs Brajesh Mishra and R.K. Mishra, under the guidance of their common Superior, what of India's Independent Foreign Policy, as the second largest Arms Importer of the world, what of our Energy Security in a changing West Asia, when we had openly announced an Indo-US-Israeli axis, to fight Terror (the source is of common origin, we said), what of the shouting from the roof-tops about Cross Border Terrorism, which is specially sponsored in the Kashmir Valley by more than one Party interested in the Valley, what of the tight embrace in which the Defence, Security and Intelligence apparatus of the State finds itself in (the world-wide experience is that, these embraces and 'sharings' are followed by overt/covert interventions), is prejudicial to National Security itself, and if any lesson is to be learnt at all from countries like the former Soviet Union, Chile, Latin America, African nations, Angola et al. Food Trade, GM Foods/Seeds, Patent Laws' Amendments etc., may be omitted at this juncture, but to dismiss recent defections in the RAW as 'routine and a global happening, a happening common in Foreign Intelligence Agencies', is not only facile, but an attempt to pull wool over others' eyes. Silence, rather then comment, may have been advisable.

It would be prudent, if the new Government puts its heads together, to make a damage assessment, and decides on a step by step, carefully calibrated approach, to limiting the damage/ cutting down the losses, and 'rebuilding India's Defences, with the intellectual, administrative, and personnel resources, that we can mobilize from within, than to keep on clutching at borrowed ideas and Advisers on loan from Extra-National Agencies and bodies. Never in the world history has the latter brought any good to any nation or to its people.

20

Perpetual War for Perpetual Peace

Limits to Power

"There will be no peace. At any given moment, for the rest of our life-time; there will be multiple conflicts in mutating forms around the globe....violent conflicts will dominate the headlines."... Paul Wolfowitz and Richard Perle in the Preamble, a prelude to the draft of the *'Project for the New American Century',* in 1992, during the heady days when the CIA's subversion project, post 1947, of the Soviet Union, had finally borne fruit. The same CIA is now being made the scapegoat for the quagmire, that has bled and enfeebled Iraq (bled by 12 years of sanctions) by war and occupation.

It may be worthwhile, elaborating what the policy determinants then said, particularly as the Indian Establishment pursues 'friendships, alliances, strategic convergence' and the over-arching sentiment of "the two largest Democracies", instead of defining and doggedly pursuing its own vital National Interests, in other words, State-to-State relations, aimed at furthering the well-being of the vast majority of the people, as this alone can bring substance to our National Security. Studying and analyzing the Policy Papers of great and Major-Powers, near and distant, is an essential pre-requisite to such an approach. In this context, the US Defence Planning Guidance (document) developed in 1992, post the Soviet Union, goes on to state: "The Foreign Policy of the US must be unapologetic, idealistic, and well funded.

America must not only be the World's Policeman or its Sheriff, it must be its beacon and guide. Our first objective must be to prevent the re-emergence of a New Rival. This is a dominant consideration, underlying the new Regional Defence Strategy, and requires that we endeavour to prevent any hostile power from dominating a region, whose resources would, under consolidated control, be sufficient to generate Global Power. These regions include Western Europe, East Asia, the territory of the former Soviet Union and South West Asia. (China has since, been categorized as a 'Strategic Competitor' by the US Administration; the analysts did not realize that the theatre of that competition may be the Persian Gulf!) There are three additional aspects to this objective: First, the US must show the leadership necessary to establish and protect a new order, that holds the promise of convincing potential competitors, that they need not aspire for a greater role, or pursue a more aggressive posture to protect their legitimate interests. Second, in the non-Defence areas, we must account sufficiently for the interests of the advanced Industrial Nations, to discourage them from challenging our leadership, or seeking to overturn the established political and economic order. Finally, we must maintain the mechanisms for deterring potential competitors from even aspiring to a larger Regional or Global role."

Perhaps, even the most partisan analysts and commentators would concede that, the 'New World Order' has been still-born. Quite apart from the ruinous deprivation of livelihoods and jobs in the Developing World, the fate of the common man in the Rich Nations has been only marginally better, with the remnants of a Social Security System, that sustained it, and that which was built up over a century of struggle, is in tatters, not even destined for a decent burial, because the Savings, Pension Funds, Health Insurance, Medicare, Unemployment Compensations are all mortgaged to profits for a tiny number and growth strategies, which are for the satisfaction of the Stock Markets, FIIs, big Banks, and Currency Trading Speculators. All this has a cause and effect relationship, with the big games/happenings, the big picture, and the strategy planning, that is reflected in the Chinese saying, "there is great disorder under the Heavens!"

"A Clean Break—A New Strategy for the Realm", advocated Richard Perle, in 1996 (to secure Israeli Security), "Permanent large military presence in the Gulf, transcends the issue of Regime Change of Saddam Hussein", he articulated, conceptualizing the need. Whereas, only some 16 months ago, the 'American Enterprise Institute', a major influence on successive administrations, had called for 'a focus on bold vision of the Post-War (Iraq) Agenda, Radical Reforms of the UN, Regime change in Iran, Syria, and 'Containment' of France and Germany, for reshaping of the political landscape of the Middle-East.

"Iraq is not just about Iraq," said Karl Rove, a pivotal figure in Washington DC. While the Global Corporate Media (from which most Indian Corporate Media draws its sources and cues) projects its news and op-eds, as if that was the truth happening around the world, and in the Middle-East in particular, whereas events on the ground appear to be evolving differently...providing indications that, there are limits to Power, specially the use of Military Power.

Apart from the Kean's Commission, and the Butler Committee Report, both sophisticated, white-wash jobs, not unlike some of our own discussion and debates do not appear to be coming to an end, on trivializing the great issues of War and Peace, that 'decorate' the years since 1991. The underlying fundamentals are neatly given the go-by the policies arising from Corporate Imperial Ambitions and these are not even mentioned. Notice how all discussions neatly turned on Intelligence Failures, the inadequacy of Military Strength, Resources and the alleged brutalities of uncivilized Insurgents.' The Oil Corporations don't figure, the Vice-President's National Energy Policy Document (NEPD) is mentioned in whispers, the Private Military Companies (PMCs) that directly serve the Corporates, it is suggested, are beyond the 'Rule of Law', everywhere, in Eurasia, West Asia, West Africa, or other 'trouble spots' in Latin America, Asia, Africa, or East Europe. Let us for a moment presume that *Operation Iraqi Freedom* or 'Afghanistan' was perfectly implemented, intelligence et al; if the Iraqis had not stood up as one, as they have, would any Super Army with super low Radiation Weapons like 'Depleted Uranium' munitions, air strikes on call round the clock have succeeded in delivering 'Iraqi Freedom'? Robert Fisk, of the *Independent* newspaper UK, in an interview, on August 6, 2004, (he is perhaps one of the few journalists who reports with his feet on the ground) said that, the writ of the Bremmer-(CPA)-Appointed Provisional Government, does not run beyond the 'Green Zone' even in Baghdad, that, the Resistance, though not under unified command, has control of the rest of Iraq, and has put out of action, the Northern Pipelines, and frequently disrupts the Southern Pipelines, to the export outlets. The War against the people of Iraq is amongst the major factors, along with 'Peaking of Oil' in Saudi Arabia, the four times revised Oil Reserve figures of Shell (*a la* Arthur Anderson audits on Enron), Yukos, and the troubles in Darfur, Nigeria, Venezuela, the Caspian Basin-eyhan axis, Equatorial Guinea etc., for the record breaking rise in Prices of Oil.

What General William E. Odom says, is relevant. The General, an Army veteran, one time college Professor, long time Washington-hand (served on President Carter's National Security Council), was Director of the National Security Agency, bigger, more heavily funded, and better provided for, than the CIA; capable of the most comprehensive Electronic Monitoring of Ether, Cyberspace, Codes, Communications, and eves-drops on just about everything on the wires and wireless world. On "Staying the Course", and reordering the Middle-East, building a friendly Democracy in Iraq, he says, "We have failed". General Odom talks straight like a soldier..."The issue is, how high a price, are we going to pay...less, by getting out sooner, or more, by getting out later?''...."Longer the US troops hang tough", he reasons, 'the more isolated America will become. That in turn will place increasing strain on International Economic, and Security institutions, that have undergirded the emergence of 'America's Inadvertent Empire'...I don't know that, the UN, IMF, the World Bank, or NATO, can survive this" *(Wall Street Journal,* April 28, 2004).

At this inflexion point in history, there are some objective processes, that appear to supercede the perceptions, and the vision of individuals and groups, however powerful they may be, with armies and unlimited WMDs at their command. By their very nature, sometimes these become unuseable, which is of course, not saying that their use can be ruled out! Notwithstanding the billions of accounted and unaccounted dollars, that are being spent by the 'Coalition of the Willing', for developing Fourth Generation, 'useable' Nuclear Micro-nukes, with Private Sector's reported participation, like that of the Carlyle Corporation, in developing the 'trigger mechanisms', and participating in the scenario building and 'targeting list' exercises, alongside the Military's Strategy and Operations, high level authorized groups, held in secret locations, like the Offut Military Base, 2003.

There are developments, that appear to have overtaken the planners, including the 'Office of Special Plans', set up by Donald Rumsfeld, to by-pass the NSA, CIA and the DIA, to make a 'cast-iron case', for the Invasion of Iraq, and the Invasions to follow, against the countries designated as 'Axis of Evil', by pre-determination. (In other words, Intelligence was not used to make a decision, to go to War, it was used to deceive the public). When the Corporate Media joined in, Paul Krugman wrote in the *New York Times*, that, after the Operation was disabled by the victims of the 'genocide by sanctions' and 'Operation Iraqi Freedom', that Rupert Murdoch had dreamed and articulated that, "the greatest thing to come out of this (Operation), for the world, would be the US$ 20-a-barrel of Oil." Even Murdoch must be eating his own words! US Oil today is at US$ 55.0, and Brent Crude at US$ 52, and a few Cents and threatens to cross US$ 70. Speculators, using Pension and Hedge Funds, are aggressively dealing in Oil 'futures' markets, to push prices skywards! Though Japan, China (with a 40 per cent rise in Energy Consumption in the first six months of this year alone), and India, along with the Developing Countries, suffer the most, the NYSE too is fearful, the US-EU economies are headed for a continuation of the 2001 Recession, call it 'Double-Dip Recession', if it eases the pain. War, disruption of oil supplies, lowering estimates of Oil Reserves, peaking of oil and erosion of existing Oil, Wells by water injection, and Bottle Brush Secondary Extraction Technologies, is not helping in Saudi

Arabia, and operationalizing the new fields will take much more time. The US Election Campaign is becoming partial to alternative Energy Projects, Energy Saving, and Energy Conservation and by default 'Global Warming' and 'Climate Change' are inching towards the front burner, recommended by expert studies, commissioned by the Pentagon/DoD!

Will the US Vice-President's secret NEPD, predicated on "hands on the spigot" or control of the Energy Resources everywhere in the world, work? Even Russia, which people thought was paralyzed and subservient to the 'Reforms' Process, imposed by the IMF in 1992, and implemented by such figures as Jeffrey Sachs and Richard Armitage's teams of Advisers, in the post 1992 period, has asserted its temporarily forgotten Sovereign Rights, in disallowing such proxies for the Oil Majors, as Khordovsky of Yukos, who bought this Oil Giant at 'garage sales', with the connivance of the bureaucrats of the erstwhile "communist" apparatus, who knew how to subvert and bend all the rules, to loot and dispose off public property under Yeltsin.

The consequence is that, 'Resource Wars' have stepped up in South-west and West-Africa. Suddenly, Darfur is up on the headlines as a major story, a cover-up for an impending Oil Grab! Away from the headlines, Political-Military rivalry has sharpened in the southern periphery of the erstwhile USSR, even as, some of the new Republics are hosting the Caspian-Ceyhan Oil and Gas Pipelines. Military Bases are being pre-prepared as Launch Bases, stretching from Georgia, breakaway Abkhazia, Ossetia, the Caucasus, Azerbaijan — sold out by one time rising star, Gaider Aliev, named to succeed Leonid Brezhnev, General Secretary of the Communist Party of the Soviet Union in 1980s, also former Politbureau figures as Karimov and Nazarbayaev, the first to lease out Military Bases to the US, appears to be regrouping. Turkmenistan, Khazakstan, Kyrgistan have agreed in principle with Russia to form a new 'Common Energy Union'. In the western region Russia, Ukraine and Bylorus are in the process of getting back together a political and economic union, depending on the results of the forthcoming presidential elections in Ukraine. In the Eastern territories, both China and

Japan are in various stages of forming state-sponsored 'private-public' joint ventures, basically to out-source energy, minerals and timber from Siberia.

Afghanistan too is in bit of a grind, though reports indicate that gas pipelines from Central Asian Region/Caspian Sea Basin, through Afghanistan to the Pakistani Ports /coast, are progressing well. However, the duality of the Afghan 'Poppy' production which contributes handsomely to the major World Banking Systems, and eventually, Heroin's retail takings help put up the stock prices of major corporations, remains a highly contentious issue, both inside Afghanistan, and as a major trading commodity and currency propellant. The UK's All Party Foreign Affairs Select Committee's recent assessment is, 'that Afghanistan could implode, if more troops and resources are not sent immediately to support the British Government's Counter Narcotics Strategy to reduce Poppy cultivation by 75 per cent, by 2008, and eradicate it completely, by 2013.' Undoubtedly, the Parliamentary Committee is concerned over 'Heroin on the Streets', in the UK. However the Opium-Narcotics Trafficking, Processing and Retailing, Money Laundering, and Bank-Parking business, ultimately to create marketable investments has many God-fathers, and cannot possibly run without the active collusion of Private Banking and Correspondent Banking' Money Transfer Channels, now given so much respectability that 'no questions are asked, none are provided'.

Most agencies mandated with Surveillance, Monitoring, Tracking the 'Drug Trade' with direct links to Arms Transfers, Gun-Running, and Terrorist groups of various varieties, find themselves a 'part' of it, in due course.

Principally, Saudi Arabia — exporters of *Wahabism,* and connected in the past to *Mujahideen* in Afghanistan, Chechenya, Kosovo, and other unlikely places the biggest importers of Arms (lying unpacked in crates for as long as 30 years!), to recycle part of its 'Petro-Dollar' earnings, as part of the 1946 Agreement, post World War II. It has a 10 million population, which is largely illiterate, unemployed, whose social security benefits are now being steadily eroded. The official Saudi Budget has been running a deficit for years! Yet, the Regime is reported to have more than a trillion dollars in the US stock markets and bonds, and another trillion dollars in the US banks. It has, like Kuwait, UAE, Oman and Qatar, a 50:50 sharing of profits, with the Oil Majors. (Most Fortune 500 toppers make their profits, not from their core manufacturing industries, but from 'Financial Services', which could mean anything!) If the Saudis, for example, need US$ 25 billion worth of New Armaments each year, for defending their kingdom, the Oil and the people, then in that order, the larger question is, how much more will buy them security, and yet, the Saudis are getting messages to reform, and could well be on a hit-list of some Oil Tzars or hawks!

Nearer home, the last seven years have seen strange happenings and goings on, from Kashmir to the North-East, and across the country, at some internal, well financed and well organized groupings with various types of covers, are actually colluding with Foreign Agencies, with a long history of covert operations in South Asia. The Pakistan Government/Army, and its second power centre the ISI, was set up by the former colonial rulers and the CIA respectively, so that, we can have our own version of the 'perpetual War for perpetual Peace' in the sub-continent. A former Defence Minister of this country, while Kargil Anti-Intrusion Operations were being executed by our valiant Army, was giving 'certificates of Good Conduct and Innocence', publicly, to the ISI. This is probably without precedence in International Relations! Hardly a day passes, when Pakistan, now a 'Most Important Non-NATO Ally', is now showered with praises from responsible levels of the State Department and the DoD, for its creditable Anti-Terrorist contributions to the 'War on Terror'. We have a Proxy War, and well funded Terrorist groups, of various hues, inciting violence and creating an environment of violence, as the Supreme Court said so explicitly in its judgement in April, 2005. We have moles and 'sleepers' by the dozens, if not hundreds, at all levels. One of them 'escaped' in June, 2004, and we still don't know how this man, under watch for months, just disappeared! If our Agencies are infiltrated at the staff and field levels, specially so in the course of the last six years, as they had the 'green signal' to collaborate and nurture an intimate intelligence relationship to do so, what of the ISI? It has a history of 57 years of 'incestuous relations' with its creators. Is there anyone appointed to the operational levels of the ISI, or who participates, in short and long term operational planning and operations, who is not beholden to, or obligated to the parent organization, and who will not do its bidding? While the people and leaders of both countries take measured and calibrated steps, to ease tensions, every nation and every people have a right to defend their vital national interests, and not only through purchases of armaments, but protecting their financial, and economic life-lines also which run through the Banking Systems, Financial Institutions, Capital Controls, making stronger our Defences against International Speculators, and their financial instruments, their confidential private understandings and agreements, in secret, with comprador elements. If the country's Border and Territorial Integrity is sacred, and if it is our duty to defend them; then it is equally vital for us to watch the new 'Financial Predators' — the ones who bleed us every hour. Let us take counsel but learn lessons from such nations as, Malaysia (in 1997), and not from China, as the latter is the new 'poster boy' of Global Finance Capital. India faces attacks and subversion on its economic front on a daily basis and Military Invasion only once in several years. Our history is not replete with Military Defeats because we lacked strength, (with one exception in the Battle of Calicut, 1498, when the Zamorin's Fleet could not follow up on its victory, by destroying the European adversary, by giving it chase in the ocean, as one Dignitary opined the other day, it is splattered with betrayals, signed and sealed, behind closed doors; and in a few cases, by poor leadership.

Let our National Grand Strategy, Doctrine and Operational concepts reflect our historical experience, our vision for the well-being and future of all our people in the context of the Global Project of International finance capital and its predatory instruments.

Note

**1 Former US Treasury Secretary, Peter O' Neill writes, in his *Memoirs*: "In February 2001, the US National Security Council staff were already drafting a document (directive), detailing how the Administration should divide up the Iraqi Oil Fields, amongst the Major Western Oil Companies, after the invasion". Former Counter-terrorism Chief, Richard Clarke, confirms that, Iraq, not Terrorism, was the Administration's first priority, in his just-published book, "Against All Enemies". Defence Secretary Rumsfeld, and Paul Wolfowitz, have confirmed that, "Iraq was on the Hit List, from day-one". In the words of Condoleeza Rice, "We don't want a smoking gun to become a mushroom cloud" and the US Vice President preordained that, "We know Iraq possesses WMDs. We even know where they are hidden."

**2 Sudan's Oil Export Pipeline to the Red Sea, was completed in July 1999. Oil reserves estimated in 1999 have since doubled in 2001. Crude Oil Production is currently at about 350,000 barrels per day, (bbl/d) and is expected to go up to 500,000 bbl/d by 2005. The Oil Fields are mainly located in Southern-Sudan, where the trouble has been incited. China's CNPC, and India's 'ONGC Videsh', along with Petronas, are partners for prospecting and production. (The US imposed Trade Sanctions, on Sudan in 1997 and economic sanctions in 2001, the latter temporarily held in abeyance).

21

Credible Nuclear Deterrance

Seven Years After

A little short of seven years, after *Pokhran II,* may be an appropriate time to review how the National Interest has been served, by exploding some devices in the Kiloton Throw-Weight Class, and claim that, we also demonstrated a Megaton Class Capability, both without a credible delivery vehicle on May 11, 1998. Though, Nuclear Weapons Capability is primarily an added Weapon, in the arsenal of diplomacy, to be kept in the scabbard. Our then Honourable Home Minister lost no time in using language against our lesser neighbour in the West, which amounted to a threat to settle all outstanding issues, from a position of strength. Followed soon a series of Nuclear Devices exploded by the neighbour, in the Chagai Hills. Then the Spin-Doctors, even of the Nuclear establishment, took over to make claims and counter claims, as to the actual yields obtained. These were devices yet. They had not been shaped into War-Heads, matched to a vector, or specific delivery vehicles. In this War of Words on 'yields' perhaps, the lone Superpower knew a little more, as there had been reports of Nuclear Monitoring Devices, planted not too distant away from the site, in the desert, which one arm of the Government may have permitted, without quite appreciating the implications for the future!

The new Government made claims that it had proved its man-hood, its Nationalist credentials with *Pokhran II*. The story goes that, it had given similar orders to the same people in May 1996, when it piloted the 13-day Government, but it was too short a time to set up the logistics then. Later statements, implying that similar intentions to test the Devices in 1995, and even nearly 10 years earlier, had been aborted, because the then Leaderships 'funked' and pulled back. This Government was made of different mettle.

Nuclear Devices were surely demonstrated in 1974, and we were ready for exploding them, even a few years earlier, but the Policy of 'Ambivalence' was preferred by deliberate logic, than the one embarked via Pokhran II. What else was the *raison de etre* of India's resolute position on the Non-Proliferation Treaty, that we will not sign it until there was an Agreement on Universal Disarmament of Nuclear Weapons, without exception. The Governments of the day had resisted all pressures to sign on the dotted line, through nearly three decades.

Pokhran II was claimed to be a great success for the new Government, internationally, and with the Superpower. Paradoxically, village folk living in the proximate neighbourhood were not impressed, and instead voiced their unfulfilled needs for Water and Livelihoods!

It suited the US and its allies to announce some sanctions on items, which in any case were never permitted by the US Department of Commerce, even earlier, as they were either in the London Club 'Trigger' list, or Missile Technology Control Regime (MTCR), or simply classified as 'Dual-use' Technologies, or items in hi-tech list, or items not to be exported to non-allies. Multi-axis Lathes or Electronic Devices were examples, since India was in the suspect list of countries, which passed on Western Industrial Secrets to the USSR. Certain Public Sector Units and scientific establishments were specially listed, for scrutiny of their Import Lists. (The Aircraft Numerical Code of the LCA got stuck in the US for months, because no one remembered to retrieve it, when the Pokhran decision was conveyed to the Scientific Adviser.) This had always been so.

We had created quite a mess for ourselves. Publicly we said Pakistan was put in its place, yet Pakistan had in place an

Arsenal of tried and tested medium, and Short-Range Nuclear Capable Missiles, under proper Military command, more or less ready to shoot. The Prime Minister wrote off a confidential, or is it secret, letter to the US President Clinton, giving the reason for *Pokhran II* ... China, he pleaded, hoping that it would place India in the US's good books, and they would happily live thereafter as 'natural allies', vis a vis China. President Clinton had the contents of the letter released! We now had a public position that, our baby Nuclear Weapon System, with untested development-stage Missiles, was pitted against China! That is not a satisfactory position in games that Nuclear Weapon Powers play. The United States had kept track of our Nuclear Weapons and Support Systems Programmes, through moles in all sorts of places, and through Third Country Operations in New Delhi, Bombay, and other places. The US was pretending to be alarmed. Why would it jump with joy, when China had MFN Status since 1973, both enjoying the benefits of a roaring trade, China's hostility to the Soviet Union since 1962, its permitting Electronic Monitoring Facilities in the North, to monitor Soviet Programmes, and it semi-official designation as the 'NATO of the East', had won it special affection in vital echelons of the US System. The US never counts on friends, only those who serve its interests.

It may be useful at this point to recap some Flag-Posts on the Road Map, since *Hiroshima* and *Nagasaki,* the Nuclear Weapons supremacy has been used for blackmail. It was so, when the Americans threatened their use, to deter the Soviets advancing on Japan, in 1944-45, from Iranian Azerbaijan in 1948, during the Berlin Airlift. All this got the Soviets to accelerate their Hydrogen Bomb. The Cuban Missile Crisis found the US ahead in Submarine based, Second Strike Capability, while the USSR was trying to catch up. Concurrently, the Soviets put a man in space first, with the US screaming 'foul', as they had always planned for the Military uses of Space-based systems! The famous "Missile-Gap" was invented to accelerate Military Programmes, as both Superpowers went on to a 'draw' in 'Mutually Assured Destruction' (MAD).

From here on, it was a race to 'Mega-Mega tonnes' and Multiple Independently Targeted Re-entry Vehicles (MIRV) with algorithm-driven, computer-generated programmes, whose trajectories in space and targeting, always surprised the adversary. There was an equally vital race to penetrate, subvert and damage the 'Command & Control' System of the other, secretly, with Viruses and Bugs in the Central Nervous System, penetration of 'Discrete Protocol Devices' in the Defence and Civilian Telecom System, and real time monitoring by CGHQ, Cheltenham, UK, and the National Security Agency, (NSA), which has much greater resources than the CIA, and is credited with all kinds of fantasies and Real Location/Monitoring Devices, which would place us all, certainly the 'Developing' Nations, on thin ice. The natural corollary of all these complimentary developments were efforts to duplicate, triplicate, and put in place Multiple Command, Control, Communications & Surveillance Intelligence (C4SIR) systems, which would provide redundancies to secure the Nuclear Weapon State. The assessed costs of providing a degree of reliability, and redundancy to such support-systems and sub-systems, to enable a survivable, credible, strike capability is as high as 50 per cent of the total Strategic Systems Budget. The announcement, therefore, by the Government that, it was committed to a 'No First Strike' Policy, left those who know what is in the tombs of Nuclear Theology, wonder struck. This became even more intriguing, when know-all of Nuclear matters, and semi-official began to suggest a Policy of 'Recessed Deterrence' to be adopted, and this concept was floated in the South Block. Recessed deterrence was a unique Nuclear 'Readiness/Response' methodology, wherein the vector or delivery Vehicles, and the Warhead, were to be kept hundreds of miles apart in time and space, each under a different Command. The Warheads were to be kept with a Civilian-Scientist group. This was to ensure 'safety' of the Arsenal! No one was asking what happened to the Response Times, which could run into many hours, particularly under the "No First Strike Doctrine", announced by the Government! It was not unreasonable in the circumstances, to infer that, this was coming out of the Jaswant Singh-Strobe Dialogue. Strobe Talbot, experienced in the subversion of the Soviet Union, and an acknowledged authority on Strategic Negotiations, with a battery of Advisers, could hardly have been matched by Jaswant Singh, a new comer. (Strobe Talbot's book, co-authored with Bechloss, *"In the Highest Places"*, is a classic on the US role, in the ultimate subversion of Gorbachev & Co.) A publicly declared 'No First Strike' Policy, when we did not have even a nascent Second-Strike capability, and a very fragile Nuclear Weapons Delivery Capability, was untenable. "Recessed Deterrence (RD)", is a complete negation of Nuclear Capability, like *Karna* the warrior of *Mahabharata* epic, taking off his *Kavach* (talisman). Simultaneously, despite India's declared position on not signing the NPT and its new *'Avatar'* the CTBT, made clear by Arundhati Ghosh, on instructions from H.D. Devegowda, the then Prime Minister of India, the BJP's Nationalist Prime Minister, presumably in consultation with India's *'Loh-Purush'* (Iron-Man), was announcing on every platform and occasion, and our Parliament was certainly not informed or consulted, that India was ready to sign the CTBT by September 1998, four months from *Pokhran II*, when neither the internationally accepted norms of Testing Nuclear Weapons, nor the minimum 12 successful Tests, with accuracies (Circular Error of Probability CEP), established in each class of Missiles. Without stable, tested and assured, measured-yields, the Government of India, under pressure from the United States, announced a Unilateral Moratorium on further Testing! China, against whom Vajpayee had written to Clinton, as the objective of our Weaponization, was continuing its Tests in 1998, 34 years after it had first exploded its first Nuclear Device. On the other hand, there were reliable reports that, the US was transferring Micro-Nuke Simulation Testing labs to China to facilitate its Nuclear Arsenal to be kept modernized. The Head of India's Nuclear establishment and the Scientific Adviser to the then Defence Minister, were being cajoled at this time, to make public statements that India's Nuclear capability was fully tested, no more Tests were necessary, and all was well for India's Nuclear future, to be signed away in the CTBT. However, miracles sometimes do happen. To the country's great good fortune, the US Congress and the Senate, vetoed the US Governments proposal to sign the CTBT stating categorically that 'Simulation Laboratory' Testing was not adequately established, and that, continued and periodical Under-Ground Tests were necessary, to maintain a credible US Nuclear Deterrent, so as not to compromise US National Security. The US in the preceding 53 years, had carried out hundreds of Nuclear Tests. It had carried out 'numerous Test Launches of its Ground, Air and Submarine-based ICBMs, IRBMs with MIRV Warheads, and was experimenting with ABM and Space-based Nuclear Systems, yet, they were not considered adequate to maintain US Nuclear Security, while India was ready to sign the CTBT and further *ipso facto* negate its internationally defended position on the NPT.

At a Seminar held at the ICSSR, under the Chairmanship of the Late Prof. L. M. Sondhi, in 2000, both Prof. Bharat Karnad and I, spelt out the ingredients of the 'minimum credible' Defence posture of a Nuclear Weapon State, arguing that, without a survivable, Submarine-based Nuclear Capability, and adequately tested weapons and platforms, the country was likely to be vulnerable. In the limited context of our Western neighbour, our position was compromised because that country had categorically declared its intention to use its Nuclear Weapons, if the Indian Forces assembled to attack it, as indeed it repeated, to deter and negate 'Operation Parakrama'. When learned Indian Generals, Strategy Specialists, Civil Servants, and Foreign Policy Experts, acting as Spin-Doctors in the media, orchestrated the triumph of 'Coercive Diplomacy' at its best, they were perhaps kidding themselves, certainly not anyone in the Nuclear and Defence establishments, around the world. Prof. Bharat Karnad has exhaustively dealt with these issues in details in his recent book, specially in the context of Range, Mega-Tonnage, Types of War-heads, to state that these may be just enough to improvise to meet Pakistan's challenge. He asserts that, they are nowhere near adequate, to deter and defend India vis-a-vis the US, which is not only an Indian Ocean Nuclear Power but increasingly established in West-Asia and Central-Asia. The present Government enjoys its friendship and talks regarding the US, as a Natural Ally, a Strategic Partner, and so on. There is, however, one abiding and immutable purpose of US Policy, and that is, to defend/extend its interests, which is now to establish a 'New World Order', under the 'Project for the New American Century' (PNAC), and in this, it knows no 'friends', only subordinates. It is hard to see the US as Santa Claus, ready to bestow gifts on 800 million impoverished people, when its direct and indirect Military Expenditures are eating away its own people's Social and Welfare Programmes, who like Oliver Twist in Charles Dicken's novel, says, "Please sir, may I?" The intervention of the then US President Bill Clinton in July 1999, asking Pakistan to withdraw, and India to not cross the International Border, gave the US another opening to become Advisers to both the Governments on 'Kashmir'. The US orchestrated the campaign that, 'Kashmir' was the most dangerous part of the world, a potential Nuclear Flash-point, and this has seen another pressure-point, at which the Indian Government has to listen attentively, to the numerous Delegations, which visit New Delhi every month, if not every week.

A prima-facie weak and vulnerable Command & Control System is the *Achilles heel* of a Weak-Muscled Weapon System. China's C&C Centres are reported to be located in mountains, inside 12 feet of hard rock, another reason for the US, trying out 'Bunker Busters' in Afghanistan. Vested interests, like in the case of the aborted Chemicals Weapons Programme, on signing the 'Ban on Chemicals Weapons Treaty' in 1997, may be burying their heads in the sands, like the ostrich, brave pronouncements at the Ministerial level, of having established various 'Commands', notwithstanding.

If the US quest for a New World Order can draw up plans to denuclearize Russia, or RSFR by 2010, after effectively doing the same in the former Soviet Republics, like Ukraine, does it not have a warning/message for both India and Pakistan?

21

Private Military Companies in the New World Order

Pirates, mercenaries, armed gangs of War-lords, have been part and parcel of history. The French Foreign Legion, operating in Francophone Africa, the erstwhile colonies of Metropolitan France, may have had a certain elan and sophistication, but they were essentially storm-troopers, to facilitate and keep in power, dominant French and Belgian Economic and Mining interests. Leaving aside Latin America for the moment, and its 'Death Squads', post the ouster of the then President Goulart in a coup by the Generals, allied with the oligarchy in 1964, the historical record of Africa, Asia, and the *Nazi* East-Europe, is replete with private armies, funded by the former colonial powers and/or commercial interests, largely Oil and strategic Raw Mineral Mining and Trading interests, that funded predatory, heavily armed and funded groups, like Mobutu in Congo, who cruelly murdered a Democratically-elected Prime Minister, on the directions of the Katangese Mining Companies, and some Intelligence Agencies, as revealed by Rajeshwar Dayal, the then Under Secretary General, UN, Incharge of Congolese Affairs. There is the whole history of Jose Savimbi's UNITA, financed by the White Regime in South Africa, and the Agencies, which brought death and destruction to the Angolans and Namibians, struggling to get on their feet. All this was justified in the name of the US-Soviet rivalry, of the Cold War. We can go on quoting names and nations across the world, where people became victims of these funded 'Liberators', acting as Non-State Actors, on behalf of the Metropolitan Centre or the Colonial Powers, new and old. The Whites had launched a 7-Nation Army, to squelch the Soviet Revolution in 1917, with the UK and France leading.

However, it is the 1990s that has given the Private Armies, now structured and run professionally, and managed by 'Private Military Companies' (PMCs), that deserve our attention. For, if they operate under various covers, disguises in other countries today, there is the probability that they may disrupt Peace and Development on this vast sub-continent too. They are close partners, and enjoy a coalition of interests with the Drug Trade, Gun-Running, Money Laundering, Terrorist organizations, both state and Non-State Sponsored. It is a heady cocktail, funded by part of the $ 700 billion Drug Retail Market, and an estimated $ 1.7 trillion Criminal Money in the Global Economy, handled by the mafias, with close links to political parties and individuals, operating as Fixers/Middle-Men, Private Banking Managers, mostly dressed in Saville Row tailored suits, moving in the glamour world of the nation's establishments.

While most of the Activists in the Disarmament circuit attend World Conferences on Nuclear Weapons, the big bombs, and campaigns against big ticket Conventional Weapon Systems, that are traded between the Arms Manufacturers and Third World Countries, where people are largely hungry, diseased or mal-nutritioned, and live a sub-human existence, *unterm ensch en,* is the German word; the trafficking in Drugs, Guns, Women, and Children, is often financed by Criminal Money and Diverted Public Funds, is passing on Small Arms, Land Mines, Explosives, Improvised Explosive Device Manuals, Training and Expertise in exterminating Minority Groups and their shops/dwellings. This is big business, and even big politics, complimenting Depleted Uranium Munitions in use, and Genetic Bombs in the offing. The political formations, which don't want to see beyond their noses, or even after knowing the criminal agendas, act as compradors and collaborators, are part of this coalition of the willing.

Since this is the coming big business, 'PMCs' have been the natural successors to the relatively unorganized, or poorly organized Non-State Actors. Military Expertise, experience of Intelligence Operations, Logistics and Special Operations, Transportation, high level Political Contacts are integrated into the enterprising PMCs, who have lobbies in the corridors of power, and are handy, ready tools of the Oil Majors, and mining companies, established or establishing business operations in Central Asia, Afghanistan, Azerbaijan, Georgia, East Europe, Colombia, Venezuela, Angola, Equatorial Guinea, Sierra Lone, or — Nigeria the new west-coast of African Oil Paradise. Zaire, Congo, Liberia, and the Central African Republic, retain their roles as Bases/Launch Pads for intervention in the neighbourhood. As this article is being written, news comes in of the farm house of a white farmer in South Africa, being used as an Assembly and Planning-Base for a PMCs/Mercenary Groups being readied for Equatorial Guinea (EG), now being designated 'Gulf of Guinea'. (Just two Helicopter Gun-ships, piloted by South-African Mercenaries, had been used some years ago to support and oust another faction). Mozambique, Rwanda, and Zimbabwe, have been earlier and is now, a happy hunting ground for executing 'Regime Changes'. Inciting Civil War, destroying the local Food Economies and capturing the Food Markets of these hapless peoples. A little muscle to help train the local Goon Squads, Small Arms, and the Poison of Tribalism, goes a long way. The mainstream media, hardly or never tells the reasons why violence or civil strife erupted, it keeps away the PMCs, the back-room boys from the TV channels, and it gives the impression that African people are blood-thirsty tribals, always ready to slit their neighbour's throats.

Somalia in 1993-94, was a great looting opportunity for Brown & Roots, now re-christened as Kellogg, Brow-Roots, in Iraq. From drinking water for the UN Forces, at the start, mainly for the US, to oil, lubricants, ready-to-eat meals, and so on, that this firm did not handle. They got all their reimbursements. (The Indian Navy deployed ships at 2000 miles from home, off-Somalia, but never got a penny from the UN Fund). In Iraq, an estimated 10 per cent of the Security Personnel are being provided by the PMCs, (namely ERINYS South-African British Company). Security of the Oil-Fields is also in the hands of the

PMCs. Halliburton, Vice President Dick Cheney's previous company, has been in the news, for fudging accounts and bills on the Pentagon. One can visualize an increasing dependence on the PMCs in such operations, as this helps to exclude body bags, pensions and disability awards from the Veterans' Funds. A great part of the US logistics in Iraq and the Middle-East, specially after Donald Rumsfeld's interventions, are now handled by the US Corporates, who in any case are dominant in Iraq and Afghanistan.

The PMCs are not just US based. UK PMCs are on the quick take-off runway. They are semi-legalised and work on a wink and a nod from White Hall.

Military Outsourcing is the buzz-word in the 'War Against Terror', and the ideology of 'Perpetual War for Perpetual Peace'. The small US contribution to defending 'Democracy and Freedom' in Sierra Lone, was not executed by elite formations of the US Army, Navy or Marines. It was accomplished through a private Oregon-based company, International Charter Incorporated of Oregon(ICI), managed by the former US Special Forces Operatives. ICI is US State Department contracted, to go into regions, areas, States, where it is not political or diplomatic to commit the US military, like Haiti or Liberia, and such places!

Mercenaries may be outlawed by Article 47 of the Geneva Convention... but, who is to regulate? A majority of the Members of the UN are too preoccupied with their crises and concerns at home, to try and raise their heads above the water. PMCs are motivated solely by profit and, therefore, fit the definition of Mercenaries, but the PMCs are a multi-billion dollar business of War, and no one will bell the cat, specially because they are Headquartered in the 'Mother of Democracies'.

The International Consortium of Investigative Journalists, ICIJ, of the Center for Public Integrity, reports that, since 1994, the US Defence Department has signed 3,061 Contracts, with 12 of the 24 PMCs identified by the ICIJ, valued at $ 300 billion. More than 2700 of these Contracts were to just two companies: Kellogg Brown & Roots, and Booz Allen Hamilton. This was pre-2003 and Operation 'Iraqi Freedom'. Then Defence Secretary, Dick Cheney, had paid Brown & Root Services, $ 3.9 million, to produce a classified report how Private Companies could help provide Logistics to the US troops, in potential War-zones. The emphasis is on 'potential' War-zones. Recall the PNAC: Rebuilding America's Defences, was being processed amongst a close-knit thinktank. Later, the Pentagon gave Brown & Roots, now named KBR, another $5 million, to update the Report. KBR is a subsidiary of Halliburton Corporation of Iraq-fame, which Dick Cheney headed in 1995 to 1999. It had already got Contracts in former Yugoslav States, under the 1995 Dayton Accord, of $ 2.2 billion, to be paid by the Liberated States of Serbia, Croatia, Herzegovinia etc. Frank Carlucci, a successor Defence Secretary, is still Chairman of the Carlyle Group, by now famous for its star cast. Many years ago, the Vinell Corporation had trained the Saudi Arabian National Guards, which protects the Saudi Oil Fields for its Government, and the 'Seven Sisters', the Oil Majors. Later, Vinell got another $ 500 million, as a subsidiary of BDM, to provide logistics and other support to the Saudi Air Force. The point to be noted is that, the names have a certain importance, but it is the interlocking directorships, share-holding pattern, and the profile of key Administration officials of Cabinet rank, which demonstrate the integration of the PMCs in the System. Vinell, part of the BDM, became part of the Carlyle Group with a revenue contribution of $ 774 million, in 1994.

According to the International Consortium of Investigative Journalists (ICIJ), stocks of PMCs increased in value, by more than twice the average rates, at Dow Jones. Estimated before the Defence Spending in Iraq began, in 2002-03, the International Security Market was projected to increase from about $ 56 billion in 1990 to $ 200 billion in 2010. Stock Prices of PMCs rose many times over, after 9/11, and the 'Pre-emptive' War Doctrine became public, through the NSSD 2002. Armor Holdings, a Florida-based company, became one of "America's 100 Fastest Growing Companies", in 1999.

Implicit is the 'privately' held view in the Defence establishments, that PMC soldiers may really be more useful, than the 'blue-helmeted' UN Forces, to manage Politico-Military situations, arising in the coming years, and the clout of the PMCs, as emerging major Corporations, closely integrated functionally, policy and plans wise, with the mega-corporations, is important, and needs recognition. They are in fact, a National Resource.

If they are served by, like the Virginia-based MPRI is, by a President, Carl Vuono, who was the US Army Chief of Staff, 1987-1991, by Ed Soyester, a former Head of the Defence Intelligence Agency, and General Crosbie Saint, former Commander, US Army Europe, they are in auto mode, to serve their own and national interests, and must have a recognized role/place in the scheme of things. MPRI's role has been the subject of scrutiny in a Congressional Sub-Committee Report on what it did, secretly, in Bosnia, Croatia, Kosovo and Sandzak.

Be it offshore Oil Fields, or Nigeria (The Army Chief of Staff, General Victor Leo Malu was replaced for objecting to MPRI's requests for certain documents, and information on the proposed overhaul of the Nigerian Military), UAE, Kuwait, Qatar, Saudi Arabia, and the Carribean, where OFCs and OCBs abound, the PMCs, small or big, can be presumed to be there. They may operate behind the scenes, or under the table, but they are there, where Criminal or Drug Money is generated or trafficked, where Gun-Running, Diamonds and Money Laundering Operators or their patrons have to be protected. There is little regulation and less oversight. If there is a Congressional Investigation, it gets underway when the horses have bolted from the stables. This, when the International Traffic in Arms Regulation Law (ITAR) requires the PMCs to obtain approval from the US State Department. PMCs can, and do sell their services through the Defence Department's Foreign Military Sales (FMS) programme, with which we are quite familiar, in the South Block. PMCs prefer the FMS route to bypass the ITAR.

The ICIJ Report quoted above, in turn quotes the US General Accounting Office (GAO), May 2002 Report, to say that, no one in the Defence Department knew the number of 'Contractors' in the Balkans, and what they were contracted to do, or the Governments, obligations to them and vice-versa. Some were obviously what in Indian parlance are termed, "Cost-Plus" Contracts, that are often inflated by the Contractor, and later approved by the Government, as a *fait accompli.* If media reports on issues raised by the US Congressmen and Senators are to be believed, this happening is 'happening' in Iraq, at an unprecedented scale, and has become a major Campaign issue, with Halliburton, has been forced to withdraw, at least till the cloud blows over.

The perspective is that, the PMCs appear to be taking the 'Driver's Seat' in certain Politico-Military situations and conflicts, that protect and advance the interests of the big Oil Majors, Mineral Corporations and Commercial, Companies, poised to capture markets, by placing pliant individuals or political groups in power in the 'New World Order'. It would be worthwhile for us to keep track of their intentions, plans, operational methods and track records.

Index

Abdul Kalam, APJ, Indian President, 34, 117
ABM Defence, 19
Abraham, Spencer, 139
Abu Gharaib, 58, 75
Accession
  of Jammu and Kashmir, 128
  to India, 153
Adampur (Punjab), 187
Administrative Reforms Commission, 203
Advani, LK, 155
Aerial—Sensors, 46
Afghan
  and Iraqi Nationalism, 23
  Camps, 79
  Fighters, 38
Afghanistan, 13-17, 19, 22, 23, 26, 38, 43, 44, 53, 55, 59, 65, 80, 83, 87, 136, 141, 146, 152, 153, 157, 166, 168, 172, 174, 176, 179, 187, 188, 211, 221
  and Iraq, 12, 15, 16, 53, 55, 83, 87, 164
  in Iran, 65
  Poppy Production, 211
Afghanistan's Mountain Cavers, 110
Africa, 14, 15, 23, 59, 86, 96, 98, 143, 182, 222
African
  Opportunity Plan, 140
  States, 140
Africans, 144
Agent Orange, 16
Agent Orange Poisoning, 171
Agostas and Scorpenes (Submarines), 119
Agricultural Economy, 35
AIDS, 93, 95, 184
  Epidemic, 166, 188
  Virus, 14, 15
Air Bases, 78
Air Defence, 191
Airborne Early Warning (AEW), 191
Akhromeyev, Marshal, 40
Al Qaeda, 38, 80, 144, 145, 146
Alaska Natural Wild Life Resources, (ANWR), 87
Allawi, 67
Aluminium Rods Case, 74

American
  Enterprise Institute, 63
  Great War Veterans' Association, 170
  Way of War (AWW), 56
AMOCO, 39, 146
Andhra Pradesh, 146
Andropov, Yuri, KGB Head, 175
Anglo-German Rivalry, 137
Anglo-Iranian Oil Competition, 137
Angola, 96, 97, 98
ANSWER Coalition in US, 158
Anti-Hijacking Drill, 33
Anti-Insurgency and Counter Terrorism Operations, 76
Anti-Mafia Commission, 39
Anti-Piracy Patrol, 46
Anti-Taliban Forces, 54
Anti-Terrorist Operation, 47
Arab Oil Sheikhdoms, 103
Arab/Afghan Fighters, 146
Argentina, 69
Argentina—Africa, 59
Armed Forces, 41, 53, 67, 68, 76
  and Military System, 114
  Modernization, 117
Arms Imports, 20
Arms Trade, 21
Arms Transfers, 211
Army War Room, 116
Army's Bio Warfare Laboratory, (Maryland), 15
Asia, 143
Asia, Africa and Latin American Countries, 85
Asian Security Diplomacy, 56
Atomic
  Bombs, 115
  Energy, 116, 117
  Energy Commission, 184, 199
  Secrets, 111
  Weapons, 138
Australia, 119
Australian Bases, 81
Avantipur (J&K), 187
Avian Bird Flu, 16
AWACS, 29, 30
Axis of Evil, 15, 74, 53, 159, 209
'Azad Kashmir', 132
Azerbaijan, 61

Baghdad, 58, 208
Baghdad and Kabul, 166
Balkanization, 38, 130, 145, 150
Balkans, 37, 69, 61
Bambo Curtain, 99, 100
Ban on Chemical Weapon Treaty, 221
Bangladesh, 13, 45, 74, 128, 151
  and India, 138
  Intelligence, 151
Banking and Insurance Funds, 104
BARC, 184
Basel Convention, 162, 177
Basra, 55
Battle Lines in Palestine—Philippines, 143
Battle of
  Calicut, 213
  Plassey, 21, 125
Belgium, 182
Bengal, 21, 124, 125
Berlin Plus
  Arrangements, 61
  Project, 86

Bhuj (Kutch-Gujarat), 187
Bhutto, ZA, 129
Big Bang Wars, 85
BJP, 74, 77, 154, 156, 184, 199, 219
  BJP Manifesto, 30, 198
  BJP-NDA
  Govt., 130
Black Money Economy, 39, 40
Blackout Bombs, 17
Blair, Tony, British PM, 43, 148, 175, 1719
Bohai Bay, 103, 137
Bolivia, 140
Bolivia and Philippines, 161
Bougainville—Afghanistan, 91
Border Security Force (BSF), 46
Border Surveillance, 156
Borneo, 96
Bosnia, 38, 39, 146, 227
  and Herzegovina, 61, 146
  Oil Exploration in-, 146
Brazil, 69, 92, 97, 161
Brazil—Kenya, 97
Bretton Woods, 162, 177
  Institutions, 63
  International, 175
Brezhnev, Leonid, 210
Britain
  Aerospace Weapons, 124
  Army, 55, 97
  Empire, 137
  Expeditionary Force, 125
  Fleet, 137
  Imperialist, 153
  Policy, 132
  Rule, 22, 125
Buddhism, 91, 128
Bunker Busters, 110, 159, 221
Bush, George, US Pres., 73, 81, 82, 98, 105, 139, 153
  Administration, 13, 160
Bush-Manmohan—Agreement, 26
Butler Committee Report, 207

Cabinet Committee on Security, (CCS), 46, 49, 50, 62, 80, 116, 123, 142, 187, 202
Campbell, Dr. Kurt, 56
Capitalist System, 175
Carnegie Endowments for Peace, 63
Casino Capitalists, 162
Caspian
  Basin, 137
  Gas, 141
  States, 95
  Oil and Gas, 103
  Oil Region, 44
  Sea Basin, 62, 94, 103, 211
  Sea Basin Reserve, 140
  Sea Region, 69, 136, 188
Caspian-Ceylon Oil and Gas Pipelines, 210
Castro, Dr. Fidel, 163
Caucasus and Baku Oil Fields, 137
Cayman Island, 178
Ceasefire, 131
Cebrowski, Admiral, 33
CENTO, 153
Central Asia 13, 23, 44, 73, 92, 101, 188
Central Asia—Nigeria, 224
Central Asian Islamic Teachings, 128
Central Europe—Latin America, 146

Centre for Strategic and International Studies, (CSIS), 56
Chad, 98
Chagai Hills, 215
Charles de Gaulle, 182
Chavez, Pres. Venezuela, 65, 94
Chemical, Biological Weapons, 149
Cheney, Dick, US Vice President, 13, 87, 103, 139, 225
Cheney Energy Report, 88, 139
Cheney Plan, 139
CHHQ, 218
Child and Women Trafficking, 148
China, 28, 29, 44, 48, 66, 68, 84, 92, 99-113, 136, 137, 147, 157, 182, 209, 213, 217
  and India, 69, 139
  and Tibet, 129
  and US, 109-111
  China, Japan, UK, 56
China's
  CNPC, 214
  Imports, 93
  Military Power, 107
  Oil Imports, 136
  Political and Military Leadership, 108
China—European Union, 162, 163
China—South Korea, 15
Chinese
  Agrarian Based Revolution, 99
  and Japanese Economies, 77
  Communist Party, (CCP), 107
  Congress Party, 97
  Economic Diplomacy, 113
  Leadership, 112
  Military Academy, 105
  Military Commission, 108
  Political and Economic Systems, 112
  Political System, 44
  Populations in-, 101
    Indonesia, 101
    Malaysia, 101
    Philippines, 101
    Singapore, 101
    Thailand, 101
  Space and Nuclear Scientists, 111
Chitral, Gilgit and Hunza Central Agency, 129
Challabis and Allawis, 54
CIA (Central Intelligence Agency), 11, 16, 28, 52, 53, 60, 75, 79, 87, 93, 151, 156, 172, 173, 177-179, 186, 205, 208, 209, 212, 218
  Reports, 83
CISDS, 59
Clinton, Bill, US Pres., 98, 110, 186, 217, 221
Clive, Robert, 125
Coalition Forces, 65
Coast Guards, 46
Cold War Proxies, 57
Collective Security Treaty, 95
College of Combat, 197
Colonial Arms, 148
Combating Terrorism and Security Sector Reforms, 61
Comintern, 107
Command and Control System, 47, 115, 218
Common Foreign and Security Policy, (CFSP), 59

Communist Party, 105
 of Soviet Union, 210
Competition Policy, 41
Computer Aided Design (CAD), 196
Computer Design Manufacturing, 196
Congo and Zaire, 88
Conventional Weapon System, 116
Cooper, Robert, 43
Corporate Fascism, 149
Counter Computer Warfare System, 29
Criminal
 Justice System, 36, 147
 Political Mafias, 148
Croatia, 146, 227
Croatia and Slovenia, 38, 145
Crosbie Saint, US Gen., 227, 228
Cross Border Terrorism, (CBT), 46, 49, 79, 186, 204
CTBT, 44, 45, 105, 111, 115, 185, 219
Cuba, 159
Cuba—Iraq, 182
Cuban Missile Crisis, 217
Currency System, 36
Cyber Space, 32, 208
Cyber Terrorist, 32
Cyber War, 27

Dayton Accord, 146
Death Squads, 222
Defence
 Deals, 48, 49
 Plans, 201
 Procurement Board, 200
 Services Pensions, 199
Delhi/Amritsar, 142
Deng Xiaoping, 105, 109, 110, 182, 183
Depleted Uranium Afflictions, (DU Afflictions), 14
Depleted Uranium Munitions, (DU Munitions), 15, 16
Devegowda, HD, 219
Diego Garcia, 81, 85
Digital Data Technique, 195
Directive Principles, 8
Disarmament Operations, 61
Dixit, JN, 130
Dixon Agenda, 132
Domestic US Military Law, 164
Dr. Kurian, 36
DRDO, 33, 48, 117
Drug
 and Human Trafficking, 46
 Lords, 40
 Money, 175
 Money Laundering Operation, 178
 Trade, 150, 211, 223
 Trafficking, 38, 146
DU
 Bombing, 166
 Burns, 167
 Exposure, 166
 Munitions, 15, 16, 164-167, 172, 187, 188, 207
 Weapons, 84, 165, 166
Dual Use of Technology, 123, 216

East Asia
 and Europe, 77
 Market, 103
East Europe, 130
East Europe—Kazakistan, 177
East Pakistan, 128

Eastern Europe, 63
East-West Centre (US), 115, 183
Economic
  Decision Making, 42
  Development, 132
  Policies, 7
Economy, 20, 150, 184
  Market, 105
  Political, 114, 190
Edible Oil
  Banks, 36
  Technology Mission, 36
Eisenhower, Dwight, 24
Electro-Magnetic Weapons (E Bombs), 17
Electronic Commission, 201
Electronic Sensors, 72
Energy Resources War, 188
Energy Security, 204
Ethnic Cleansing, 146
European Committee on Radiation Risk (ECRR), 165
European Union, 38, 43, 60-62, 86, 101, 146, 177

Fallujah, 83
Fascism, 147, 149, 156, 157, 175
Fascism, Global, 149
FBI, 45, 156, 196
Financial Services Building Allocation, 198
Fissile Material Control Treaty (FMCT), 185
Flora and Fauna, 188
Food Corporation of India (FCI), 36
Food for Work Program, 36
Food Trade, 41
Force Mix and Architecture, 201
Foreign Policy Centre London, 175
Four Great Modernizations, 101
France, 69, 119, 222, 223
France and Germany, 207
Fratricidal War, 151
Free Market Economy, 37
  Reforms, 13
Free Trade, 148
Freedom Fighters, 153
Freedom Movement, 126
French Air Force, 119
Fundamentalist Groups, 91
Fundamentalists, 42
Future Combat System, 17

G-7 (Countries), 50, 92, 94, 138, 173, 184
  Agenda, 161
  and WTO, 163
Gammon, John C, 93
Gandhi, M.K., 134
Gandhi Non-Violence Freedom Movement, 175, 160
Gandhi, Rajiv, 184, 197
Gandhi, Sonia, 130
Ganga, 78
GATT, 119, 147
Gene Warfare Project, 110
General Command HQs (GCHQs), 28
Geneva Conventions, 76
Georgia and Azerbaijan, 95, 210
Georgia—Kirgizia, 62
Georgia—Turkmenistan, 74
German Foreign Policy, 61
Germany, 69, 119, 182
Ghosh, Arundhati, 219
Global
  Criminal Economy, 39, 40

Economic Agenda, 41
Economic System, 55
Economy, 41, 223
Energy, 93
Energy Demand, 87
Energy Resources Base, 87
Positioning System (GPS), 13, 14, 29, 32
Warming, 210
Globalization, 8, 41, 55, 64, 66, 68, 70, 143, 144, 146, 148-150, 154, 156, 158, 161, 163,
Globalizaton, Liberalization and Privatization, 119, 130
Golden Triangle, 40
Gorbachev, 40, 65, 99
Grain Banks, 36
Great Game II, 90, 95, 98
Great Power Yalta Agreement, 138
Great War II, 84
Green Zone, 208
Gujarat, 47
Gulf and the Caspian, 96
Gulf of Ghana, 224
Gulf War, 15, 16, 18, 28, 88, 170
Gulf War Syndrome, 165, 171
Gulf-Caspian—Central Asian Region, 95
Gun Running, 21, 39, 77, 151, 152, 211, 223, 227

HAARP, 19
Hague Convention, 164
Haiti, 225
Hari Singh, Maharaja, 92, 126
Harkat-ul-Ansar, 80
Hate-Politics, 42
Hawk Jet Trainer, 122
Helsinki Headlines Goals, 60
Herzegovina, 39
High Frequency Active Auroral Research Program (HAARP), 15
Hijacking of IA Flight, 80
Hindu Mahasabha, 126
Hindu Militia, 149
Hindukush, 147
Hindutva, 156, 157
Hiroshima and Nagasaki Bombs, 175
Hitech Coalition Armed Forces, 18
Hitler, 156, 158
Holland, 119
Homi Bhabha, 115
Human Resource Development Program, 112
Human Rights, 96, 98, 100, 160
Human Rights Conventions, 167
Hurriyat, US Supported Outfit, 46
Hydrogen Bomb, 217

IMF(International Monetary Fund), 39, 148, 177
and World Bank, 37, 38
Loans, 37, 75
Imperialism, 158
Improvised Explosive Device Manual, 223
India and Pakistan, 86, 129, 133, 185
India and US, 78, 81
India-Bangladesh, 149
India-Nepal Relationship, 45
India's
Foreign and Defence Policies, 183, 187
Freedom, 126
Oil on Shore—, 203

Operation Parakrama, 20
Security, 41
Indian
Armed Forces, 47, 76
Army, 127, 128, 135
Army Division in Iraq, 187
Bengal, 151
Independence Act, 126
Intelligence Agencies, 64
Military, 72
Navy, 74, 77
Ocean, 111, 147
Ocean Nuclear Power, 220
Ocean Rim, 46
Oil Export Pipeline, 214
Security, 62
Indians and Africans, 144
Indigo—Land Tax, 22
Indonesia, 87, 96, 97, 101
Indonesian Military, 53
Indo-Soviet Treaty, 100
Indo-US
Civilian Nuclear Energy Agreement, 45
Defence Agreement, 45
Defence Framework Agreement, 7, 62
Defence Pact, 25
Israeli Axis, 204
Military to Military Relations, 69
Nuclear Agreement, 7, 78
Relations, 64, 70
Strategic Pact, 25
Strategic Partnership, 82
Indus Water Treaty, 35
Industrial Nations, 206
Infiltration, 42
Information Technology, 42
Information Warfare Centre (China), 29
INS Delhi, 192
Instrument of Accession, 127
International
Atomic Energy Agency (IAEA), 60, 74, 115
Court of Justice, (ICJ), 50
Criminal Court, 49, 76
Law, 150, 164
Law of the Sea, 50
Military Education and Training (IMET), 72
Oil Trade Pact, 159
Police Academy, 69
Security Program, 56
Trade, 41
Iran, 7, 45, 74, 139, 159
Iran, Syria, 207
Iranian Azerbaijan, 138
Iraq, 7, 15, 17, 23, 45, 65, 83, 85-87, 96, 136, 137, 139, 146, 158, 159, 167, 172, 179, 208, 209, 224
and Afghanistan, 58, 67
and Niger Uranium Case, 74
and Palestine, 76
Invasion, 142
Iraqi Cities, 75, 83
Mosul, 83
Najaf, 83
Ramadi, 83
Iraqi National Assets, 66
Iraqi Nationalism, 65
Iraqi Oil, 103
ISI, 73, 146, 212, 213
Islamic Countries, 45
Islamic Oil World, 85
Israeli Advisors, 156

Israeli Security, 207
ISRO, 183, 193, 199
Italian Parliament, 39
Italy, 69

Jakarta Peace Consensus, 158
Jal Bahini, 128
Jammu and Kashmir, 45-47, 78, 80, 91, 115, 126-130, 132, 186, 187
    Militia, 127
Jan Sangh, 126
Japan, 68, 84, 89, 101, 119, 137, 209, 210
Japan, South Korea and China, 101
Japan—Latin America, 84
Jarring Report, 132
Jaswant Singh, 43, 44, 62, 110, 185
Jaswant Singh-Strobe Dialogue, 218
Jehadi Forces, 55, 73
Jinnah, MA, 127

Kabul and Baghdad, 15
Kargil, 45, 129, 178, 203
Kargil Anti-Intrusion Operation, 212
Karimov, 210
Karzai, Afghanistan Pres., 58
Kashmir, 43, 44, 45, 81, 92, 126-128, 130-135, 142, 152, 153, 156, 177, 200, 212
    see also Jammu and Kashmir
Kashmir Study Group, (KSG), 44, 45, 129, 130, 155, 185
Kashmir Valley, 153, 155, 185, 204
Kashmiris, 127, 128
Kazakistan, 176
Kazakistan's Caspian Coast, 94
Kean's Commission, 207
Kerala, 146
Kermit Roosevelt (CIA), 65
KGB, 99
Khalistan Liberation Army (KLA), 146, 152
Khandelwal, JIC Chairman, 174
Killer Squads, 156
Kissinger, Henry, A, 35, 56, 94
KMT Regime, 107
Koirala, Girija Prasad, Nepal PM, 45
Korea/Vietnam, 17
Korean War, 107, 108
Kosovo, 15, 16, 148
Kosovo to Kashmir, 131
Kosovo—Uzbekistan, 90
Kosovo Liberation Army (KLA), 38, 40
KPMG Scandals, 162
Krishnamachari, TT, 203
Kurdish Factions, 54
Kuwait, 159, 227
Kyoto Protocol, 50
Kyrgistan, 210

La Fontaine, Air Chief, 197
Labour Policy, 41
Lahore, 45, 129
Lahore Talks, 185
Land Attack Cruise Missile, 29
Land Reforms, 127, 153
Latin America, 73, 143, 222
Latin America, Mexico and Russia, 154
Latin America—East Europe, 207
Latin American Nations—Africa, 20

Latin American Politics, 40
Latin America—Russia, 178
Law Enforcement Forces, 86
Liberalised States of Serbia, 226
Liberalization, 41, 145, 148, 150
Liberia, 225
LIC-Mundhra Matters, 203
Line of Control, 186
Line of Control in Jammu and Kashmir, 72
London Club Trigger List, 123, 216
LTTE, 151, 153, 174
Lugano Report, 42

Mafias, 36, 40, 144
Malacca Straits, 46, 74, 77, 94, 111
Malaviya, KD, 203
Malaysia and Indonesia, 74
Malaysia, 188
Malu, Victor Leo, Gen., 227
Manhattan Project, 165
Manmohan Singh, Indian PM, 25
Mao Tse Tung, 109
Mao Zedong, 105
Maritime Security, 188
Marshall Tito, 85
Masstricht Treaty, 59
McArthur, Gen., 107, 198
McNamara, 25
Mehar Singh, 127
Menon, Krishna, 115, 128, 131, 132
Mercenaries, 146, 225
Mercenary Terrorism, 150
Mexican Infiltration, 72
MFN (Most Favoured Nations), 100, 113
  China, 217
Micro-Electro-Mechanical System (MEMs), 17, 29, 32, 192
Micro-Nukes, 105, 158, 169
Militarization, 11, 89, 143, 148, 149, 156, 158, 163
Military
  Airfields, 46
  Alliance System, 128
  and Civil Intelligence Agencies, 45
  Bases, 44, 210
    India, 156
    Iraq, 85
  Industrial Complex, 24, 112
  Junta, 151, 152
  Planning, 18, 19
  Technology, 19, 71
  to Military Relations, 52, 64, 70, 71, 76, 81, 82, 95
Ministry of External Affairs, 126
Ministry of Finance, 200
Minority Community, 169
MIRV (Multiple Independently Re-entry Vehicles), 217, 220
  Ballistic Missile, 84
Mishra, Brijesh, 74, 204
Missile Delivery System, 47
Missile Technology Control Regime, (MTCR), 216
Mobutu (Zaire), 97
Mobutu in Congo, 222
MOD Deals, 48
Modernization, 108, 192
Mohamad Mahathir, PM Malaysia, 145, 162
Money Laundering, 37, 40, 148, 154, 211, 223, 227
Monopoly Trade, 137
Mountbatten, Lord, 127
Mujahideens, 128, 153, 211
Mukherjee, Pranab, 82
Mukti Bahini, 128

Multinational Corporations (MNCs), 8, 37, 41, 57, 104, 160, 175
Multiple Conflicts, 11
Musharraf, President Pakistan, 55, 130, 186
Mussolini, (Italy), 156
Mutually Agreed Destruction (MAD), 217
Muzaffarabad, 127
Muzaffarabad-Srinagar Bus, 130
Myanmar, 74, 152

Naga and Mizo Fronts, 153
Nagas, Manipuris and Zomis, 152
Nagasaki and Hiroshima (Japan), 115
Nambiar, KA, 124, 198
Nanda, Admiral, 48
Nano-Technology, 17
Napalm, Daisy Cutter, 159
Narasimha Rao, PV, Indian PM, 49, 75
Narco Trade, 152, 157
Narcotics, 21, 39, 77, 152
National Atlantic Treaty Organization (NATO), 23, 26, 28, 37, 38, 42, 61, 62, 65, 73, 128, 145, 157, 177, 208, 217
  Forces, 83, 187
  in Afghanistan, 142
  in Brussels, 182
Nuclear Arsenals, 182
  Operations, 59
National
  Conference, 127
  Defence System, 201
  Defence Union, 71
  Defence University, 70
  Endowments for Democracy, 63
  Energy Policy Document (NEPD), 207, 210
  Geospatial Agency, 28, 173
  Intelligence Council, 52, 59
  Lawyers' Guild (US), 152
  Mapping Agency, 28
  Mapping and Imagery Agency, 173
  Maritime Program, 108
  Missile Defence Program, 71
  Policy Goal, 117
  Security, 30, 34-36, 37, 43, 114, 120, 204, 205
    Adviser, 15, 49, 62, 155, 209, 218
    Advisory Board, 62, 142
    Agency, 28, 33, 42, 208
    and Economic Policy, 49
    Council (NSC), 173, 184
    Decision Directives (NSDD), 37
    Document, 39
    Policy, 15
    Policy Document, 34
    Strategy Document, (NSSD), 12
Nationalized Banking Sector, 38
Nawaz Sharif, Pak. PM, 185
Naya Kashmir, 92, 127
Nayyar, KK, 185
Nazarbayaev, 210
Nazi, 75
Nazi Army, 85
Nazi Fascist Army, 107
Nazi Germany, 112, 137
Nazi Movement, 149
Nazi Party Swastika, 154
Nazis/Fascist Atrocities, 69

NDA Govt., 184, 189
Nehru, Jawaharlal, 115
Nepal, 13, 35, 45, 74, 152, 157
Nepalese Gurkha Soldiers, 97
Nevada Test Site, 165
New Energy Policy (NEP), 139
Next Step in Strategic Partnership (NSSP), 62
Nicaragua, 50
Nigeria, Mali, Malawi, 35
Nixon, US Pres., 100
Non-Aligned States, 70
Non-Military NATO States, 182
Non-NATO Ally, 26, 141, 212
Non-Nuclear Weapon States (NNWS), 49
Non-Proliferation Treaty (NPT), 108, 184, 216
North East, 80, 91, 187, 200, 212
North East India, 151, 152
North Korea, 86
North Korea, Taiwan, 103
North Pole, 108
Northern Alliance, 54
NSSD, 72, 83, 106, 119, 142, 147, 181
NSSP, 77, 78
Nuclear
  Bomb, 100
  Club, 105
  Command and Control System, 44
  Development Program, 23
  Doctrines 44
  Flash Point, 115, 131, 221
  Micro Nukes, 209
  Monitoring Devices, 215, 216
  Power Plants, 165, 166
  Submarine, 104, 119, 198
  Submarine Project, 108
  Tests, 45
  War, 166
  War Heads, 141
  Weapons, 43, 141, 165, 169, 185, 216, 217, 220, 223
  Weapon Capacity, 215
  Weapon System, 115, 120, 149, 217
  Weapons State, 60, 220
  Weapons Tests, 165
Nuremburg Principle, 51

Odom, Gen., 208
Offshore Corporate Bodies (OCBs), 37, 40, 148, 162, 227
Oil and Gas
  and Mineral Resources, 92
  and Natural Gas, 93
  Fields, 87
  Giants, 70, 210
  Imports, 136
  Pipelines, 103
  Rich Nations, 143
  Resources in-, 137
    East Indies, 137
    Indonesia, 137
    Jawa, 137
    Oman and Qatar, 212
ONGC Videsh, 214
Operation
  'Save Pakistan Freedom', 74
  Artemis, 61
  Iraq Freedom, 172, 209
  Parakrama, 79, 116, 189, 220
  Phoenix, 145
Opium Production and Exports, 83
Opium War, 107
Opium-Narcotics Trafficking, 211

Osama Bin Laden, 91
Ottoman Empire, 137
Owens, William, Admiral, 27

Padmanabhan, S, 20, 188, 202
Pakistan, 13, 44, 46, 55, 73, 78, 80, 81, 111, 115, 126 129, 130-133, 159, 176, 177, 186, 212, 216, 221
 and India, 168
 Army, 128, 187, 203
 Army Units, 127
 as a Terrorist State, 44
 ISI, 151, 152
 Military, 73
 Occupied Kashmir (PoK), 129
 Ports, 211
 Regulars, 127
Pakistan-Afghanistan Caspian Basin, 142
Pakistan-Based Terrorist Group, 80
Pakistan—East Europe, 69
Palestine, 65
Palestinian, 45, 148
Pant, KC, 50
Patent Law Amendment, 204
Patriot Act, 176
Peace CBMs, 130
Peaking of Oil, 56, 208
Peasants Struggle, 157
Pehlavi Industry, 137
Penal System, 40
Pension Funds, 68, 206
People Liberation Army (PLA), 28, 107, 113
People Liberation Army (Navy), 108
Persian Gulf, 206
Petro Dollars, 45, 56, 68, 84, 159
Philippines—Latin America, 69
Pinter, Harold, Noble Prize Winner, 25
Pipeline Project, 136
Plassey, 21, 22
Plebiscite, 130, 132
Pokhran, 45
Pokhran-I, 184
Pokhran-II, 44, 115, 183, 184, 201, 215, 216, 219
Political and Economic Development, 150
POTA (Prevention of Terrorist Act, 2002), 154
Powell, Colin, 70, 31, 131
POWs, 129
President Clinton's Commission on Critical Infrastructure Protection, 32
Presidential Commission, 29, 172
Private Military Companies (PMCs), 17, 68, 84, 90, 93, 95, 96, 146, 150, 163, 207, 223-226, 228
Privatization, 35, 38, 40, 67, 145, 148, 150, 151, 154, 193
Project for the New American Century (PNAC), 11, 12, 25, 73, 83, 106, 110, 119, 143, 147, 150, 157-159, 168, 169, 175, 193, 221, 226
Proxy Operations, 128
Proxy Wars, 58, 95, 186
Public Accounts Committee, 199
Public Distribution System (PDS), 36
Purulia Arms Drop Case, 91

Qatar, 227

Radcliffe Award, 129
Radiation and Public Health Report, 166
Radioactive Depleted Munitions, 141
Radioactive DU Anti-Tank, 141
Rajeshwar Dayal, 222
Ram Naik, 136
Rand Corporations, 63, 184
Reading University, UK, 57, 59
Reconfiguration Technology, 195
Red Indians, 144
Red Sea, 214
RED Team, 32
Reforms, 7, 8, 13, 75, 112, 210
Republic of Congo, 61
Research and Analysis Wing (RAW), 79, 142, 174, 204
Resource Wars, 210
Revisionism, 100
Revolution and Military Affairs (RMA), 109, 210
Revolutionary United Front (RUF), 96, 97
Rickover, Hyman G, Administrator, 193
Right to Accession, 127
River Water Sharing, 35
Robert Clive, 22
Robot-Bugs, 29
Rogue States, 53
Roosevelt, Kermit (CIA), 65
Royal Military Academy, Sandhurst, 55, 56
Rumsfeld, Donald, 49, 81, 82, 214
Russia, 13, 44, 59, 60, 62, 95, 95, 159, 210
Rwanda, 97
Saddam Hussain, 159, 207
Sangh Parivar, 46, 154
Sankhya Vahini, 47
SARS Invasion, 105
SASO, 54
Saudi Arabia, 45, 93, 142, 159, 160, 210, 211, 212, 227
Saudi Arabia, Exporter of Wahabism, 210, 211
Saudi Arabia National Guards, 226
Saudi Arabia—Zaire, 84
Saudi Armed Forces, 56
Saudi Intelligence, 153
Saudi Oil Peaking, 140
SDI or Star War, 19
SEATO, 131
Security,
  Council, 104
  Council Resolution, 128, 132
  Economic, 36, 39, 114
  Energy, 34, 114
  Financial, 34
  Nutrition, 35, 114
  Nutrition and Livelihood, 114
  People's, 36
Seed/GM Food Companies, 190
Service Protection Act, 49
Shah Commission, 51
Shanghai, 102, 107
Shanghai Communique, 100, 113
Shastri, Lal Bahadur, 41, 203
Sheikh Abdullah, 92, 127, 133, 134
Sheikh Mujibur Rahman, 151
Shell BP's Oil Reserves, 87
Shenzen, 102
Shevarnadze, Pres. Georgia, 95
Shia, Sunnis and Kurds, 84

Shimla Agreement, 129
Siberia, 103, 211
Sierra Leone, 95-97, 225
Sikh Separatist, 153
Singh, SK, 185
Sino-Indian Border, 101
Sino-US Trade, 113
Slave Labour, 149, 152
Slave Trafficking, 38
SMART (Shipboard Modular Arrangements), 195
Smurfing, 40
Social Market Economy, 99, 102, 105, 109, 112
Social Security (Pension) Funds, 103
Social Security System, 206
Society, 29, 36, 93, 147, 149
 American-Jewish, 155
Somalia, 224
Sood, VK (LG), 189
Soros, George, 63
South Africa, 90, 95, 96
South Africa Arms Manufacturers, 96
South Asia, 147, 149-151, 153, 154, 157, 184
South Asian
 Market, 148
 Societies, 154
South China Sea, 94, 101
South East Asia, 86
South East Asian Economies, 36
South Korea, 68, 84, 119
South West Asia, 12, 206
Soviet Union, 11, 12, 40, 47, 85, 99, 100, 107, 110, 130, 138, 138, 204, 205, 206
 Economy and Policy, 40
 Military Supplies, 100
 Revolution, 1917, 175, 223
Space Technology, 183
Special Operation Command (SOCOM), 54
Spy Satellite Imagery, 80
Sri Lanka, 45, 74, 150, 151, 152
Stability and Support Operation (SASO), 23
Star War Program, 148
Stat Wars, 27
Straits of Hormuz, 94
Structural Adjustment Program, 45, 119
Submarines, 122
Sub-Sahara Africa, 61
Sub-Sahara State, 98
Sufism, 91
Suharto, 97
Sun Tzu, 105
Sundarji, Gen., 197
Surveillance Agency, 28
Swadeshi, 122, 124, 199
Sweden, 119
Syria, Iran, North Korea, 15

Tahiliani, Administrator, 197
Taiwan, 68, 100
Talbot, Strobe, 44, 50, 62, 185
Taliban, 46, 79, 80, 144, 179
Taliban/Northern Alliance Govts., 141
Tariq Aziz, 130
Tax Amnesty Schemes, 154
Technology Export, 185
Tehelka Tapes, 48
Tengiz Oil Fields, 94
Terrorism, 13, 21, 59, 71, 77, 80, 91, 92, 150, 154, 155, 161

Terrorism and Insurgency, 77
Terrorism, Economic, 37
Terrorist
  Attack on Indian Parliament, 155, 188
  Brigades (Pak), 153
  Groups, 152, 211
  Organization, 80, 146, 223
  Outfits, 152
Theocracy, 76
Third World, 55, 145, 180
  Air Force, 30
  Countries, 119, 223
  Leadership, 28
Timor, 96
Tora Bora, Kabul, Paktia, Karises, 167
Trade Policy, 42
Trafficking in-, 223
  Drugs, 223
  Guns, 223
  Women and Children, 223
Trans-Afghanistan Energy Pipeline, 147
Transfer of Technology, 47
Transnational Companies (TNCs), 58, 110, 148
Trifurcation of Jammu and Kashmir, 185
Trilateral Commissions, 63
TRIPS, 41, 148, 160, 184
Tripura, Assam and West Bengal, 151
Trojan Horse, 31, 48, 166
Turkmenistan, 210
Two Nation Theory, 131

UAE, 159
UK, 25, 28, 43, 45, 50, 59, 61, 90, 119, 120, 223
  And US, 18, 126
  France and Israel, 119
  Immigrants, 156
  Private Multinational Corporations, 225
  UK's All—Committee, 211
Ukraine, 221
Ukraine, Russia and Bylorus, 210
Umm Qasr Port, 159
UN, 13, 20, 60, 74, 83, 95, 128, 131, 170, 179, 207, 222, 225
  Charter, 128, 129, 150
  Commission for India and Pakistan (UNCIP), 132
  Forces, 224
  General Assembly, 39, 145
  Security Council, 50, 60, 128, 131, 172
  Resolution, 95
  System, 25
  UNCLOS, 50
Unemployment Compensation, 206
UNICEF, 35
University of Michigan, 56
Unmanned Aerial Vehicles, (UAVs), 17, 29
Uranium Wars, 167
Uruguay GATT Agreement, 75
US, 12-14, 16, 19, 20, 23, 25, 28, 30-35, 38, 43-46, 50, 52, 55-61, 63, 64, 66-69, 72-76, 79, 80, 82, 83, 85, 88, 92, 94, 95, 100-106, 107, 109, 115, 128, 129, 131, 137, 146, 148, 149, 151, 152, 153, 155, 156, 158-162, 165-169, 172, 176, 181, 183, 185, 187, 193, 203, 205, 216, 218, 219, 220

Administration, 63, 75, 88, 94, 107, 111, 147, 153, 186, 206
Air Force, 119
Air Force Strategic—, 16
And Israeli Intelligence Teams, 45
And Pakistan, 115
And UK, 81, 112, 131, 146, 154, 178
Armed Forces, 75, 75, 85, 86, 89, 200
Army, 13, 16, 84
Army War College, 54
Attack and Invasion of Afghanistan, 141
Banks, 68, 159
Borders, 165
Cities, 108
Defence, 13, 14
Advisory -, (DARPA), 17, 27
Budget, 84, 98
Planning Guidance, 205
Policies, 181
Department of Energy, 93
Drug Enforcement Agency, 45
East-West Centre (Honolulu), 34
Economic Aid, 73
Economy, 77, 101, 106, 112, 159, 160
Election Campaign, 210
Electronic Spy Stations, 109
European Union Economies, 209
Fifth Fleet, 94
Forces, 13, 73
Forces in Iraq, 83
Foreign Policy, 11, 88
Game Plan, 45
Imperialism, 158
In Iraq, 65
Industry, 193
Information Centre, 80
Institute of Peace, 91
Israel and India, 155
Joint Force Command, 17
Logistic in Iraq, 225
Market, 103
Militarization, 26
Military, 16, 29, 31, 58, 73, 74, 86, 88, 98, 139, 160
Bases, 62, 173
Budget, 147
Forces, 76
Intervention, 66
Leadership, 86
Policy, 65, 168
System Design, 123
National
Energy Policy Dev.Group (NEPDG), 139
Intervention, 67
Security, 220
Security Advisor, 188
Security Agency, 173
NATO's Allies, 14
Navy, 33, 46, 74, 191
NSSD, 110
Nuclear Submarine Project, 193
Nuclear Threat, 108
Occupation in Iraq, 84
Oil Imports, 139
Pacific Fleet, 71
Policies and West Asia and Africa, 178
Policies Towards China, 101
Policy, 72, 73
Policy Makers, 140

Presidential Doctrine, 49
Security and Military Policy, 139
Space Command, 144
Stock Markets and Bonds, 212
Strategic Military Covert Doctines, 76
Submarine Ring, 137
Supreme Court, 127
Trade Administration, 190
Transnational Corporations, 161
Treasury Bonds, 68, 77, 101, 112
Troops, 170, 208, 226
Troops and Military, 158
Uranium Medical Res. Centre, 15
Vital Interest, 181, 190
War, 84
US-India Defence Relations, 70, 72
US-India Military Alliance, 111
US-Mexican Border, 46
US-Nepal Anti-Terrorist Pact, 157
US-Soviet Dialogue, 174
Usman, Brig., 127
USSR, 44, 65, 99, 101, 108, 109, 129, 182, 216, 217

Vajpayee, Atal Behari, 70, 110, 156, 185
Venezuela and Mexico, 140
Vietnam, 16, 22, 50, 53, 75, 101, 108, 159, 182
Vietnam War, 85, 150
Virtual Reality Displays (VRDs), 29
Vo Nguyen Giap, 25
Voice Recognition Transcript, 28
Volcker Report, 7

Wakkan Corridor, 109
Wall Street, 14, 67, 110, 159, 175
Wall Street Bankers, 65
War Breaker Technology, 28
War by Other Means (WOMs), 31
War in Shadows, 75
War on Terror, 16, 55, 56, 64, 70, 77, 79, 82, 90, 143, 148
Warfare,
Bio-Chemical, (BCW), 15
Biological, 169
Command Control, 31
Counter Information, 32
Cyber, 15, 30-33
Digital Data, 30
Economic, 20
Electronic, 30, 80, 105
Gene, 169
Germ, 169
Information, 28, 30, 33
Low Intensity, 55
Network Centric, (NCW), 17
Radiation, 105
Robotised, 17
Wars in Shadows, 87
Water Purification Plant for Iraq, 35
West Africa, 207, 210
West Africa Oil, 103
West African Countries, 146
West Asia, 15, 23, 56, 73, 207
West Asia—Indonesia, 138
West Asia—Philippines, 110
Western Alliance System, 123

Western Intelligence Community, 21
Westmoreland, Gen, 16
White Revolutions, 36
White Slave Trafficking, 146
WHO, 164
Wilson, Harold, British PM, 173
WMD (Weapons of Mass Destruction), 15, 60, 164, 169, 172, 179, 209, 214
World Bank, 98
World Bank and IMF, 161, 162
World Bank-Transnational, 35
World Energy Consumption, 93
World Trade Organization (WTO), 40-42, 60, 102, 105, 119, 147, 148, 175
Patent Regime, 190
Regime, 161
World War I, 137, 212
World War II, 63, 69, 111, 120, 137, 160, 175, 211

Yalta, 138
Yalu River, 107
Yangtze, 107
Yeltsin, 210
Yeltsin Regime, 40
Yugoslavia, 37, 39, 59, 85, 130, 145, 146

Zamindari, 125
Zamrin's Fleet, 213
Zbigniew Brzezinski (ZB), 15, 175-177
Zhou-en-lai, Chinese PM, 108
Ziang Zamin, 182
Zuckerman, Sir Solly, 120